THE REFORM JUDAISM READER

North American Documents

MICHAEL A. MEYER

AND

W. GUNTHER PLAUT

UAHC PRESS

NEW YORK, NY

Photographs clockwise from top:

Ordination of Rabbi Sally Priesand by Dr. Gottschalk. Courtesy the Jacob Rader Marcus Center of the American Jewish Archives.

Israel rally, New York.

Confirmation class, Temple Beth-El, San Antonio, Texas. Courtesy Temple Beth-El.

Simchat Torah, Rabbi Michele Medwin, Temple Sholom, Broomall, PA. Photo by Steve Medwin.

Social Action, UAHC. Photo courtesy the Jacob Rader Marcus Center of the American Jewish Archives.

Synagogue Affiliation Commission Meeting, Temple Emanuel, Denver, CO. Barbara Shuman, Rabbi Howard Jaffe, Rabbi Steven Foster, Myra Ostroff. Courtesy of the UAHC William and Lottie Daniel Department of Outreach.

Sukkot, Rabbi Norman Lipson, Temple Dor Dorim, Weston, Fl. Courtesy of Rabbi Norman Lipson.

Baby-naming. Photo courtesy of the Spector family.

Library of Congress Cataloging-in-Publication Data

The Reform Judaism reader : North American documents / [compiled by] Michael A. Meyer and W. Gunther Plaut.

    p. cm.

Includes bibliographical references and index.

ISBN 0-8074-0732-1 (pbk.)

    1. Reform Judaism—United States—History—Sources. 2. Reform Judaism—Canada—History—Sources. 3. Judaism—History—Modern period, 1750—Sources. I. Meyer, Michael A. II. Plaut, W. Gunther, 1912–

BM197.R393 2000

296.8'341'0973—dc21

                                 00-041765

10 9 8 7 6 5 4 3 2 1

Contents

Preface   v

Historical Introduction   vii

1. **The Heritage of German Progressive Judaism**   1

   Israel Jacobson   2

   Zacharias Frankel   4

   Abraham Geiger   6

   Samuel Holdheim   12

   Leo Baeck   15

   Ismar Elbogen   18

2. **The Major Institutions of Reform Judaism**   21

   The Union of American Hebrew Congregations   22

   The Hebrew Union College–Jewish Institute of Religion   25

   The Central Conference of American Rabbis   29

   The World Union for Progressive Judaism   32

3. **Theology   36**

   Introduction   37

   A Growing God   38

   Ethical Monotheism   40

   The God of the Covenant   41

   A Feminist Concept of God   44

   Revelation   47

4. **The Realm of Public Prayer   55**

   The Need for a Minyan   56

   The *Kippah* Syndrome   59

   The Changing Prayer Book   62

   Gender Sensitivity   67

   Prayers for Healing   70

   Musical Diversity   72

   A Revolution in Worship   75

5. **Shabbat and Holy Days   78**

   Saving Shabbat   79

   Enhancing Shabbat   84

   The Holy Days   88

   Pesach   91

   Old and New Observances   93

6. **Life-Cycle Events   99**

Entering and Affirming the
   Covenant 99
Women's Life-Cycle 106
Marriage 108
Divorce 109
Dealing with Death 111

7. **The Halachah of Reform
  117**
New Approaches 118
Abortion as a Flashpoint
  123
The Need for a Guide 125
The Ground of Mitzvah
  126

8. **Zionism and Israel 132**
Official Opposition 133
Early Reform Zionists 134
Official Reversal 138
Zionist Activism 139

9. **Social Justice 145**
The First Social Justice
  Platform of the CCAR
  146
The First UAHC Statement of
  Basic Principles on the
  Synagogue and Social
  Action 147
Vietnam 150
Three Specific Issues 153
Jewish Faith and Social Justice
  156
Social Justice Dilemmas
  159

10. **Outreach 161**
Mixed Marriage 161
Conversion to Judaism 173
The Role of the Non-Jew in
  the Synagogue 179

11. **Education 182**
The Goals of Jewish Education
  183
Reform Jewish Day Schools
  185
The Influence of NFTY
  186
The UAHC Torah
  Commentary 189
The Educated Reform Jew
  191
Torah at the Center 192

12. **The Platforms of American
  Reform Judaism 195**
The Philadelphia Principles
  (1869) 196
The Pittsburgh Platform
  (1885) 197
Guiding Principles of Reform
  Judaism (1937) 199
Reform Judaism—A
  Centenary Perspective
  (1976) 203
A Statement of Principles for Re-
  form Judaism (1999) 208
Epilogue 213
Suggestions for Further Reading 215
Index 219

Preface

One of the earliest and most significant characteristics of the Reform movement has been its awareness of historical change and development in Judaism. Today it has its own history, stretching back nearly two hundred years in Europe and only slightly less than that in North America. Contemporary Reform Judaism is far different from what it was in the beginning, and even from what it was a generation ago. In its organizational structure, its theologies, activities, problems, and aspirations, Reform Judaism remains in flux.

Self-knowledge therefore seems crucial in order to guide Reform Judaism safely into the future. We have undertaken this collection of significant documents in order to advance our movement's understanding of its history, its present status, and its current direction.

This reader primarily addresses Reform Jews in the United States and Canada, and therefore—with the exception of the opening chapter and the material relating to the World Union for Progressive Judaism—we have limited our sources to those originating in North America. We have attempted to use documents that are either fundamental to Reform Judaism, such as its organizational purposes and its platforms, or portray particularly well the principal areas of Reform concern. On a number of live issues we have either presented opposing points of view or called attention to controversies in our introductions.

In most cases we have included only excerpts from lengthier documents, indicating omissions by ellipses. Footnotes that occur within some of the documents have been excluded. The source of each document is noted, for anyone desiring to read the documents in their entirety. For readers who wish to pursue their study of Reform Judaism further, we have provided guidance with "Suggestions for Further Reading" in narrative form.

Our work on this reader has been a most pleasant collaborative effort. We have met in person on more than one occasion and corresponded (often daily) by e-mail in order to work out its scope and determine its content. Both of us wish to thank Rabbi Hara Person of the UAHC Press for initiating the project and helping us to carry it through. Liane Broido, Debra Hirsch Corman, and Rick Abrams also deserve our thanks for all their efforts. As we send this volume out into the world, we trust that it will be used both by individuals and by study groups in universities and in synagogues. It is our hope that it will aid in the process of self-reflection essential to any movement that seeks a meaningful future.

Michael A. Meyer
W. Gunther Plaut
Cincinnati and Toronto

Historical Introduction

There is a sense in which Judaism was always Reform Judaism and Orthodoxy represents a deviation from tradition. Biblical prophets attacked condoned inequalities, and rabbis in the talmudic period sought to preserve the spirit of biblical law by circumventing its letter. But in the course of time, innovation and flexibility in law and custom diminished as each succeeding generation became less willing to alter the status quo. When the Reform movement began in Central Europe during the first decades of the nineteenth century, the earliest Reformers sought to bring new life to a faith grown stagnant and losing its appeal to growing numbers of acculturating Jews. Seeking continuity with tradition, the earliest Reformers were not only moderate in their proposals but sought to tie them to the tradition of Jewish legal interpretation, introducing changes in custom, but not in halachah.

However, the gradual emergence of a Reform movement, and eventually of a Reform denomination, was prompted mainly by a shift in Jewish status determined by external factors and not immediately linked to historical precedent. By the end of the eighteenth century the more welcoming cultural and social environment of the European Enlightenment induced an increasing number of Jews to internalize its universal values, which they found to be in conflict with existing forms in Judaism. Once centralized states took away instruments of Jewish social control, notably the *cherem* (the ban) that rabbis had been able to level against religious dissenters, these Jews could flout traditional Jewish beliefs and practices with impunity. The early Reform movement was directed toward the growing numbers alienated from a Judaism with which they could no longer identify, not at those who remained committed to tradition.

The first practical religious reforms, undertaken in Germany at the beginning of the nineteenth century, ranged from aesthetic to ideological. Least controversial was the institution of decorum and of edifying sermons in the language of the country. More disputed was the introduction of vernacular hymns and organ music. Most radical were changes made in the liturgy itself, concentrating on passages that expressed hope for a return to Zion and the reinstitution of the ancient sacrificial service. Such changes were not simply motivated by newfound concerns about how Judaism would be regarded by non-Jews at a time when Jews were looking toward political emancipation. More fundamentally, the younger generation was internalizing aesthetic values and political loyalties that made it difficult for them to engage in religious services that reflected an atmosphere and a liturgy that did not speak to their sensibilities and religious hopes.

Although religious reform in varying degrees of moderation or radicality spread throughout Central and Western Europe in the nineteenth century, it achieved its greatest European success in Germany. There scholarly study of Jewish tradition emerged as the basis and justification for reforms. There reform-minded rabbis gathered in rabbinical conferences in the mid-1840s to discuss fundamental issues of Jewish observance. And there "Liberal Judaism" (a relatively conservative expression of Reform ideas and practices) became the dominant form of Jewish religious expression.

It was also in Germany, in the first half of the nineteenth century, that the basic principles of Reform Judaism were laid down. Of these, among the most significant were the ideas that Judaism was by nature dynamic, rightfully changing in response to an ever clearer perception of God's will, that religion was not merely a service of God, but rather intended to elevate the moral and spiritual life of the individual, and that Judaism was ultimately universal in its aspirations, aiming at a messianic goal that embraced peace for all humanity.

These ideas were brought to America by German-Jewish immigrants, rabbis and laypeople alike. Although religious reform in the United States had begun with a small Sephardi "Reformed Society of Israelites" in Charleston, South Carolina, in 1825, it was in the wake of the growing number of Jews from Germany that existing congregations began to institute reforms and new ones, dedicated to change, were established in all major American cities beginning in the 1840s.

Two rabbis, representing very different approaches, gave direction to the early movement in America. David Einhorn (1809–1879) was a man of considerable philosophical learning and deep convictions. A radical reformer, he insisted on principle above practical success, on taking sides on moral issues—such as slavery—regardless of the consequences. His influence was initially limited by lack of flexibility and elitism, but it was his more thoroughgoing variant of Reform Judaism that became dominant in the decades after his death. Isaac Mayer Wise (1819–1900) was made of very different stuff. Energetic and gregarious, motivated by grandiose ambitions, Wise was willing to compromise principles for the sake of practical achievements. His goal was to unite American Jewry on a broad basis that embraced a spectrum from modern Orthodox to radical Reform. It was Wise who was directly or indirectly responsible for creating all three of the major institutions of Reform Judaism in America: a congregational union, a seminary, and a rabbinical association.

However, Wise's vision was too broad to be practically sustainable. It soon became apparent that no program and no institutions could serve both the most radical and the most conservative factions. After the uncompromising Pittsburgh Platform was adopted in 1885, earlier supporters of Wise broke with him and created an emergent Conservative Judaism. What remained could only claim to be one denomination among the three that crystallized in the United States early in the twentieth century.

The movement now entered a radical phase, which retrospectively became known as "classical Reform Judaism." It stressed universalism over particularism, found little value in rituals, paid virtually no attention to halachah, and rejected Zionism as undermining the "Mission of Israel" to advocate for ethical monotheism in a providentially ordained diaspora. Focused on American society, it both equated American values with Jewish ones and began to direct the movement toward a "prophetic" critique of economic inequalities. Its adherents were almost exclusively Jews of German origin whose Reform loyalties represented a religious differentiation parallel to the social one that set them apart from East Europeans, who were arriving in larger numbers beginning in 1881.

By the 1930s, however, the heyday of classical Reform was ending, though it continued to attract a diminishing share of adherents among both rabbis and laity. A gradual shift had begun that would affect both the social composition and the ideology of the American movement. During these years the first significant numbers of East European Jews affiliated with Reform congregations and became their rabbis. They brought to the movement a deeper sense of worldwide Jewish solidarity and a closer familial relationship to Jewish traditions. These years of the Great Depression also sharpened social consciousness, especially among the rabbis, while Nazi Germany's increasingly severe anti-Jewish measures began to dampen the unbridled optimism with regard to human potentialities that had earlier characterized the movement. Zionism, hitherto a minority position, now captured a growing majority of both the rabbis and the lay leadership. Ritual practices once abandoned, such as blowing the shofar and building a sukkah at the synagogue, were gradually reintroduced by individual congregations. The trend of emphasizing faith and morality over ritual and observance was beginning to reverse itself. The movement's new platform, adopted by the rabbis in Columbus, Ohio, in 1937, reflected this profound transformation.

The first two decades following World War II were a period of extraordinary growth for the Reform Judaism in America. As Jews moved to the suburbs in increasing numbers, they established new synagogues alongside churches. Joining in the general religious revival in the United States during the Eisenhower years, they affiliated also to express their identity as Jews and to provide for the religious instruction of their children. The membership of the Union of American Hebrew Congregations (UAHC) rose from 400 congregations in 1949 to over 600 in 1960. Sisterhoods, men's clubs, and youth groups flourished. Social justice programs were instituted in local congregations, and the movement established a Religious Action Center in Washington. Interfaith activities expanded following Vatican II, and Jewish religious thought attracted new attention as a "covenant theology" began to seriously challenge the religious rationalism that had earlier been dominant.

However, by the mid-1960s the period of rapid growth had come to an end, theological doubts troubled many rabbis, and the movement was divided on the question of how to deal with the increasing incidence of mixed marriage. The focus of Jewish life moved away from the synagogue toward the Jewish Federation as concerns of the united community, such as Israel and Soviet Jewry, engulfed narrower denominational ones. Ethnicity prevailed over religion.

The movement seemed to be losing its self-confidence and its sense of unity when, in the mid-1970s, the publication of new prayer books, the creation of its own Zionist organization, and the adoption of a new platform that embodied the concern for Jewish survival gave it new impetus. In succeeding decades American Reform Judaism began to grow once more.

By the end of the twentieth century the UAHC had more than 850 congregations, the Hebrew Union College–Jewish Institute of Religion (HUC-JIR) could boast four flourishing campuses with a variety of programs for rabbis, cantors, educators, Jewish communal workers, and lay leaders, and the Central Conference of American Rabbis (CCAR) could claim more than 1,700 members, with a rapidly increasing percentage of them women. Synagogue auxiliaries—the Women of Reform Judaism, the National Federation of Temple Brotherhoods, and the North American Federation of Temple Youth—engaged the movement's expanding membership. Sociologists were agreed that Reform Judaism was the fastest growing Jewish denomination in America, already the largest in identification, though perhaps not yet in affiliation. In the last year of the century, its rabbis adopted a new platform that emphasized the idea of holiness, giving expression to the movement's renewed concern with individual religious experience. Jewish education for adults as well as children became the highest priority of the UAHC. A movement that valued both tradition and individual choice, it was realized, required thorough grounding in Jewish texts.

THE HERITAGE OF GERMAN PROGRESSIVE JUDAISM

✦ The beginnings of the Reform movement were not in North America but in Europe, particularly in Germany. There in the second decade of the nineteenth century, laymen established the first Reform temples. There, as well, talented thinkers forged the ideology of the movement, which to a large extent characterizes it to this day. The early leaders of Reform Judaism in the United States were nearly all immigrants from Germany, who had learned its principles in their native land and carried them across the Atlantic.

In Germany, unlike any other European country, Progressive Judaism, along a spectrum ranging from a dominant conservative liberalism to radical reform, captured the allegiance of a large majority of the Jewish community. From its ranks came outstanding rabbinical intellectuals who combined significant historical scholarship with active lives as pulpit rabbis. They raised issues that have received recurrent attention since their time and to this day: How does one reconcile biblical criticism with faith in the sacred nature of the text? What is the enduring value of Shabbat, and how can contemporary Jews best observe it given their involvement in non-Jewish society? What can we believe about Creation and Revelation? And what is the role of the Jewish people in the world?

The German Reformers were pioneers in modern Jewish theology, in creating a revised, intellectually more acceptable liturgy and more aesthetically pleasing synagogue music, in giving women a greater measure of religious and educational equality, and in finding a larger religious purpose for Jewish existence. In these ways and others, they were intent upon making Judaism personally meaningful to Jews who had become alienated from traditional forms. Their battle was not only—perhaps not even principally—with Orthodoxy, but with the ever more powerful forces of secularism that captured the souls of modernizing Jews, leaving little room for religion. By the early twentieth century non-Orthodox German Judaism was undergoing a limited religious revival, which deepened under the pressure of Nazi restrictions. In the wake of the Holocaust, the principles of the German Reform movement, which had begun to pass to the New World a century earlier, became its living legacy.

Israel Jacobson (1810)

In 1810 the wealthy Israel Jacobson (1768–1828) dedicated a "temple" in the little town of Seesen in Westphalia where students at a school he had founded there and their parents could pray in a decorous service that included a German sermon, some German hymns, and organ accompaniment. His dedication address, directed to Jews, Christians, and God, reflects the influence of the rationalism and universalism of the German Enlightenment. Its emphasis on the "fatherhood of God and the brotherhood of man" remained central in the Reform movement.

It has been left to the tolerance of our days to bring about and to make possible that which only a little while ago would have appeared impossible. In building this edifice, it has not been my intent to bring about a complete religious unification of all religions. One accomplishes nothing at all if one desires everything or too much at one time. What is needed is gradual and slow development as is demonstrated by nature itself, when it brings forth its greater spiritual and physical accomplishments. Any divergence from this wise procedure of our common mother Nature which human stubbornness or frivolity might suggest, would only be followed by failures or even by the very opposite of that which was desired. What I had in mind when I first thought about building this temple was *your* religious education, my Israelite brothers, *your* customs, *your* worship, etc. Be it far from me that I should have any secret intention to undermine the pillars of your faith, to diminish our old and honored principles through the glitter of new opinions, or that, because of some hidden vanity, I should become a traitor to both our religion and you. You know my faithful adherence to the faith of my fathers. I need not protest it. My actions will witness for me more than my words. But if I do seek here first some rapprochement between you and our Christian neighbors, I would ask more for your gratitude and honest help than for your criticism or even opposition. For your true and progressive enlightenment depends upon this rapprochement. On it depends the education of your spirit for true religiosity and, at the same time also, your future greater political welfare. Who would dare to deny that our service is sickly because of many useless things, that in part it has degenerated into a thoughtless recitation of prayers and formulae, that it kills devotion more than encourages it, and that it limits our religious principles to that fund of knowledge which for centuries has remained in our treasure houses without increase and without ennoblement. On all sides, enlightenment opens up new areas for development. Why should we alone remain behind?

Let us be honest, my brothers. Our ritual is still weighted down with religious customs which must be rightfully offensive to reason as well as to our Christian friends. It desecrates the holiness of our religion and dishonors the reasonable man to place too great a value upon such customs; and on the other hand, he is greatly honored if he can increasingly encourage himself and his friends to realize their dispensability. Our ecclesiastical office, the Israelite Consistory [the governing council for Westphalian Jewry], is willing to help us, is greatly concerned with the improvement of our synagogues and schools, spreads more correct principles abroad, and will, without partisanship, do the best for us even if at the moment we cannot see the flowers or fruits of these efforts.

And you, my highly honored other friends, who in name and in some aspects are different from my faith, I hope I have the full agreement of your sympathetic hearts in the principles I have set forth of the intent of this temple building, and of the hope for a happier future for my compatriots. There is nothing in this intent that in any way contradicts the principles of pure religion, of the demands of general morality, of reason, or of your own humanitarian attitude. I trust, therefore, that you will be far from receiving my brothers coldly. I trust that you will not reject them, as did your forebears only too often, but rather, that you will accept them with love into the circle of your society and business; that you will solicitously stretch out your hand to us in that rapprochement which I have sketched in its ideological outline, and for the sake of which partially I have dedicated this temple. Accept, therefore, my deepest and most devoted thanks for your warm interest in this rare celebration which you have so obviously manifested for me and my friends through your precious presence and through the expression of your sentiments.

And Thou, O God, whose mighty hand has lifted up our people once again after such long debasement, just as it happened once after a long imprisonment; Thou, O God, whose goodness has made it possible to complete the work of several years and bring it to a happy ending—grant unto us further, we pray, that we might sense the glorious traces of Thy love, of Thy benevolence, of Thy protection, both in the faith of our compatriots as in the results of this temple building. But with this confidence let us not be guilty of the indolence of delay, of the embarrassment of indecisiveness, of the mystical hope of the superstitious, and merely hope for Thine assistance. May we, conscious of our dignity, never forget *man*, the high destiny of a being whom Thou hast gifted with reason and freedom, that he might think for himself, act for himself, and whom Thou didst destine not to be a soulless machine in the plan of Thy creation. Let us never despair of the good cause of religion and mankind. Let us not lose heart when new obstacles will be thrust across our path, when we find that any beginning, like the uplifting and enlightenment of a dispersed people, can proceed but slowly and with many difficulties, and can mature only after centuries. Above all, O God, make us vividly conscious that we are brothers with all the adherents of other divine teachings; that we are descendants of one humanity which adores Thee as their common Father; that we are brothers who must learn love and gentle tolerance; brothers, finally, who under Thy guidance walk toward a common goal and who, in the end, when the mist will have been dispelled from before our eyes and all the errors gone from our spirit and all doubts removed from our reason, will meet each other on one and the same road. Amen.

Source: Israel Jacobson, "Rede des Herrn Präsidenten Jacobson," *Sulamith* 3.1 (1810): 298ff., trans. in *The Rise of Reform Judaism: A Sourcebook of Its European Origins,* ed. W. Gunther Plaut (New York: World Union for Progressive Judaism, 1963), 29–31.

Zacharias Frankel (1844)

Until his break with fellow Reformers over the question of whether Jewish tradition absolutely required use of the Hebrew language in prayer, Rabbi Zacharias Frankel

(1801–1875) represented the moderate wing within the German Reform movement. Here, in 1844, he expresses his conservative philosophy according to which the slowly changing views of the community, rather than principles espoused by rabbis, should determine the pace of reform. Conservative Judaism in America later came to regard Frankel as its spiritual progenitor.

Time hurries onward and radical reforms are demanded, but we do not want to forget that not all demands of our time are justified. But on the other hand, we cannot overlook the fact that the long-standing immobility of the past needs rectification. Until a few decades ago, Judaism had for a long period been in a state of total immobility. It satisfied the people and, therefore, their teachers did not have the right to introduce reforms even if they had been able to transcend their age. The great gap between yesterday and today has still not been bridged, and the will of our people is still firmly rooted in the past. As long as this will still pulsates strongly, we cannot and will not touch it; rather, it must be the desire of our teachers to gain the confidence of the people by leading them gently, so that ultimately they may be granted the right to reform.

Will these reforms then be valid? When the will of the people is expressed through these teachers, when they make reforms in full knowledge of their time and in the spirit of the people—what dictum, what authority could deny them this right? The will of the people, this strong power which Judaism recognizes, this will validated by history and science and represented by teachers of truth and loyalty to our faith—would not these be valid? For some time now it has been suggested that a Synod be called where theologians would agree on reforms. But a time for such a realization has not come as yet. The theologians do not express the will of the people, for they have not gained their general confidence, partly through their own fault, and partly because the popular will cannot be expressed as long as there is inner strife and as long as the struggle between the old and the new is fought so fervently. But time will heal and help to fill the gap between yesterday and today. The teachers will find in their own lack of success a new challenge to fulfil the duties which their position imposes upon them. Thus, they will become conscious of the will of the people and will become truly living representatives, and reforms will come, not out of the people's illness, but grow from living principles.

Representation of the total popular will and of science—these are the two main conditions for a reform of Judaism. Next to faith, the Jew puts his confidence in science. His whole past history of study and mental orientation guarantees that, without a genuine science of Judaism, our theologians will never have any influence upon the people. In such a science, history too will find its just tribute and due recognition.

It would be too bold to anticipate the shape of a future which perhaps is not far away, and to determine whether it will find a common way for both faith and life. But at the same time it would be a total misreading of the great ferment of our time if on one hand one criticizes the status quo and on the other the lack of definitive reform. The opposites do not as yet permit of a compromise. Either reform will break itself on the wall of opposition, or it will dissolve tradition without displacing it and will destroy it without maintaining it through progress. We aim at a worthy representation of the total will of the people and at a science of Judaism. These will lead us to our goal and aid us to find that measure for reforms which live not only in abstraction but can be translated into reality. Our slogan is *Moderate Reform* which, properly understood, will be Judaism's saving force and will contribute to its eternal continuity.

Source: Zacharias Frankel, "Ueber Reformen im Judenthume," *Zeitschrift für die religiösen Interessen des Judenthums 1* (1844): 26f., trans. in *The Rise of Reform Judaism: A Sourcebook of Its European Origins,* ed. W. Gunther Plaut (New York: World Union for Progressive Judaism, 1963), 24–25.

Abraham Geiger

Abraham Geiger (1810–1874) was the central figure in the history of the German Reform movement. As a rabbi, he served Jewish communities in various cities; as a scholar, he made major critical contributions to Jewish historical research; and during the last years of his life, he was a teacher at the Liberal rabbinical seminary in Berlin. A letter, written in 1836, indicates that his early rabbinical years in the small town of Wiesbaden were troubled by doubt as to whether Judaism would be able to meet the challenge of modernity. In 1869, after serving as rabbi in Breslau and Frankfurt, Geiger returned to Wiesbaden to dedicate its new synagogue. His dedicatory sermon attests to Geiger's growing appreciation for emotion as well as reason, for the Judaism of the prophets, and for the solidarity of the Jewish people. Although Geiger did not write a work of systematic theology, he did address issues of faith. In the third passage, taken from popular lectures he first gave while a rabbi in Breslau in 1864, Geiger presents his understanding of Revelation.

---

1. The Youthful Rebel (1836)

The course to be taken, my dear fellow, is that of critical study; the critical study of individual laws, the critical examination of individual documents—this is what we must strive for. The Talmud, and the Bible, too, that collection of books, most of them so splendid and uplifting, perhaps the most exalting of all literature of *human* authorship, can no longer be viewed as of Divine origin. Of course, all this will not come to pass today, or even tomorrow, but it should be our goal, and will continue to be so, and in this fashion we are working closely with every true endeavor and movement of our day, and we will accomplish more by study than we could by means of a hundred sermons and widespread religious instruction. For the love of Heaven, how much longer can we continue this deceit, to expound the stories of the Bible from the pulpits over and over again as actual historical happenings, to accept as supernatural events of world import stories which we ourselves have relegated to the realm of legend, and to derive teachings from them or, at least, to use them as the basis for sermons and texts? How much longer will we continue to pervert the spirit of the child with these tales that distort the natural good sense of tender youth? But how can this be changed? By driving such falsehoods into a corner, of course; by clearly revealing this paradox both to ourselves and to others; by pursuing into their secret hiding places all those who could seek to evade the issue, and thus eventually helping to bring about the great cave-in which will bury an old world beneath its ruins and open a new world for us in its place. . . .

Source: Abraham Geiger, "Briefe an J. Dérenbourg," *Allgemeine Zeitung des Judenthums* 60 (1896): 164f. (trans. Ernst J. Schlochauer), in *Abraham Geiger and Liberal Judaism,* ed. Max Wiener (Cincinnati: Hebrew Union College Press, 1981), 86–87.

2. The Rabbi (1869)

August 24, 1869

Inasmuch as Israel is and should remain unique, it is a spiritual bond that unites Israel. It is a spiritual life all its own which embraces all its members, and which will remain unchanged even under the most diversified circumstances—through all the changes of rushing events which crowd one upon the other, in the most distant lands and in the midst of differing ideologies and varying convictions. But if you should ask me: "What is the content of this ideal that binds us together with so indissoluble a bond?" I will have to answer you that man has not been endowed with the ability to give an exhaustive portrayal of a spiritual life. . . . What is true of the knowledge of God applies here also. Who would presume to set forth what God is, to seek to confine His essence into one single exhaustive concept? All we can say is that He exists and that He is the original cause of all of life. He is the All-Wise One. But it is only the traces of His infinite wisdom that we behold in that masterpiece which is the world. He is the Almighty. His rule is evident everywhere. It is he Who maintains the Universe and provides it with power to continue growing and developing. Thus you may see God even if you are not capable of grasping His essence.

. . . Of Israel's spiritual life, too, we can only say that it exists and that it manifests itself as a basic force. . . . An emanation of the Divine spirit, Israel was imbued with a creative spirit all its own and has been so to this very day. The other religious creeds are its daughters . . . and the best that is in them they owe to the spirit and tradition of Israel. Israel worked as a basic force in history. Israel exists; at first it was a small family, then it grew into a tribe and thereafter it became a whole state. And when its spirit became separated from the political state, might one not have assumed that it would vanish and that its body would disintegrate into its original components? But this never came to pass. It was only then that Israel's soul truly blossomed forth and entered into all parts of the world; and now the strength of Israel has proved itself everywhere. Even as it did not cease to grow in days of oppression, so it will not disintegrate in freedom; it will not dissipate itself into atoms to join alien configurations. To the outside, of course, in civic affairs, it will join with other elements and merge into the national life that surrounds it; but it will always retain its own spirit: it will continue to exist.

Of course, Israel is not like a stone which endures through millennia, rigid and unchangeable, which then is smashed and broken apart when the elements sweep over it. . . . No, Israel is wise; its life is a life of knowledge. Its faith, likewise, is not fixed, bound or rigid—for that would not be wisdom and eternal spiritual life. No, Israel heeded the call: "*Know* the God of your fathers and serve Him." Listen and choose for yourself; test it and see for yourself. It was not the outward, rigid law that made Israel indestructible; it was the winged message of the prophets that rendered Judaism inviolable. The lightning flashes of the spirit did not emanate from Sinai only; they flared forth also from Israel's great men, the prophets. In a world of paganism and idol worship, their message became a life-giving spiritual sun.

In later times, too, Israel remained loyal to that spirit and to knowledge, never attempting to confine freedom. . . . To be sure, the sons of Israel were part of the times in which they lived and could not rise above the level of their contemporaries in knowledge and perception. . . . But even in the darkest days, there was an inner strife and stirring which preserved the real life of Israel in strength and vigor. . . . And was it not in the darkest ages that the brightest luminaries shone forth from Israel, of all peoples? That which a great medieval thinker plainly set forth was felt by all, even unawares: faith is not an empty phrase, a formula or an assertion which you must accept unquestioningly. . . . No, faith is an idea which, rooted deep within your heart, must constitute the foundations of your spiritual being, the flower of spiritual life, the noble fruit of genuine conviction. . . . Israel never gave recognition to any belief that would not be consistent with understanding; it never worshiped as a sacred mystery that which was in contradiction with what could be comprehended by human reason.

"Faith and Reason are two beacons," each shedding its own light, but both ultimately meeting and fusing into one bright beam. This is the doctrine of Israel; this is its wisdom and this is the guarantee for its continued survival. In our days, much that blossomed in times gone by has faded away, and minds frequently are divided. But do not despair, my friends, for Israel's spiritual life remains unified. Scholarship may move along the most divergent paths; trends may split up into a host of shadings and partisan factions; yet, do not lose courage; only *one* spirit is now and shall ever be within Israel. . . . Spiritual life undergoes manifold changes in its outer manifestations, and the Divine spirit, too, reveals itself in many different forms. But it is precisely the varied nature of its manifestations that marks the existence of a genuine spiritual life in the midst of Israel.

Thirdly and lastly, my dear friends, Israel is "mighty." Israel is endowed with a vitality that ensures its survival. By this I do not mean the kind of might that relies on the strength of the arm. . . . Israel's vitality has always consisted in the endeavor to fight for that which is Divine. . . . It has given its all, and suffered without flinching or hesitation for its God and for its faith. . . .

Israel's vitality is derived from its readiness to make sacrifices when it is called upon to defend all that is great and good. . . . A testimonial of this ready devotion is also this new House of God in all its splendor and magnificence; it is a testimonial of honor for Israel, a badge of honor for this congregation, and a memorial to the noble and cheerful spirit of those who gladly gave of their own possessions for its construction.

... Israel has always distinguished itself by its good deeds and will continue to do so in unflagging zeal. In this respect it always was one whole, one unit, and has remained so to this day. No call for help from afar is allowed to go unanswered. All hasten to stretch forth the hand of brotherhood; the warm heart does not grow cool along the way, nor does it ever cease to beat. We are one, and we belong together. The good Jewish heart is the bond that unites us. Many things may have departed from our midst; many an outward ritual, many an obsolete statute has vanished from the scene. But the fountainhead still remains in full vigor; the good heart is still beating and will not die. And as long as you, my people of Israel, can say of yourselves: *Even when I seem to be asleep my heart is still awake,* then you, too, will live and survive, inviolable, eternal. . . .

―――――――――

Source: Abraham Geiger, *Nachgelassene Schriften* 1 (Berlin, 1875), 436ff., in *Abraham Geiger and Liberal Judaism,* ed. Max Wiener (Cincinnati: Hebrew Union College Press, 1981), 262–64.

3. The Theologian (1864)

Generally speaking, we may distinguish in man two mental processes—a twofold attribute with which man has been favored: we differentiate between talent, on the one hand, and genius on the other. These two may touch at some points, yet they are forever essentially different and apart from one another. This difference is not simply one of degree, but of actual essence. Talent is the gift to comprehend ideas easily and quickly, to assimilate them and then skilfully and adeptly to communicate them. However, talent is based on that which is already in existence, on past achievements and on such riches as have already been acquired. It does not create anything original. Not so genius. Genius does not lean upon anything; genius is creative. It discovers truths which were previously hidden and reveals laws which have not heretofore been known. It is as if there were revealed before it in brilliant clarity, and in their context according to their orderly interplay, those forces which work deep within the core of nature. It is as if these forces were tangibly real, as if the spiritual impulses both within the individual and within mankind as a whole have unveiled themselves before genius, so that it may peer into the inmost recesses of the soul and from there single out the driving forces which motivate the human spirit. Talent may be cultivated; it may be acquired by effort and diligence. But genius is a free gift, a favor, a mark of consecration which is imprinted upon man; if it is not present in him, he can never acquire it on his own. . . .

The Greeks boasted of having been autochthons, of having been born in and of their own soil. Whether this claim is justified is a moot question. But another claim, which may perhaps reflect its deeper meaning, may surely be acknowledged, namely, the autochthonous nature of their mind, the originality of their particular national tendency. The Greeks had neither patterns nor teachers for their art and learning. They served as their own mentors and masters, and presently they shone forth with a perfection which made them the teachers of mankind in almost every age. . . .

Does not the Jewish people, too, have such a genius, a religious genius of this type? Was it not also an original force that enlightened its eyes so that it could look more deeply into the higher spheres of the spirit, that it could discern more clearly the close relationship between the spirit of man and the Universal Spirit, that it could grasp the higher challenge of human existence and perceive the profound ethical quality in man with greater clarity and intensity, expressing it as its unique insight? If this is indeed so, then this intimate contact of the spirit of the individual with the Universal Spirit, this illumination of individual minds by the all-encompassing force so that they could break through their finite barriers, is—let us not shy away from the word—revelation as manifested in the people as a whole.

Not all the Greeks were artists, they were not all Phidias or Praxiteles, and yet the Greek people as such had the gift of producing great masters. The same was true of Judaism. Certainly not all the Jews were prophets, and the verse *Would that all the people were prophets!* was no more than a pious wish. Another verse, *I shall pour My spirit over all flesh,* is a promise which never became reality. Nevertheless, the Jewish people is the people of the revelation which subsequently gave birth to the select instruments of that revelation. They were scattered sparks of light, as it were, which, gathered together by those chosen to proclaim the revelation, shone forth fused into one single bright flame. There is no reference to the God of Moses or to the God of the Prophets; our literature speaks only of the God of Abraham, Isaac and Jacob, of the God of the entire race, of its patriarchs who showed this same predisposition, that of introspective vision. This is the revelation which lay dormant in the people as a whole and then found a unifying focal point in certain individuals. It is a truism of profound significance that even the greatest prophet of them all left his work unfinished. He was not to stand out like Atlas who bore the world upon his shoulders, carrying out a task without participating in it—inspirer and executor at once. . . .

Truly, Judaism originated with the people of the revelation. Why, then, should we not be allowed to use this term when we speak of penetration to the deepest foundation, of an illumination emanating from the higher spirit, which cannot be explained and which, though subject to later evolution, was not evolutionary in its origin? . . .

We have no intention of limiting and narrowing the term in a dogmatic fashion. It may be interpreted in many ways; but its essence always remains the same—the contact of human reason with the First Cause of all things. Notwithstanding the high regard in which the teachers of old held the concept of revelation, they never sought to deny its relationship to human endowments. The Talmud teaches that the spirit of God will rest only upon a wise man, upon a man of moral strength who is self-sufficient because he is content, having overcome all ambitions and lusts. Only a man of inner stature who senses the Divine within himself will be capable of absorbing the Divine. He must not be a mere mouthpiece through which the message is transmitted, through which the word is spoken without his being aware of it. He must be a man close to the Divine in the truest sense of the word, and therefore receptive to it. . . .

Source: Abraham Geiger, *Das Judenthum und seine Geschichte* 1 (Breslau, 1864), 27f., in *Abraham Geiger and Liberal Judaism*, ed. Max Wiener (Cincinnati: Hebrew Union College Press, 1981), 180–82.

Samuel Holdheim

In nineteenth-century Germany, Samuel Holdheim (1806–1860) represented the radical wing of the Reform movement. Unlike his rabbinical contemporaries, he eschewed compromise for the sake of unity, preferring to express his views boldly. In the first passage he insists that the gulf between tradition and present belief must be fully recognized, thus avoiding the pitfall of pretending that the Talmud is a modern document. In so doing, he speaks against the position of the moderate Reformer Levi Herzfeld (1810–1884). In his remarks at the third conference of German rabbis, in

1847, Holdheim presented a conception of the Sabbath based on sanctification rather than physical rest. Given the economic integration of German Jewry that created pressure to work on Saturday, he also argued that the only way to preserve the valuable idea of the Jewish Sabbath was to observe it on Sunday.

---

1. The Authority of the Present (1845)

Reform must avoid as much as possible to press the banner of progress into the rigid hands of the Talmud. The time has to come when one feels strong enough vis-à-vis the Talmud to oppose it, in the knowledge of having gone far beyond it. One must not with every forward step drag along the heavy tomes and, without even opening them, wait for some innocent remark, therewith to prove the foundations of progress. Incidentally, the Talmud has found its own nemesis; for exactly what the Talmud once did with the Bible, the rabbis of today now do with it. The Talmud, too, was cautious and anxious because it did not have a real, strongly founded, invigorating, reforming principle. Therefore, constantly, with every single step it glanced back at the Bible and, without having recognized that the Bible only spoke from a theocratic point of view, the Talmud superimposed upon the text of the Bible those reforms which changed circumstances had forcibly brought into existence.

Dr. Herzfeld and many others do exactly the same. They speak from their own present day ideology and yet do not trust it quite completely. They, therefore, imagine erroneously that their ideology is founded in the Talmud. But just as the Bible, if one understands it correctly, earnestly rejects all talmudic re-interpretations, so must a more exact knowledge of the Talmud earnestly and decisively reject these modern ways in which the Reformers treat it. Dr. Herzfeld should not place before us so absolute and general a statement as: "The Talmud is right." Rather, he should say, *"The Talmud speaks with the ideology of its own time, and for that time it was right. I speak from the higher ideology of my time, and for this age I am right."*

Source: Samuel Holdheim, *Das Ceremonialgesetz im Messiasreich* (Berlin & Schwerin, 1845), 48ff., trans. in *The Rise of Reform Judaism: A Sourcebook of Its European Origins,* ed. W. Gunther Plaut (New York: World Union for Progressive Judaism, 1963), 123.

2. The Essence of the Sabbath (1847)

All our efforts for the restoration of a dignified Sabbath observance are in vain, and unfortunately there is no radical means to settle the conflict between Sabbath celebration and the demands of civic life, other than changing the former to some other, occupationally unencumbered day. I protest against any concession which seems thereby to have been made to Christian principles. I have in mind only the possibility of a dignified Sabbath celebration. The wounds from which our religious life suffers cut deeply into all our hearts; and helplessness will be the mark of all our endeavors until the time comes when the only possible cure for the disease will have been prescribed.

The difficulty of changing the historically transmitted day of rest to some other day does not lie merely in the purely religious significance of the Sabbath, but rather in the symbolic biblical statement that God had rested on the seventh day, having completed all creation, hallowing and blessing the day of rest. This was tied later to the commandment to rest, which assured that this commandment referred precisely to that certain seventh day, the *Shabbat bereshit,* and that day alone has, indeed, been celebrated in Israel all along. Thus, the observance of a definite seventh day in creation is connected closely with its symbolic significance. The celebration of that day in ages past allegorically described its basically differing Jewish religious concepts vis-à-vis paganism. However, apart from the ideas which we gained elsewhere and made our own, the Sabbath can no longer have any significance for its own sake. From the narrative which tells that God had rested on the seventh day, we can, if we wish to avoid anthropomorphisms, gather only that God, after creating the universe, manifested himself as the Creator in His absolute distinction from the world. We take for granted that these and all other manifest religious truths which we have accepted are no longer symbolized by man as before, namely, by resting. It says in the Bible: Man shall hallow the Sabbath, which really means that on the Sabbath *man shall consecrate himself.* In other words, he shall celebrate the Sabbath not merely by resting but rather by actively consecrating and dedicating his existence. In this way every reason for observing that particular day ceases to exist by itself, and the purely religious meaning of the Sabbath can no longer contain any religious impediment for its modification, provided such change is governed by other religious motives.

Since the Sabbath is of crucial importance for the preservation of religion, the reasons for changing it to another day must be sought and found exclusively in the needs of preserving our religion. The Sabbath finds itself in conflict with civic life; experience shows that, in this contest, it loses ground daily and there is no hope that we will see it emerge victoriously. The Rabbinical Conference has made it its worthy task to achieve a peaceful compromise in this contest. Should it succeed in solving this problem it would not dream of lessening the importance of the Sabbath. However, if there is no other means of settling the dispute peacefully, our religion will be threatened by the greatest danger, and for the sake of its self-preservation it will and must demand imperatively the changing of the Sabbath to another day, this being the only expedient. Thus, the religious reasons for implementing a change are none other than to rescue our religion from certain perdition.

Source: Samuel Holdheim, *Protokolle der dritten Versammlung deutscher Rabbiner, vom 13. bis 24. Juli 1846* (Breslau, 1847), 70ff., trans. in *The Rise of Reform Judaism: A Sourcebook of Its European Origins,* ed. W. Gunther Plaut (New York: World Union for Progressive Judaism, 1963), 193–94.

Leo Baeck

The last great representative of Liberal Judaism in Germany was Rabbi Leo Baeck (1873–1956), who led German Jewry during the dark Nazi years. As the first passage, from his major work, The Essence of Judaism, *indicates, Baeck saw in Judaism a religion of ethical deeds performed in response to the Divine command. In the second selection from the same book, Baeck recognizes that the unfathomable but loving Creator God is the other aspect of the morally demanding God of Revelation. Miraculously, Baeck survived internment in the Terezin concentration camp. After the war, he continued to serve for ten years as president of the World Union for Progressive Judaism, the international body of the Reform movement. Baeck's thought, along with that of his contemporaries Hermann Cohen, Franz Rosenzweig, and Martin Buber, continues to influence Reform Jewish theology today.*

1. The Commandment (1926)

There is a certain danger in attributing to religious experience the decisive religious value. Religion can no more be built on it than it can be built on mere prayer; it is only a means of becoming aware of religion. For the religious experience is not yet religion itself. The religious life will never be able to dispense with this experience, for in it faith raises itself, if not to its summit, then to a sacred height. Yet man lives neither for nor on his emotional moods. "To indulge in pious reveries is easier than to do what is right," and in the past men have had slight difficulty in reconciling pious reveries with deeds that were not right. Such moods of religious emotion may mislead one to suppose that they in themselves already constitute complete religion.

Judaism teaches that religion must not be a mere internalized experience, even of the most intense kind, but rather the very fulfilment of life. Though this may seem a mere verbal distinction, it is really a distinction within the soul. Only the right deed places man in the presence of God at all times and only it can be demanded of him at all times. Through it alone can man reach that deep inner unity with God, as well as that other unity with his fellow man. If the ideal embraces everybody and imposes its demand upon all, then men are brought together into a community of God. In the pious deed is the sustaining foundation of the confession of faith. It provides the secure religious foundation, common and equal to all, for the love of God and the trust in God. We cannot truly believe in what we do not practice. He who has not become sure of God by *doing* good, will not achieve a lasting realization of God's being through a mere inner experience. It is through man's deed that God reveals himself in life. "We will do and we will hear" (Exod. 24:7), says the old phrase in the account of the revelation in Exodus, with a meaning which overflows the vessel of its words. And as the Talmud later expresses it, "Take the commandments of God to your heart, for then you will know God, and you will have discovered his ways." Knowledge too proceeds from the will—from the will for the good.

Judaism also has its Word, but it is only one word— "to do." "The word is very nigh unto thee, in thy mouth, and in thy heart, that thou mayest do it" (Deut. 30:14). The deed becomes proof of conviction. Judaism too has its doctrine, but it is a doctrine of behavior, which must be explored in action in order that it may be fulfilled. Hence there is no doctrine in Judaism other than the expression of the divine *command*. "The secret things belong to the Lord our God: but those things which are revealed belong unto us and our children for ever that we may *do* all the words of this law" (Deut. 29:28).

Source: Leo Baeck, *The Essence of Judaism*, rev. ed. (New York: Schocken Books, 1948), 55–56 (trans. Victor Grubenwieser and Leonard Pearl).

2. Mystery Joined to Commandment (1926)

If the feeling of having been created by God is the first fundamental feeling of Judaism, then the awareness of man's own creative power for doing good is its second fundamental experience. And thus a great unification is effected. To the mystery is joined the explicated; to the secret of his origin the path that he should travel; to the reality created by God the reality which man himself should create; and to the certainty of the secret the certainty of the commandment. If the former awareness gives man his place in the universe, this second awareness lifts him out of the universe and enables him to gain knowledge of that world which is to belong to him. If at first there came the searching query with its Where, How, and Why, now there comes the decisive answer with its Thou shalt, and Thou art able. If in the beginning religion showed the way from God to man, it now shows the way from man to God. Secret and commandment are united, for only the two together give the full meaning of life. The unity of both is religion as Judaism teaches it.

Thus there comes into religion the second great paradox: Man is created and yet creates; he is a product and yet produces; he belongs to the world and yet is above it; his life exists only through God and yet possesses its independence. From this contrast between miracle and freedom, between the bondage of the unfathomable and the emancipation achieved through the moral command, there arises a spiritual unity which is an answer to life's problems.

And it is in Judaism's unification of these seemingly disparate concepts that it is different from all other religions. For all other religions only affirm and cause man to experience the feeling that he has been created; they do not stress that he exists upon earth in order himself to create. They foster the first religious idea that man is dependent upon the eternal and the infinite, but since they give this a disproportionate emphasis they allow the idea of fate, a doom enclosing all phenomena, to creep into religion. And then the miracle means everything and the deed seems insignificant by comparison. For these religious faith knows only that each life has an allotted destiny to which man is elected or from which he is rejected; they do not see man himself as molding or choosing his own life so as to fashion his own destiny.

But Judaism balances in an even rhythm the sense of man's having been created by God and man's own ability himself to create. Though Judaism sees the world as laying hold of man, it also sees man as laying hold of the world. Though man may experience the meaning of the world through faith, he gives meaning to the world through his action. He has received his life, but he has to fulfil it.

Only now does the relationship between man and God attain its full significance. Having learned that he has to realize the good, man also discovers that God stands before him as the Commanding One, the Judging One and the Just One; he sees that God demands of him the moral deed and puts the command before him so that it may be fulfilled. "He hath shewed thee, O man, what is good; and what doth the Lord require of thee . . . " (Mic. 6:8). "And now, Israel, what doth the Lord thy God require of thee . . . " (Deut. 10:12). The God who creates and grants love is at the same time the ethical holy will; he is the God of the commandment who demands righteousness. Just as divine love gave and created, so divine justice commands; it places unconditional duty in the forefront of man's life. If love tells man what he is because of God, then justice tells him what he ought to be before God. And only the two together are a full revelation of the One God; only the two together disclose the full meaning of human existence. Through their unity is revealed the deepest content of the unity of God. It is a special characteristic of this unity that the hidden and unfathomable elements of our life tell us of the love of God while the clear and definite elements tell us of God's commanding justice. It is man as an individual who experiences all this; the commandment speaks to his personality. He hears the question put to him by God, "Where art thou?" To the individual man God appears as a personal God. All thought of God becomes the word with which he speaks to us and to us alone; it becomes the expression of the obligation which we feel toward him. If man's yearning first expressed itself by turning to God with questions and hopes, by exclaiming "my God," the soul now learns to reply to God with the understanding that God demands and expects. The word of God enters the life of man, demanding a decision from him: "I am the Lord thy God, thou *shalt.*"

Source: Leo Baeck, *The Essence of Judaism*, rev. ed. (New York: Schocken Books, 1948), 120–22 (trans. Victor Grubenwieser and Leonard Pearl).

Ismar Elbogen (1931)

Summing up the history of the Reform movement in Germany in 1931, Ismar Elbogen (1874–1943), a professor at the Liberal seminary in Berlin, pointed to its shortcom-

ings. Liberal Judaism had succeeded in altering theology and liturgy, but it had not sustained religious fervor. Elbogen's critique remains relevant for the contemporary Reform movement.

The real nature of Reform does not consist of shortening prayers and giving second place to Hebrew, but of those changes in the text which proceed from dogmatic considerations and from opposition to or differential interpretation of religious teachings. The main issues have been the doctrine of bodily resurrection and the belief in a personal Messiah with whose appearance are connected the restoration of the Temple and of the sacrificial cult, the ingathering of the dispersed people of Israel and their return to Zion—doctrines which were reflected in the prayers. In contrast to the demand for other changes (introduction of sermons, use of the vernacular) which were understood by almost everyone, most dogmatic reservations were brought forth primarily by men with theological training and never enjoyed great popularity. Very little interest was elicited by changes which went beyond those already made in the Hamburg Temple.

This dichotomy between the interests of the theologians and the understanding of the congregations provides an important reason why the success of the Reform movement stands in no real relationship to the expenditure of care and energy and the ensuing upheaval of congregational life. In their idealistic enthusiasm the leaders of the Reform movement lost the perspective for the realistic situation. They vastly overestimated both the general progress of their age and the growth of religious education amongst the Jews. Just as little as the revolutionary promises of the year 1848 initiated the hoped-for time of mankind redeemed, so little did the opinions which were expressed in the rabbinical assemblies bring about a fundamental enlightenment amongst our co-religionists. The thin upper layer of the intelligentsia who adopted those theories was preoccupied with its interest in general culture. Its members remained rather indifferent to the religious movement and proved to be a weak staff of support for it. The broad masses, however, whose life was rooted in the views and forms of the past went forth empty-handed. Theological reform could not capture their emotions and its dogmatic decisions did not have the power to evoke enthusiasm.

Besides, the circumstances of the time were not too favorable. They directed the main attention of men toward a chase for acquisition and pleasure and turned them far away from the pursuit of a Messianic ideal. The

Reformers, confident of their example and their doctrine, proved their courage and decisiveness by proceeding, without long theoretical considerations, to jump quickly into the fray and try to change life itself. But the disadvantages of such precipitated procedure were soon in evidence. Reforms were made with cool and calculating reason and much of the poetry and the feeling content of the service were sacrificed to sober rationalism. The scientific justification of the new views had been undertaken only a short time before, but theology quickly committed itself to opinions which did not always prove to be scientifically sound and which met with decided opposition in the congregation. History has rendered its negative verdict on all radical innovations; it justifies only a steady development which builds upon the past.

The mistakes which were made in the beginning of the movement damaged its development permanently, even though there are signs that now its situation is more favorable. There is enough work to do. Little is accomplished by changing and shortening prayers, if enthusiasm and understanding for the service itself cannot be awakened at the same time. But this above all has been missing so far, and least of all has the Reform movement reached this, the most prominent of its goals. It has not succeeded in bringing the hoped-for freedom into its worship forms because its followers lacked the necessary appreciation and a deep, loving comprehension. Even the dangers of externalization were not spared the Reform service, for it has evidenced the same rigidities as had the old services. Finally, the fear which was expressed a hundred years ago at the beginning of the movement has fulfilled itself in frightening fashion. Despite the simplification of the service there has been no corresponding familiarity with it. Indifference towards its institution has grown and is in fact greatest where the demands for "timely" change have been most completely satisfied.

Precisely here lies the most important task for the future, that is, to reawaken the fervor of prayer and the enthusiasm for divine worship. The service must become once again what it was to our fathers—the center of religious life and the place for religious contemplation and dedication.

Source: Ismar Elbogen, *Der jüdische Gottesdienst,* 3rd ed. (Frankfurt, 1931), 441ff., trans. in *The Growth of Reform Judaism: American and European Sources until 1948,* ed. W. Gunther Plaut (New York: World Union for Progressive Judaism, 1965), 304–6.

THE MAJOR INSTITUTIONS
OF REFORM JUDAISM

✦ Although American Reform Judaism has numerous institutions and organizations, with differing constituencies and purposes, four are primary: the Union of American Hebrew Congregations (UAHC); the Hebrew Union College–Jewish Institute of Religion (HUC-JIR); the Central Conference of American Rabbis (CCAR); and the World Union for Progressive Judaism (WUPJ).

The first to be established, in 1873, was the UAHC. Although the idea of a congregational union had long been championed by Rabbi Isaac Mayer Wise of Cincinnati, the final impetus for its creation came from laypeople, especially the president of Wise's congregation, Moritz Loth. Its initial activity was almost exclusively focused on maintaining the first successful rabbinical seminary in the United States, the Hebrew Union College, established under Wise's leadership in 1875. In 1922 Rabbi Stephen S. Wise established the Jewish Institute of Religion, a rival liberal seminary in New York. Not until 1950 did the two institutions merge fully to create HUC-JIR.

Once there were sufficient rabbinical graduates, Isaac Mayer Wise, in 1889, organized them into the CCAR, which was at first a regional organization but soon became a national entity. Ever since, these three institutions, representing the laity, scholarship, and the rabbinate, have directed the course of American Reform Judaism. Not until 1926 did the American Reform movement join with its counterparts elsewhere to create the WUPJ, at first centered in London and today in the State of Israel.

The following selections are taken from different periods in the history of each institution so that the reader can gain awareness both of the initial purposes of each and of how those purposes have changed over the years.

The Union of American Hebrew Congregations

As the first selection, taken from the Proceedings of the first General Convention of the UAHC, indicates, the earliest member congregations were greatly concerned to maintain their autonomy within the UAHC, and that continued to be the case when a new constitution, reflecting a fresh order of priorities, was adopted in 1946. The current version indicates a broader view that looks beyond institutional concerns, while the preamble to the report of the UAHC long-range planning commission lays out a high-minded vision of the ideal Reform Jew.

---

1. Objectives of the UAHC (from the first constitution, 1873)

It is the primary object of the Union of American Hebrew Congregations to establish a Hebrew Theological Institute—to preserve Judaism intact; to bequeath it in its purity and sublimity to posterity—to Israel united and fraternized; to establish, sustain, and govern a seat of learning for Jewish religion and literature; to provide for and advance the standard of Sabbath-schools for the instruction of the young in Israel's religion and history, and the Hebrew language; to aid and encourage young congregations by such material and spiritual support as may be at the command of the Union; and to provide, sustain, and manage such other institutions which the common welfare and progress of Judaism shall require—*without, however, interfering in any manner whatsoever with the affairs and management of any congregation.* *

Source: The Union of American Hebrew Congregations, *Proceedings of the First General Convention*, 22–23.

2. From the New Constitution of the UAHC (1946)

Preamble

The congregations represented in this Union of American Hebrew Congregations affirm their faithful attachment to Judaism and their adherence

---

*Italicized in the original text.

to its liberal interpretation, and unite to discharge their responsibilities under the protection of benign Providence.

Objects

a) To encourage and aid the organization and development of Jewish congregations.
b) To promote Jewish education and to enrich and intensify Jewish life.
c) To maintain the Hebrew Union College.
d) To foster other activities for the perpetuation and advancement of Judaism.

Congregational Autonomy

Nothing contained in this Constitution or the By-laws shall be construed so as to interfere in any manner whatsoever with the mode of worship, the school, the freedom of expression and opinion, or any of the other congregational activities of the constituent congregations of the Union.

Source: The Union of American Hebrew Congregations, *71st–73rd Annual Reports,* 287.

3. Mission Statement from the Amended Constitution (1995)

The mission of the Union is to provide vision, leadership and programmatic support to Reform Jewish congregations and to perpetuate and advance Reform Judaism. To fulfill its mission, the UAHC has four major goals.

a) To promote the enrichment and growth of Judaism through Reform Jewish congregations.
b) To foster the vibrancy of Reform Judaism through Torah (lifelong Jewish education), *Avodah* (worship of God through prayer and observance) and *G'milut Chasadim* (the pursuit of justice, peace and deeds of loving-kindness).
c) To support the Hebrew Union College–Jewish Institute of Religion, enabling it to train rabbis, cantors, educators and other professionals and scholars who are essential to the spiritual and educational life of our religious community.
d) To be supportive of the State of Israel and the Jewish people and foster

the development of Liberal Judaism worldwide under the auspices of the World Union for Progressive Judaism.

Source: UAHC website, www.uahc.org.

4. Preamble to the Report of the UAHC Long-Range Planning Committee (November 1995)

It is our goal that future generations of Reform Jews be characterized by the following:

1. Faith *(Emunah):* Jews who share an awareness of God's Presence in their lives through cultivating a sense of the sacred *(k'dushah),* through embracing religious and moral obligations (mitzvot), and through the commitment *(b'rit)* between God and the Jewish people.

2. Study *(Talmud Torah):* Jews who learn and teach our sacred texts, our history, and/or traditions, listening to the voice of God that addresses the individual heart and mind.

3. Prayer *(T'fillah):* Jews who value and practice individual and communal prayer on a regular basis, seeking through prayer to relate their lives to the Divine.

4. Observance and Celebration *(Sh'mirah Vachagigah):* Jews who sanctify and enhance their communal, family, and personal lives by the rhythm of Jewish observances and celebrations in both the synagogue and their home.

5. Morality *(Musar):* Jews who reflect high moral standards in their career and personal life and who advocate those same values in our society and world.

6. Social Justice *(Tikkun Olam):* Jews who take personal responsibility for mending our world through individual and collective religious action—the quest for social justice, the enhancement of individual dignity and freedom, the pursuit of peace, and the preservation of a habitable planet for future generations.

7. Love of the Jewish People *(Ahavat Yisrael):* Jews who actively promote the welfare of all Jews *(k'lal Yisrael)* throughout the world out of a sense of love, mutual responsibility, shared history, and common destiny.

8. Love of Zion *(Ahavat Tzion):* Jews who, even as they build a vibrant Jewish life in North America, affirm their historic and spiritual bond

to the Land of Israel and work to strengthen the hands of those Jews who strive to build a democratic, just, and religiously pluralistic society in the State of Israel.

9. Reform Judaism *(Yahadut Mitkademet):* Jews who are wholeheartedly and actively committed to Reform Judaism — in its religious philosophy, its synagogues, its national and international institutions — finding in the Reform movement the best means for instilling spiritual content and moral purpose into their lives as Jews and as human beings.

Source: The Union of American Hebrew Congregations, "Teaching Teachers Reform Judaism," *Torah at the Center* 2, no. 1 (Rosh Hashanah 5759), 9–10.

The Hebrew Union College—Jewish Institute of Religion

The first published catalogue of the Hebrew Union College, issued for the academic year 1894-1895, seeks to attract a wide range of students. Fifty years later, its catalogue looks back on the first half century and stresses the new tasks laid upon the college by the developing Holocaust in Europe. The Jewish Institute of Religion's Announcement for the year 1923–1924, probably written by Rabbi Stephen S. Wise, reveals his intent that JIR be open to the expression of contradictory points of view. The most recent HUC-JIR catalogue reflects the commitment of the College-Institute and its president, Rabbi Sheldon Zimmerman, both to Reform Judaism and to academic integrity.

---

1. From the Programme of the Hebrew Union College (1894–1895)

According to its organic laws, the Hebrew Union College imposes no test whatever besides competency on its members, either teachers or students. Every person coming up to its standard of admission . . . is accepted among the regular students, and receives free of expense the tuition, use of the library—including text-books—and all other benefits the College affords. It furthermore limits personal freedom of thought, speech and action only by the dicta of common morality, the laws of the land, and the diciplinary regulations of the Institute. It is strictly free to all denominations, and moral, law-abiding persons, and invites all to come and learn.

Source: Programme of the Hebrew Union College, 1894–1895, 10.

2. *From the Catalogue of the Hebrew Union College (1944–1945)*

This College, the oldest Jewish theological school in the Americas, is dedicated to the preservation of Judaism, its great historic ideals and its traditional institutions. It holds that Judaism is both in spirit and fact a continuously progressive religious discipline, and that it must be kept constantly liberal and spiritually alert. It believes that if Judaism is to live and expand here in America it must be open to every positive influence of modernism, must square itself with every advance in scientific thought, and must engender that type of religious devotion which will evoke the uncompromising loyalty of every Jew.

In accordance with these basic principles the Hebrew Union College has carried on its work. Its first sessions were held in the vestry rooms of Congregations B'nai Israel and B'nai Yeshurun. The original teaching staff consisted of Rabbi Wise and one assistant. Seventeen students responded to the first call. The Library in those days contained little more than a few Bibles and prayer-books hastily gathered from nondescript sources. From these modest beginnings the College has grown steadily under the leadership of its successive Presidents, Isaac M. Wise (1875–1900), Moses Mielziner (1900–1903), Gotthard Deutsch (February 1903–June 1903), and Kaufmann Kohler (1903–1921). Today its Faculty consists of one professor emeritus, eleven active professors, and nine special instructors. During the sixty-nine years of its existence it has graduated four hundred and seventy-five rabbis. Its Library, now one of the three largest Jewish libraries in the world, contains approximately 100,000 volumes and 2,500 manuscripts. Its staff consists of a Librarian and six assistants. It has its own bindery and photostatic department. The College is housed in five stately buildings upon its own tract of land, consisting of approximately eighteen acres, situated on Clifton Avenue opposite beautiful Burnet Woods. . . .

Today the Hebrew Union College is conscious that the greatest challenge in its history lies before it. Jewish life and scholarship in Europe have been crushed or rigidly circumscribed. The future of world Jewry, certainly for our generation, rests in America. No one at this hour can question this fact. American Jewry, and particularly the Hebrew Union College, is preparing itself to give to Jews, wherever they may be, the spiritual and religious leadership they must have, in order to survive.

This College has already reared three generations of American Jewish leaders who have gone into the communities of the United States, into

Canada, Cuba, Panama, England, Palestine, South Africa, and have fought for the ideals of religion and social justice in accordance with Judaism's prophetic tradition. They have been a positive force for truth, justice and social betterment among Jews and non-Jews in every community where their voices have been heard.

Today during this crisis, created by the second World War, the College has anticipated its historic obligations by appointing to its staff eleven distinguished Jewish refugee scholars from all parts of the war-torn world, giving them the opportunity to carry on their scientific studies in the quiet and security of free America.

Jewish scholarship, communal leadership, and religious idealism have been the guiding principles of this College throughout the past and will be fostered with even more determined purpose in the future which is dawning for the Judaism and Jewry of tomorrow.

Source: Catalogue of the Hebrew Union College, 1944–1945, 1–2.

3. From the Preliminary Announcement of the Jewish Institute of Religion (1923–1924)

The Jewish Institute of Religion is founded in the conviction that the large Jewish population of America, now more than three and one-half millions, requires additional institutions for the training of men for the Jewish ministry, research and community service. The logical centre for this institution is New York City, which today contains approximately one-half of the Jews of the United States and one-tenth of the Jews in the world. This large Jewish community, largest in the history of Israel, constitutes an unequalled laboratory for study, training and research. Here men will be able to acquire the necessary learning and may also study at first hand the different groups of which the Jewish community is composed and the various ways in which the Jewish spirit expresses itself.

The Jewish Institute of Religion, liberal in spirit, does not commit its teachers and students to any special interpretation of Judaism. All Jews possess in common the same literature, the same history, the same varied religious experiences, and these will be studied scientifically in the classroom. The different interpretations of the literature, history and religion, the different constructions of Judaism and of Jewish life, orthodox, conservative, liberal, radical, Zionist and non-Zionist, will be expounded to the students in courses given by men representing these different points of view.

Every member of the Teaching Staff will be free to seek and to state the truth as he sees it, and in the same way every student will be free.

The Jewish Institute of Religion will also make available to the general public a constructive knowledge of Judaism, its spiritual and social ideals, its history and its outlook, its contribution to the world's progress and store of good. It is believed that there are many, both Jews and non-Jews, who, without devoting themselves to specialized studies in Jewish literature, history and religion, would welcome an opportunity to add to their general culture through an attractive and popular exposition of subjects of Jewish interest.

Source: Preliminary Announcement of the Jewish Institute of Religion, 1923–1924, 6.

4. From the HUC-JIR Catalogue (1997–1999)

The Hebrew Union College–Jewish Institute of Religion is the intellectual, academic, and spiritual center of North American Reform Judaism. Its faculty, administration, student body, and literary resources represent our fervent hope for the future, our commitment to the present, and our continuity with all the generations of the past. A learned community and the attainment of academic excellence are essential for creative Jewish survival into the twenty-first century and beyond. We proudly take our place in the unfolding story of the Jewish people, its covenant with God, and its place in the service and history of humankind.

Sheldon Zimmerman
President and Rosh Yeshiva

The Hebrew Union College–Jewish Institute of Religion defines itself as the academic arm of Reform Judaism dedicated to the study of Jewish and related disciplines in the spirit of free inquiry, with nothing in the Jewish past or present alien to its interest. The College-Institute is committed to the propositions that it must be sensitive to the challenge of a changing world and that Jewish ideas and values are meaningful to the building of the future. Students are welcome who meet the College-Institute's standards of scholarship and who, whatever their faith, are devoted to the exploration of the Judaic heritage. The College-Institute sees itself as standing for freedom of research, publication, and instruction.

Resolution of the Board of Governors

Source: HUC-JIR Catalogue, 1997–1999, [3].

The Central Conference of American Rabbis

In his remarks to the first regular convention of the CCAR, in 1890, its president,
Rabbi Isaac Mayer Wise, stresses its role of support to individual members when their
views come under attack and its mission to advance Judaism as a universal religion.
In his presidential address almost a hundred years later, Rabbi Jack Stern chooses
instead to dwell on the nature of the contemporary rabbinical role.

---

1. From Rabbi Wise's Address to the CCAR Convention (1890)

The united Rabbis of America have undoubtedly the right—also according
to Talmudical teachings—to declare and decide, anyhow for our country,
with its peculiar circumstances, unforeseen anywhere, which of our religious
forms, institutions, observances, usages, customs, ordinances and prescrip-
tions are still living factors in our religious, ethical and intellectual life, and
which are so no longer and ought to be replaced by more adequate means
to give expression to the spirit of Judaism and to reveal its character of
universal religion. It is undoubtedly the duty and right of the united rabbis
to protect Judaism against stagnation and each individual rabbi against the
attacks frequently made upon every one who proposes any reform measure.
Let the attack be made hereafter on the Conference and let the honor of
the individual be preserved intact. All reforms ought to go into practice on
the authority of the Conference, not only to protect the individual rabbi, but
to protect Judaism against presumptuous innovations and the precipitations
of rash and inconsiderate men. The Conference is the lawful authority in all
matters of form. . . .

Whatever advances the spirit of Judaism in its true character as universal
religion it is the right and duty of the united rabbis in conference
assembled to do, and to do it well, in the name of God and Israel, for
the sake of our country and our people, for the triumph of truth,
humanity and righteousness.

Whatever the individual could not or should not do, and yet ought to be
done in support of Israel's mission or in advancement of American Judaism,
the Conference could and should do. The collective learning and piety is a
power for good by sincere cooperation. If many support one, one is a power.
If one sustains many, he becomes the wisdom and energy of many. If the

spirit of Judaism is to be developed to universal religion and provided with the forms and means to be accessible to the common intelligence—and this is our mission and duty—we must have the united rabbinate, the annual Conference, the earnest and steady work of all our intellectual forces united in one power. With this Conference we enter upon the new phase of American Judaism as the free messenger of God to a free people, a kingdom of priests to anoint a holy nation. Let the work be equal to the ideal, and the success as rich as the Lord's promise to all his anointed messengers; "Jehovah said unto me, thou art my son, I have this day begotten thee."

Source: Isaac Mayer Wise, "Historical Oration," *CCAR Yearbook* 1 (1890–1891): 19–21.

2. From the President's Message (1987)

The rabbinate is in fact a profession and in truth a calling. . . . Can we, as teachers of Torah, offer to those who are willing to learn "a spiritual force" . . . a moral compass . . . a transcendental purpose . . . a sense of their personal worth? Can we help them release their own bottled-up spiritual energy? Can we persuade them to live their lives in awareness of the One before whom all of us stand?

My answer to these questions, after 35 years in this Conference, is that every rabbi I know has stood before some kind of thornbush, its flame unconsumed. Every rabbi I know has responded to some kind of calling, and that calling is at the soul of that rabbi's life. Every rabbi I know has his or her sacred stories to tell.

We touch lives and we teach Jews—even more than we ourselves may realize: not only when the *b'nei mitzvah* [those becoming bar or bat mitzvah] stand with us in front of the ark but during the preparation time when they are sure they can never do it—and we give them the assurance that they can; not only in the moments of *kiddushin* [marriage] under the *chupah,* but when we ask them in the pre-marriage discussion why they want to be married, and sometimes for the first time they confront the holiness of that question; not only when we say *kaddish* at the graveside or give the eulogy at the funeral—but when we talk to the family in advance and one by one they weave a sacred story of love and of life.

We teach and we touch—not only the faithful who are there from Shabbat to Shabbat or from class to class, but those who are there in crisis—and not only the crises of their personal lives but also of their world: Sabra and Shatila; Jewish names in public scandals; the Friday afternoon that Jack Kennedy was killed that became the Friday night when our synagogues were thronged. They came for "transcendental purpose." For "moral compass." To be taught and be touched and be held. . . .

Human beings that we are, rabbis that we are, every time we stand before our own thornbush, something happens by the time we walk away. None of us remains the same after we officiate at the funeral of a suicide, or of a child, or when the one who lies before us was our friend. None of us remains the same when we stand under the *chupah* with brides and grooms whom we knew when they were children, or above all, when they are our own children, *im yirtseh haShem* [if it shall be God's will]. None of us stays the same after we have given a really good sermon—or a really bad one. Never the same, as our marriage blossoms with one at our side to give us strength and love—and to tell us the truth about our sermons. No rabbi remains the same after our first child is born—which is precisely the time we cease to be experts on children. No rabbi remains the same after the first trip to Israel or the second or the tenth—or whenever we breathe the air of a Jerusalem morning.

So here we are: these human rabbis with a profession and a calling. And here they are: these changing congregations with many good people, many caring Jews. Some of them in need. Some in search. . . .

My hope for our Conference . . . is to provide a network of opportunities and resources that will respond to the personal and professional needs of our colleagues. Pain can be avoided—sometimes. Confrontation can be headed off—sometimes.

Why the strain and conflicts? Sometimes, I believe, because of a gaping void on the other side: in the education and understanding on the part of our congregational leadership about their relationship to rabbis. How does the leadership of a congregation shift gears from the moment when they decide who will be their new rabbi to all of the subsequent moments when that same person (whose destiny they have just determined) now becomes their leader, their teacher, and sometimes even their critic—hopefully their loving critic? How do they then shift back again at contract time when the destiny of their leader and their critic is again in their hands? How does the leadership of a congregation respond to the new corporate mentality which prepares questionnaires, to be distributed to the entire congregation, for the evaluation of its rabbi? How should a congregation be guided to a *cheshbon* [accounting] of its own moral accountability when it considers disengaging the rabbi who has served for 20 or 25 years? How do we motivate congregational leaders who have carefully listed the rabbi's responsibilities to the congregation, to ask of that same rabbi: "And what do you expect of us?"

Ultimately, how do we construct a model, a realistic model, for rabbi-congregation relationships where mutual expectations are Jewishly appropriate and graced with integrity? . . .

At the heart of the matter is the imperative for congregations and rabbis to acknowledge that a climate of adversariness is the *failure* of the relationship and not to inherent to it, that rabbis and congregations are *shutafim*, partners, in transforming their building and themselves into what their title often claims them to be: a *K'hillah K'doshah* [holy congregation]. For all of us, may it come to pass in our day.

Source: Jack Stern, "The President's Message," *CCAR Yearbook* 97 (1987): 10–13.

The World Union for Progressive Judaism

When it was created in 1926, the WUPJ had as its principal purpose to create new congregations, especially in Europe. The move of its headquarters to Jerusalem, in 1974, indicated an expanding interest in Progressive Judaism in Israel, though not to the detriment of furthering it elsewhere around the world, especially in the former Soviet Union, where numerous Progressive congregations have come into existence in recent years.

---

1. From the Constitution of the World Union (1926)

Preamble

The World Union for Progressive Judaism, inspired by the belief of the Prophets in the mission of Israel to spread the knowledge of God, declares that that belief lays upon Israel the duty to work for a further recognition, by Jews and by all mankind, of the religious and ethical demands of righteousness, brotherly love and universal peace.

The World Union, convinced of the capacity for development inherent in the Jewish religion, declares that it is the duty of each generation of Jews to bring the religious teachings and practices of their fathers into harmony with developments in thought, advances in knowledge, and changes in the circumstances of life.

Name

The Name of this organisation shall be "The World Union for Progressive Judaism" (hereinafter referred to as "The World Union").

The term "Progressive" shall include all forms of Judaism which are in harmony with the principles of the Preamble whether designated "Liberal," "Reform," "Progressive," or by any other name.

Purpose

The objects of the World Union are:

To further the development of Progressive Judaism; to encourage the formation of Progressive Jewish Religious Communities or Congregations in the different countries of the world and to promote their co-operation; to stimulate and encourage the study of Judaism and its adaptation and application to modern life without changing the fundamental principles of Judaism, and to awaken an active interest in Progressive Judaism among those Jews who, for one reason or another, do not participate in Jewish religious life.

In furtherance of these objects the World Union will as far as possible keep its members informed of the developments of thought, and the progress in Judaism throughout the world, and in those countries in which there are no progressive congregations, the World Union may, through such representatives and organisers as the Governing Body, from time to time, appoint, co-operate with and assist residents of the said countries in organising such congregations.

Source: Constitution of the World Union for Progressive Judaism (n.p., n.d.), 91–92.

2. Excerpts from a Keynote Address by Retiring Executive Director, Rabbi Richard Hirsch (1999)

During this convention we celebrate the 25th anniversary of the transfer of the World Union's International Headquarters to Israel. In my judgment, the commitment to build a strong, indigenous, liberal movement in the Jewish state was the most consequential decision made during the last half century of Progressive Judaism. . . . This evening I would like to share with you some of the objectives which have motivated me.

Objective One: To move Progressive Judaism from the periphery to the center of Jewish life. . . .

To become major players, we were obliged to join the World Zionist Organization and the Jewish Agency for Israel, the prime international organizations of world Jewry centered in Israel. Were we aware in advance of some allegations of politicization and ineffectiveness directed against these institutions? Yes; but we dared not permit these shortcomings to absolve us from sharing responsibility as full partners in the vital tasks undertaken by world Jewry: the struggle to rescue Soviet Jewry and Ethiopian Jewry and other endangered communities; the efforts to absorb immigration; to settle the land; to Zionize Jewish education, and to enhance the quality of life in Israel. To move the International Headquarters to Jerusalem and not to join the national institutions of Jewish life would have been like ushering the bride to the *chupah* and not placing the ring on her finger. We wanted to get married to Jewish destiny.

Objective Two: To demonstrate that as a movement we need Israel as the testing ground of Reform Jewish authenticity. . . .

We dare not be oblivious to this challenge. If Progressive Judaism can develop and thrive only in a non-Jewish environment, if we cannot succeed in impacting on the lives and values of Jews living in the Jewish state, then the charges of our critics may be substantiated. Therefore, the ultimate test of Jewish authenticity for Progressive Judaism lies in our efforts in Israel. If we succeed in Israel, we pass the test. If we fail in Israel, then doubt is cast on the authenticity of our Diaspora movement. . . .

Objective Three: In the process of demonstrating that Progressive Judaism needs Israel, we shall begin to demonstrate that Israel needs Progressive Judaism. . . .

When they support our rights, Israelis are not doing us any favors. They need liberal Judaism. Just as the struggle on behalf of Soviet Jewry accelerated the attainment of democratic rights for all peoples in the USSR, just as the struggle for racial equality in America advanced the pursuit of democratic rights for all citizens, so support of our struggle is essential for the well-being of Israeli society. To guarantee rights for all streams of Judaism is to guarantee the preservation of Israeli democracy for the entire society, just as to deprive us of our fundamental rights will inevitably weaken the democratic institutions of Israeli society. Liberal Judaism is an idea whose time has come. But not only for liberal Jews, for all society. . . .

Objective Four: To participate in the ongoing process of responding to the critical question: What should be the Jewish character of the Jewish state?. . .

The ultimate goal is to impact on those individuals in search who have begun to discover that secularism and nationalism are inadequate alternatives to fundamentalist Orthodoxy. This is where we as a liberal movement enter. We are engaged in a struggle for the soul of the Jewish people. It is a struggle to win the minds and hearts of individual Jews. It is a struggle which will shape the character and fate of the Jewish state, and ultimately of world Jewry.

Source: "Excerpts from a Keynote Address by Retiring Executive Director, Rabbi Richard Hirsch," *WUPJ News,* 11 March 1999, pp. 3–7.

THREE

THEOLOGY

✦ Theology (the knowledge of God) is relatively new as a separate discipline in Judaism. While philosophers like Saadyah, Maimonides, and Judah Halevi wrote extensively about God's existence, presence, and relationship with Israel as the Chosen People, they considered themselves and were thought of as philosophers rather than theologians. The latter discipline came into its own through developments in the Christian world. Especially in the nineteenth century, scientific inquiry and the explosive impact of Darwinian theory appeared to threaten Christian teaching and dogma, and theologians attempted to firm up the knowledge of and belief in God. While Jews were affected by this confrontation, their major attention was directed to the practice or non-practice of mitzvot, rather than to matters of belief.

But in the mid-twentieth century, God-belief weakened seriously among Jews under the impact of the Holocaust. Though Christian "Death-of-God" theology found little resonance among Jewish thinkers, the diminution of faith among Jews had become real, and many had installed science as the primary guidepost of their lives.

Jewish theology now became a discipline in its own right, a development that was centered in Reform Judaism. Since the movement had abandoned the traditional assumption that compliance with halachah was demanded by God, the question naturally arose what it was that God demanded of us. This fundamental inquiry has become a fertile field for Reform Jewish thinkers, a selection of whose views is represented in the following. The reader must keep in mind that excerpts from a body of complex argumentation cannot do full justice to the author's presentation.

Introduction (1890)

Isaac M. Wise set the tone in 1890 when he addressed the CCAR on the theme "On Judaism."

We are ... agreed, I trust, that the spirit of Judaism, made intelligible to us in its literary monuments and its historical revelations, is the essence of universal religion, the future religion of mankind, as its rays of light and fructifying energy are now the underlying principles and efficient cause of the civilized world's religious systems. Human reason can conceive no idea or ideal of Deity superior to the Jehovah of Moses, the absolute Being by whom and in whom the All exists, lives and perpetuates itself in its innumerable varieties of forms; who is in His manifestations, both in nature and history, absolute power, universal and sovereign intellect, supreme love and benignity, the only perfect being. So Moses teaches and defines the Supreme Being, and this is the underlying doctrine of Judaism. None can rise higher than to the highest, hence none did and none ever will rise above the Mosaic conception and revelation of Deity. On the contrary, human speculation in theology, science and philosophy has proved itself incapable of producing or even reaching the Jehovah of Mosaic revelation; it has submerged and obscured the main ideas on the one hand in a pool of anthromorphisms and fetichisms, in order, as it is maintained, to accommodate the sublime thoughts to the weakness of human reason; and halts, on the other hand, in the professed ignorance of agnosticism or the abyss of despair of atheism. It is not unreasonable to maintain that the Jehovah of Moses is a divine revelation after we know that all mankind these thousands of years could not duplicate and not improve it. If we add thereto that all doctrines, precepts, commandments and ordinances of religion, be it form of worship, ethics, government or concerning Providence, personal immortality, reward and punishment, remission of sins, the conception of the world, the hopes and future of mankind on earth, and all other matters of religion can be derived only from man's cognition of Deity, and in rational harmony with the divine nature; admit as we must that the cognition of truth, the right, the good and the beautiful in all those matters must be in proportion to our cognition of God and his nature;

and add thereto that the Mosaic Jehovah is the highest conception of Deity attainable by man; you must admit that the spirit of Judaism is the essence of universal religion of mankind.

Source: Isaac M. Wise, "Historical Oration," *CCAR Yearbook* 1 (1890–1891): 17–18.

A Growing God (1977)

Henry Slonimsky (1884–1970), a disciple of neo-Kantian philosopher Hermann Cohen, taught at the Jewish Institute of Religion. He concluded that the traditional concept of God could no longer explain the tragedies of modern times.

Why [do] most prayers seem to go unheeded and unanswered? The answer to that is that this is not true. True prayers never go unanswered. But what is true prayer? We shall see later that it is a prayer which God Himself puts into our hearts to give back to Him enriched by our fervor, our power. That is true of all inspiration and so of religious communion with the Godhead. And the answer to such true prayer is always a gift of power, a gift from the great reservoir of power.

And if in the supremely tragic case in which it happens that man prays, and God gives, and still both together go down in apparent defeat, that defeat is inevitable in a world slowly growing, and where the forces of darkness, of blindness, opaqueness, indifference or even malice, against which God and man are together leagued and arrayed, are still in the ascendant. Moreover, that defeat itself is a spiritual victory, because it is an heroic effort, which pushes back the domain of darkness and suffuses with light and spirit the opaqueness and indifference of the lower order, and adds stature to God and man. That heroic effort on the part of man aided by God is the supreme act of spiritual creation, the creation of a new order of being.

And finally, the smart question is why we should have to pray at all to a God who should know us and who therefore should supply our wants without our troubling Him.

Our theory of the correlation of God and Man, whereby they mutually re-enforce each other in a mystic life-giving circle, growing together through each other's gift and enrichment, holds for religion as for all the major creative efforts of man—for music and poetry and the arts of beauty, as for the visions of justice and government and character and love. God is the source of inspiration, but man must do the work and give it back to Him enriched—fashioned, articulated, built. "In Thy light we see light" is the simple literal truth: inspiration is from God. But it is we who must weave that light into a fabric and utterance. God hands a chalice to mankind which mankind must hand back to Him at the end of days, foaming with its own inner saps and juices, its own sweat and blood and wine, its own infinite experience. Not the alternative of Christian theology, God's grace or man's works, but the two together is the subtle and profound position of Jewish religious thinking. Thus Akiba, the greatest of the rabbis, tell us at the end of the Mishnah tractate on Yom Kippur, as the consummating thought of that tractate, "Happy are you O Israel: before whom do you cleanse yourselves, and who cleanses you? Your Father which is in heaven." Not man alone, not God alone, but the two together confront a world which is mere material for being made divine.

And the same profound idea is embodied in the death of Akiba as contrasted with the death of Jesus. Both seem to be forsaken by God, by the God for whom they have given their lives. But Jesus cries out in his despair the agonizing words of the Psalmist, "My God, my God, why hast Thou forsaken me?" (Ps. 22:2)—and that seems to be his final utterance. Whereas Akiba, though likewise forsaken, and left to be flayed alive by the same Roman executioners, and with a similar mood of despair echoing in his ears from his disciples who stand around him and who ask, "Can this be the reward for the saint and hero?" nevertheless rises to supreme heroism, and in a world in which God seems to be woefully lacking he proclaims his belief and his companionship with God. "Hear, O Israel, the Lord our God, the Lord is One" are his last words as he breathes out his great soul. That is true religion: to insist on God in a God forsaken world, or rather in a world not yet dominated by God, and thus to call Him into being.

As similarly on an earlier plane the pagan hero Prometheus defies the god who will not help, whereas Job, though cruelly and unjustly tried, still utters the sublime words, "Though He slay me yet will I trust Him." Again the insistence on a God who as yet is sadly wanting, a God who by such faith is made to emerge. Again not God alone, not man alone, but the two together, for man gets his faith subterraneously from the hidden God.

We invoke in conclusion the name of that great rabbi who seems to us the supreme embodiment of the Jewish type. Akiba quotes and makes his own the concluding words of an utterance which occurs repeatedly in our Rabbinic writings (Yoma 23a, Gittin 36b, Shabbat 88b), and in which not merely is Jewish religiosity expressed sublimely, but which I regard as the full expression of the mood and attitude of the heroic man as such, the mood and attitude of the tragic hero in a growing world like ours: "Our rabbis have taught: those who are persecuted and do not persecute in turn, those who listen to contemptuous insults and do not reply, *those who act out of love and are glad of sufferings*, concerning them Scripture says, They that love God are like the sun going forth in its strength" (Jud. 5:31).

To act out of love and to be willing to bear the suffering which the good and true man must inevitable bear in a world like ours, in a world which is only partly divine and which must be won for God through the efforts of man—that is the deepest utterance of the rabbis and the culminating idea of Jewish religiosity and of Jewish prayer.

Source: Henry Slonimsky, "Prayer and a Growing God," in *Gates of Understanding*, ed. Lawrence A. Hoffman (New York: CCAR Press, 1977), 77–79.

Ethical Monotheism (1965)

Levi A. Olan (1903–1984), rabbi in Dallas and president of the CCAR 1967–1969, was a religious rationalist who considered human freedom to stand at the center of ethical monotheism.

The prophetic declaration of Ethical Monotheism bound Judaism to the doctrine of responsible human freedom. So long as there were many gods, conflict was inevitable and order in human events was unthinkable. Zeus could, and often did, upset the plans of other deities. A unique God, the Creator of heaven and earth, substituted cosmos for chaos, and made possible the free moral relationship between Himself and man. God and man are voluntarily covenanted, each possessed of freedom and responsibility. Freedom is not whim or caprice. Abraham boldly reminded God of His commitment to justice, even as God, through His prophets, persistently confronted man with the moral demand of their contract. The foundation stone of Ethical Monotheism is freedom. From the day when Moses revealed that man's choice between good and evil determines the issue of life and death, to Leo Baeck, who professed it and taught it to the Jews in a concentration camp, the Jewish tradition, with very rare exceptions, has remained loyal to the belief in man's moral freedom. Indeed, to forsake it is to annul the Covenant as well as the only reason for Jewish existence. . . .

There are a few basic affirmations which Judaism has jealously guarded against all processes of acculturation. Monotheism is one, and man's moral freedom, another. It rejected all suggestions that man is subject to stars or fates, to inherited sin or unalterable forces of nature and society. Its prophets discovered and revealed a God of freedom who endowed men with the capacity to choose freely between good and evil. Rabbi Pinchas of Koretz caught the spirit of our tradition. He commented upon the Biblical verse, "It is not good that man should be alone; I will make a helpmate for him," by saying "And God said: 'There can be no goodness in man while he is alone without an evil impulse within him. I will endow upon him the ability to do evil, and it will be as a helpmate to him to enable him to do good if he masters the evil nature within him. Without the evil impulse man could not do evil, but neither could he do good.' " Judaism and human freedom are inseparable.

Dostoevski, in *Brothers Karamazov,* has Smerdyakov say: "All things are permissible." This is the inevitable conclusion to the moral determinism so predominant in modern culture. The belief that nobody is ever morally responsible harbors a destructive power greater than the atom. Free men may, if they choose, control the atom. Men who are not free, cannot choose. These days summon us to be resolute in our historic Jewish conviction that men are free to choose their destiny and that God will help them when they choose to do His will.

Source: Levi A. Olan, "Freedom and Responsibility," *CCAR Yearbook* 75 (1965): 134–36.

The God of the Covenant (1977)

In the early 1950s a group of rabbis assembled at Oconomowoc, Wisconsin, for discussions on post-Holocaust theology. * *In the course of their meetings, the nature of*

Meeting at the instigation of Lou Silberman and Herman Schaalman, the participants were predominantly from the Reform movement. Among them were Eugene Borowitz, Jakob Petuchowski, David Polish, Steven Schwarzschild, Bernard Martin, Arnold Wolf, Emil Fackenheim, and Gunther Plaut. They were joined by a few Conservative rabbis (including the late Morris Adler) and one Orthodox rabbi, Zalman Schachter-Shalomi (as he later became known). The group met for several years.

the covenant between God and Israel and its central importance for modern Judaism emerged as the focal theme. In later years the participants were often referred to as "covenant theologians." The Reform participants, especially, had a significant impact as several of them assumed academic posts and/or published widely. Eugene Borowitz (1924–) was one of them. Through his many books and lectures and his long teaching career as Professor of Education and Jewish Religious Thought at HUC-JIR, he became the most influential theologian of the movement.

As against all secular interpretations of being a Jew, commitment to the Covenant insists that a relationship to God is primary to the life of the Jewish people and the individual Jew. The first concern of our apologetics, then, needs to be the recapture of the living reality of God in individual Jewish lives and thus in the Jewish community. The major target in this regard is the crypto-agnosticism with which most Jews have evaded this issue for a generation or more. In the face of contemporary nihilism, I am convinced, the old hope of serious values without commitment to God is increasingly untenable. The second concern of our apologetics is to help the individual Jew identify personally with the people of Israel. That is somewhat easier in our present time of high regard for ethnic difference and the search for one's own folk roots. Yet the primary model most people use in their thinking remains the Cartesian one of the detached self seeking truth without pre-conceptions or commitments. This has particular appeal to Jews since it immediately releases them from Jewish attachment in accord with the social pressures on any minority to assimilate to the majority.

Moreover, if there is no universalism then Jews lose whatever right they have to be part of general society. It thus becomes important to argue that all selfhood, though possessing universal dignity, is historically and particu-larly situated. Because of its uncommon worth Jews should will to make the fact of their being born into the Covenant the basis of their existence.

This construction of our situation as Jews overcomes what I take to be the fundamental difficulty with previous theories. Those which were God cen-tered were reductive of our peoplehood. Yet those which made the Jewish people central so reduced the role of God in our folk-life that they effectively secularized us. Furthermore, if peoplehood is the primary factor in Jewish existence what remains of the autonomous self? When the Covenant rela-tionship is the basis of our understanding of Judaism, self, God and people are all intimately and immediately bound up with one another. This does not settle how in any instance the self will respond to God or to the Jewish people, relationship being too fluid for that; yet Covenant sets up a constraining dialectic in place of liberal Jewish anarchy, universalism or secularism.

As to God, a new humility emerges. Persons have relationships which are deeply significant for their lives without fully or nearly understanding those with whom they have such relationships. As against rationalist models, concepts of God (clear intellectual envisagements of God) are of subsidiary interest—if not positively discouraged. Making concepts primary tends to make thinking a substitute for relating and implies a thinking humanity is God's equal. In a relationship thought is not abandoned but it must not dominate. It serves as a critic of faith and as explicator of its consequent responsibilities. This is the safeguard against superstition and cultism. At the same time there is openness to many forms of envisaging God. That is, any concept of God which makes relationship possible (or is appropriate to living in Covenant) is acceptable here. This seems closer to the traditional model of *agadic* thinking than liberal theologies have been as a result of their emphasis on an idea-of-God as the essence of Judaism. And it provided for the continuing intellectual growth in our understanding God, a characteristic of all of Jewish history, particularly in our time. Specifically, I do not see that thinking in terms of Covenant prohibits after-the-fact explanations of the God with whom one stands in relation, as an impersonal principle, or a process which has certain person-like characteristics (the conservation of values). For myself, however, the most appropriate model of thinking about the God with whom I stand in relation is a personal one. That is not to make a detached, metaphysical observation concerning the nature of God but only to say that this is the best basis I have found for drawing an analogy to the God with whom I stand in Covenant when I try to think about God. Persons being the most complex thing in creation, I find this an intellectually reasonable procedure. Further, my experience of being involved with God being a personal one, this envisagement seems appropriate. Some additional explication of what it means to say that God is person-like might, I think, be given.

The notion of relationship provides an approach to living with the problem of evil and, specifically, the Holocaust. Relationships exist not only when there is immediate confirmation of them but also in its absence. To trust means that the relationship is considered still real though no evidence for it is immediately available. One also believes such confirmation will yet be forthcoming. The practice of Judaism, the life of Torah, is an effort to build a strong relationship with God. Within the context of such closeness, Jews have largely been able to live with the evils in the world. There are special reasons why it has been difficult to continue this approach in modern times, most notably the loss of our belief in personal survival after death. The Holocaust raised our problems in this regard to an unprecedented level of tension, for some to the point of breaking the relationship with God. It remains stupefying, inexplicable. Yet, perhaps to our surprise, it has not destroyed the Covenant. For most Jews the ties with the people of Israel are far stronger than anything we anticipated. The absence of God during the Holocaust cannot be absolutized. It should not be used to deny that God has since been present in our lives as individuals and in that of the people of Israel (notably during the victory rather than the new-Holocaust of the Six Day War of 1967). The perception of a transcendent demand upon us to preserve the people of Israel, the affirmation of a transcendent ground of value in the face of contemporary nihilism, have led some minority of Jews to a restoration of our relationship with the other partner in the Covenant, God. The absence of God and the hurt we have felt are not intellectually explained. Yet it is possible, despite them, to continue the relationship. For the intellectually determined the most satisfactory way of dealing with this issue is to say that God's power is limited. For those to whom this raises more problems than it solves, there is acceptance without understanding. Both positions are compatible with relating to God in Covenant. I find myself constantly tempted to the former though mostly affirming the latter, a dialectic I find appropriate to affirming the Covenant.

Source: Eugene Borowitz, "Liberal Jewish Theology in a Time of Uncertainty, a Holistic Approach," *CCAR Yearbook* 87 (1977): 163–65.

A Feminist Concept of God (1998)

Feminist theology has brought about a new perception of the Divine. It does not refer to God in hierarchical images or terms of power (Lord, Sovereign, King of the Universe), seeing these as essentially male perceptions. Instead, feminists will speak of the Divine Presence, the Other, or Partner, whom we experience in relationships—to humans as well as to the world. In her book, Engendering Judaism, *Rachel Adler (1943–)*

describes herself as descended from five generations of Reform Jews, having lived for many years as an Orthodox Jew and having "learned both to love and to struggle with traditional texts and praxis." She brought these concerns with her when she returned to Reform Judaism. Professor Adler teaches at HUC-JIR in Los Angeles.

To acknowledge God as Other than ourselves, as creator of the universe, as the covenant partner with whom we co-create a world of law, raises questions of power, authority, and responsibility. These are questions of particular moment in a feminist theology, because theologies can be used to enforce and validate distributions of power by gender, status, and class in the social world and to teach people to perceive themselves as helpless, incompetent, or irremediably flawed. Metaphors of power and authority are particularly problematic if we believe they endorse absolutism or create castes, because, in democratic societies, we reject power distributions that disenfranchise people or that do not entitle them to equal respect.

We need to ask ourselves whether disparities of power and authority are inherently oppressive or whether it is the abuse of these disparities that is unjust. I would like to suggest several categories of relationships that necessarily involve disparities but do not require disadvantaging or degrading the less powerful or less authoritative participant. These include relationships in which one participant with specialized competence helps the other to heal, to acquire learning or skill, or to gain self-understanding or spiritual illumination. Such relationships are ethical when recipients are made partners in the process and when the goal is to benefit and empower. Indeed, if the helper were to regard the recipient as passive and incompetent, it would make it impossible for the goal to be achieved.

Other relationships where disparities exist but need not degrade or infantilize are mentoring and parenting. Good mentors and good parents take pride in the developing powers of those in whom they have invested themselves and look forward eagerly to their full flowering. When maturation is complete, a generational boundary still remains in place between parent and child, mentor and disciple. They may respect each other deeply and yet not be peers. Obligations will still bind the guided and the guide to one another, but they will have come to share a language in which they can discuss how particular obligations fit into the overall pattern of what now are shared projects and values. Their history together invests the good mentor or parent with continuing influence and respect, without any presumption of incompetence on the part of the disciple or grown child.

Images of God as experienced helper show us to ourselves as attainers of competence. What they do not reflect are our limits, our gaps, our constraints, our regrets. We act, we make things happen, but things also happen to us. As storytellers together, we and God write our lives. God presents us with inevitabilities, with opportunities and constraints. We present God with our choices and responses. Because of our power of choose, things also, as it were, happen to God. God as powerful Other, as the one who perceives beyond the bounded perspective, who permits into our stories elements we experience as disruptive, as agonizing, is the lightning rod for our rage and fear, awe and dependency. To continue to affirm that we are in relationship with this God is not to affirm God-as-power or God-as-patterner in some abstract sense, but rather to assert that we as actors have moral weight: we matter to God. This does not necessarily require from us passive acceptance of God's will. Our indignation is an equally powerful act of trust: it presumes that our covenant partner can be held accountable in relationship.

Affirming God as Other, however, still leaves the problem of gender unresolved. Some who would grant that God reveals Godself to us as an Other argue that a more truthful language would purify itself of gendered imagery entirely, presenting the divine Other in neuter terminology. This is clearly impossible in Hebrew, which has no neuter gender. Even in English, however, objections arise. Used in reference to human roles and attributes, neuter language is more abstract and hence less emotionally charged. Vivid images and powerful feelings accompany the words *mother* or *father* but do not attend the word *parent*. Moreover, in a male-dominated society, neuter language is still assumed to refer to males. If the referent is female, it is customary to signify this difference through a modifier: "a woman rabbi," or "a woman judge." God can, of course, be compared to gender-free aspects of the creation, such as rocks, hills, wells, and fountains, but anthropomorphic imagery inevitably entails gender, because the human beings reflected in it are sexually differentiated creatures.

Should anthropomorphism then be discarded as a language of theology or prayer? Marcia Falk accuses it of facilitating "liturgical idolatry."

> It is not just the exclusive maleness of our God-language that needs correction, but its anthropocentrism in *all* its ramifications. For as long as we image divinity exclusively as a person, whether female or

male, we tend to forget that human beings are not the sole, not even the "primary" life-bearing creatures on the planet. We allow our intelligence and our unique linguistic capabilities to deceive us into believing that we are "godlier" than the rest of creation.

Yet I would argue that expunging anthropomorphism from the language of prayer, even if it were possible, would be undesirable. We can still include the beautiful images of God as bird or rock or water. But these images alone are not sufficient to sustain relatedness. Anthropomorphism is necessary because stories are necessary. We know God from the stories we and God inhabit together. Stories are a human genre. For God to step into story for us, God must clothe Godself in metaphor, and especially in anthropomorphic metaphor, because the most powerful language for God's *engagement* with us is our human language of relationship.

Source: Rachel Adler, *Engendering Judaism* (Philadelphia: Jewish Publication Society, 1998), 93–96.

Revelation

1. Nothing Is More Important (1954)

A widely read philosopher of the second half of the twentieth century, Emil L. Fackenheim (1916–) considers Revelation as central to Jewish religious life.

No religious doctrine is more baffling than that of revelation; yet none is more essential.

Two alternative interpretations present themselves of which neither appears intelligible. Either revelation reveals what man may discover by means lying within his nature: but then revelation is superfluous. Or else revelation reveals what lies beyond human means of discovery: but then it would seem to lie beyond human comprehension also, and the recipient of a revelation cannot understand it. This dilemma cannot be avoided by fashionable equivocations. To associate revelation with poetic inspiration is to make it the product of man; but revelation is either the direct gift of God or not revelation at all.

Yet no doctrine is more essential than revelation, unless it be faith in God itself. Creation establishes time and history, whereas redemption consummates and redeems them. Revelation is an incursion of God *into* time and history; eternity here breaks into time without dissolving time's particularity. Creation and redemption establish the significance of time and history in *general.* Revelation establishes the significance of the *here and now* as unique; it is the religious category of existentiality as such.

If revelation is impossible then there is significance only to the human situation in general, even though God is accepted. And the law as well as the promise known to man remains in strict universality. But this makes individual men and historic moments universally interchangeable. God may then be related to man in general: He is only indirectly and accidentally related to myself, my people, my historic situation.

Existence, however, is of inexorable particularity. The moral law to which I am obligated may be universal, but the situation in which I must realize it is unique. A historic situation reflects what history as such is, but it is nevertheless something all its own. Israel is a manifestation of mankind, but what makes her Israel is unrepeatable and uninterchangeable. If there is no revelation, the particular in existence is a meaningless weight upon time and history, from creation until redemption. History in that case has meaning only at its beginning and at its end: nothing essential goes on within it. . . .

Judaism rests on the assertion of the actuality of a series of revelations which have constituted Israel as a historic community destined to serve a specific purpose. Where it speaks of mankind and the God of mankind, Judaism is nothing beyond what a universally human religion might be; only at the point where, leaping into the particular, it is concerned with Israel and the God of Israel, does Judaism separate off from universal truths of faith.

Jewish existence is established by, and responsible to, divine revelation. Hence it shares the dialectical character of all revelation. That Jewish existence has a meaning is vouchsafed by the faith which accepts the reality of revelation; of a revelation which has established Jewish existence. But the nature of that meaning is involved in the dialectic of the paradox. All revelation both reveals and conceals: thus the meaning of Israel's existence, too, is both revealed and concealed. It must remain concealed: for the divine plan for Israel remains unfathomable. Yet it must also be revealed: for Israel is to play a responsible part in that plan. Since the

Jew is to live a consciously Jewish life before God he must have at least a partial grasp of its meaning; but in its fullness that meaning is not disclosed: for his Jewishness is only partly the Jew's own doing. The Jew both makes, and is made by his destiny.

The God-man-relation demands of man a free response, the response through moral law. The God-Israel-relation demands of the Jew, in addition to the moral response, a response expressing his Jewishness in all its particularity. This response is Halakhah. Moral law, mediated through the leap of faith, becomes the divine law to man. Halakhah is Jewish custom and ceremony mediated through the leap into Jewish faith; and it thereby becomes the divine law to Israel. In themselves, all customs, ceremonies and folklore (including those Jewish, and those contained in the book called Torah) are mere human self-expression, the self-expression of men alone among themselves. But through the leap of faith any one of them (and pre-eminently those of the Torah) have the potency of becoming human reflections of a real God-Israel encounter. And thus each of them has the potency of becoming Halakhah, commanded and fulfilled: if fulfilled, not as self-expression but as response on the part of Israel to a divine challenge to Israel; as the gift of the Jewish self to God. Thus no particular set of ceremonies is, as such, divine law: this is an error flowing from the orthodox misunderstanding of the nature of revelation. But, on the other hand, all customs which flow from the concreteness of Jewish life have the potency of becoming divine law, and are a challenge to fulfillment. The denial of the religious significance of any law which is not moral is an error flowing from the modernistic misunderstanding of the nature of the concrete before God.

We have said that, as all revelation, the revelation of God to Israel both reveals and conceals; and that, correspondingly, the Jew both makes, and is made by his destiny. Thus, whether the Jew practices Halakhah is, on the one hand, not constitutive of his Jewishness; on the other, it is not indifferent to his Jewishness. If the former were the case, the Jew would wholly make his Jewish destiny; if the latter, he would be wholly made by it.

Thus the meaning of Israel's destiny is in part revealed: it is to respond, ever again, to a divine challenge; to become, of her own free choice, a people of God; to give perpetual realization to this decision in thought and practice. Situations change, and with them the content of the response they require; but the fact of challenge, and the need for response, remain the same.

Yet the meaning of Israel's destiny is also concealed. Man cannot under-stand the final reasons for the tensions of his existence; the Jew cannot understand the final reasons why he was chosen to exemplify these tensions. Hence the Jew is also unable to decide whether or not Israel will continue to exist. He is, to be sure, free to decide whether to be a devout or stiff-necked Jew, whether to heed or to ignore the divine challenge. But if it is really true that God has a plan for Israel, Israel is as little free to alter that plan as she is able to understand its final meaning.

Source: Emil L. Fackenheim, "An Outline of a Modern Jewish Theology," *Judaism: A Quarterly Journal,* summer 1954, 247–50.

2. Experiencing the Commandment (1961)

Jakob J. Petuchowski (1925–1991), Professor of Rabbinics and Theology at HUC-JIR in Cincinnati and the author of thirty-six books, considered learning to listen for the commandment the major task facing Reform Jews.

The modern Jew must regain the frame of mind in which he is able to experience the "commandment" addressed to him. It is a frame of mind which the Rabbis of old attempted to create, when they insisted that the Revelation at Sinai must be as topical to the Jew as if it had happened to him *"today."* It is also a frame of mind to which the modern Jew *can* attain, as has been demonstrated by Franz Rosenzweig, both in his thought and in his way of life.

How does one set about listening for the commandment? There could hardly be a hard-and-fast rule for this. But one of the prerequisites is undoubtedly the willingness and the readiness to shape one's whole life according to the pattern which God gives us to see. And we do not have to start from nothing! The accumulated heritage of the Jewish past is ours to select from, ours to experiment with, in our endeavor to find out what God wants *us* to do.

Consider, for example, the case of the man who, after sober reflection, has come to the conclusion that one of the ways in which he can make God more real in his life is that of self-discipline. He cultivates the habit of saying "No" to himself occasionally. He is now looking for a regimen which would place this kind of self-discipline on a more permanent basis. He might hit upon the idea of abstaining from certain kinds of meat, such as beef or lamb.

Now, if this man were a Jew, a moderately informed kind of Jew, he would find such a system of self-discipline ready-made for him in the pages of the Torah. This he could adopt as a whole, or in part. The meat from which he abstains would then not be lamb, but pork. Moreover, in addition to cultivating self-discipline for his own spiritual welfare, he would, at the same time, strengthen his links with the Jewish past and the Torah tradition. Above all, he would furnish an example of how a cold letter of dietary legislation could become a living "commandment."

It is thus clear that the modern Jew in search of the "commandment" addressed to him must, as a starting point, engage in intensive Jewish study. A daily period set aside for this task is surely within reach of all. Yet the moment a decision for Jewish study has been reached, an important "commandment" has already been accepted. Of all the things a man can do which, according to the Rabbis, would yield him enjoyment both in this world and in the next, the "study of Torah" ranks as the greatest. For, with all the emphasis which is placed on "action" rather than on "study," the latter is far from being underestimated. The Rabbis recognized that "study leads to action." It will certainly do so in the case of the modern Jew who studies *in order* to discover what to *do*.

And that is why study will have to go hand-in-hand with "experimentation." The modern Jew, fumblingly at first, and overcoming his initial shyness, will want to "try out" those practices and observances which *might* contain God's commandment to *him*. Here, practice is the only way to find out. Only by actually *trying* to observe it, will he be able to discover whether he is dealing with a "commandment," or just with another item of what is still only "legislation" to him.

Of course, all of this will be marked by a high degree of subjectivity. There is in it none of the certainty which Orthodoxy promises its adherents, none of the matter-of-factness of complying with the established legislation of a body politic. One individual's observance of the Sabbath, for example, is unlikely to be identical with that of another individual. The former might consider that to be forbidden "work" which for the latter is an indispensable ingredient of his Sabbath "delight." But this is the price which will have to be paid. For the majority of modern Jews, it will either be this or nothing at all.

It is the state of affairs well described by Franz Rosenzweig, when he said that what we have in common nowadays is the landscape, and no longer the common road on which Jews walked in unity from the close of the Talmud to the dawn of Emancipation. The best we can do today is to work at our individual roads in the common landscape. Perhaps the future will again know of a common road, or, more likely, of a common *system of roads.*

Source: Jakob J. Petuchowski, *Ever Since Sinai* (New York: Scribe Publications, 1961), 109–12.

3. The Need to Be Commanded (1967)

Arnold Jacob Wolf (1924–), a Reform rabbi in Chicago, has been a prolific theologian and critic of the Reform movement. Its adherents, he holds, need to ritualize their ethical convictions to make them truly effective.

A Jew must do whatever he can for God. The assumption is that there is a God, that there is a God who cares about what we do, that some of what God cares about that we do is "Jewish." I do not think that "Jewish" means only peculiar to Jews, otherwise keeping kosher would be a higher *mitzvah* than loving one's neighbor. The point is that the Jew helps God by loving *and* by eating. In our post-Freudian age we know how closely eating and loving are linked, how profoundly they interpenetrate. None of us would be able to say with Jesus anymore, "Not what goes into the mouth defiles a man, but what comes out of the mouth, this defiles a man." What goes in comes out!

Distinctions between "ethical" and "ritual" commandments are invariably premature if not downright useless. Religion is not only a matter of being a good boy; in fact, being a good boy is a lot harder than it looked to early Reform Judaism. The country of Kant and Hermann Cohen produced the murder camps. Everyone knew what was good, all right, but very few Germans risked doing it. The problem of religion is not saying good things but changing people. *Kashrut* may be as relevant to that task as *tzedakah;* they are finally inseparable.

More profoundly, the need of our time is the ethicizing of the apparently ritual and the ritualizing of the ethical. *Pesach,* prayer, piety are full of human, that is, ethical, consequences. But these must be recovered in the modern age. Where classical Reform fell prey to the philosophic trap, modern (romantic) Reform falls into a sociological pit. Thus Passover (!!—do we call *Shavuot* "Weeks"?) once was reduced to a kind of Freedom Charade. Now it is more likely to be manipulated into a children's bribe or a nostalgic exercise of culinary Judaism. But *Pesach* remains an ethical religious, that is, an existential, possibility. *Pesach* is a time of revolution in which the Jewish man can find his obligation to all the enslaved including himself; *Pesach* is more than I can say it is.

The Sabbath is the supreme ethical-religious moment. It is full of doing, remembering, discovering. Prayer, food, study, Exodus, community, social justice, children are all interwoven. Turn it and turn it, everything is potentially *Shabbosdik*. But Shabbat requires a good deal of preparation and concern, at least as much as a congregational membership campaign or a TV program. It takes one's thought and one's will and one's time. It has its own choreography and its own tempo. It is unmodern and therefore supremely important to modern Jews. Our fathers' fathers could have done without Shabbat; we dare not try. But who of us could say whether it is an "ethical" or a "ritual" commandment?

The apparently "ethical," on the other hand, requires ritualizing. The best example of this I know is civil rights. When it was a matter only of saying nice things or doing easy ones, we Jews were all ethical. But once the chips were down and civil rights came to mean the Negro Revolution (against, *davke*, us), Black Power, and the radical left, our Jewish liberals fled in unseemly hurry and panic. They did not have, we do not have, stamina for ethics in an urban setting. We are not willing, perhaps not even able any longer, to give up our old presuppositions, our bourgeois biases, just because they are wrong. But that means, of course, that we are no longer authentic Jews even if we think we are Orthodox.

A real Jew would have ritualized the ethical problem of equality. He would have made his moral commitment not on the basis of self-interest or emotional attachment to the suffering Negro or of his view of American self-interest. He would be with the underdog against the oppressor (even when he himself *is* the oppressor) for exactly the same reason he doesn't give a party on Friday night or eat bagels on *Pesach*—the only possible good reason being to do something for God.

Being good is largely a matter of being guilty in the right way and having the stamina to deal with one's guilt. These are both classical ritualistic problems. Reform was wrong to derogate from the sacrificial system the fasts and the confessionals. We need all the help we can get to rid ourselves of deep, corroding guilt. But we also need the *halakhah* (or at least a *halakhah*) to tell us how to channel our proper responsibility, to ritualize our personal duty. In other words, we desperately need to be commanded, and by a Commander worthy of the name.

Source: Arnold Jacob Wolf, *Unfinished Rabbi* (Chicago: Ivan R. Dee, 1998), 21–23.

FOUR

THE REALM OF PUBLIC PRAYER

✦ Perhaps nowhere else is the development of American Reform Judaism more visible than in the various prayer books and guides it has produced. Their content ranges from close adherence to traditional modes to radical innovations and sometimes back again. This continuous attention given to liturgy (the form and substance of the public prayer service) goes back to the origins of Reform in North America. It began in the early part of the nineteenth century with certain liturgical changes: the introduction of sermons in the vernacular, the institution of instrumental music, the shortening of the service, and mixed seating.

Shabbat and holiday services were the focus of these innovations, while daily worship in the synagogue suffered neglect, as did attention to private prayer. In time this was meliorated by the creation of home prayer books, which reflect a growing recovery of traditional modes. Also, new emphasis on cantorial music, congregational singing, and healing services as well as the impact of feminism brought a new spirit to the liturgical enterprise.

Still, these changes, however necessary and welcome, have thus far not managed to move most Reform Jews to worship regularly in the synagogue or to follow a routine of private prayer. While Friday night rituals, the Passover seder, and certain life-cycle events have retained their place in many, if not most Reform homes (see chapter 5, "Shabbat and Holy Days," and chapter 6, "Life-Cycle Events"), daily private prayer has suffered the gravest neglect. The movement has tried to remedy this shortcoming, at first by appending sections for private prayer in the *siddur* and then by issuing separate home prayer books.

Prayer books are sacred tools, but they have built-in limitations.

Though they exist to fill spiritual needs, in the end they will not move Jews living in a secular culture to worship unless they themselves consider worship a need and, hopefully, a mitzvah as well.

The Need for a Minyan (1992)

Jewish tradition accorded communal worship a place of special importance. Though private prayer three times a day remained an obligation, joining with the community, if at all possible with a minyan (ten adult males), was deemed preferable. Tradition reserved special parts of the service for occasions when a minyan was present. Chief among these are the reading of Torah from the scroll and the recital of the Mourner's Kaddish. The requirement was increasingly disregarded when Jews in North America moved to new or outlying communities. But the question has persisted, for being Jewish has always meant to live in community whenever and wherever possible. The Responsa Committee of the CCAR has from time to time dealt with the subject, it being understood that a Reform minyan would count women as well as men.

She'elah [Question]

A New Zealand congregation inquires about the Reform perspective on the need for a minyan, and about what should or should not be done during a service when fewer than ten are present. The rabbi writes that he "would appreciate it if you guide our ritual committee towards setting a policy."

T'shuvah [Answer]

Leaders of the CCAR have on three occasions addressed aspects of the questions asked.

R. Jacob Mann, in 1936, issued a brief responsum on the need for a minyan at Friday night services and, basing himself on an old Palestinian custom, allowed the practice of holding services without a minyan. "While every attempt should be made to have a full minyan, the importance of regular services in the Temple is such as to conduct them even when there are fewer than ten people present."

R. Solomon B. Freehof, in 1963, ruled on whether a person who could not attend synagogue services could say *Kaddish* at home, with no one else to join in the prayers. The responsum was quite detailed, permitting the practice under certain circumstances and making alternative suggestions.

R. Walter Jacob, in 1989, responded to the question: "May we conduct a service at home with less than a minyan?" This responsum, like R. Mann's, was also quite brief and allowed a minyan-less service, urging congregations meanwhile to expend extra efforts to have people come together in the synagogue.

All three were thus permissive, though R. Freehof hedged his ruling with particular cautions.

We have agreed to review the entire matter, not only in order to summarize previous and highly respected opinions, but also because we feel that the developments of Jewish life, and especially in our own movement, call for additional considerations. . . .

It cannot be denied that the rule of ten is frequently disregarded in Reform congregations, especially in small communities, but not there alone. With lessening worship attendance in general, even in places where adequate numbers of worshippers can be found, attention to the time-honored practice of requiring a quorum is rarely an issue.

Yet there are good reasons why this practice deserves our continued attention and respect, with the proviso, of course, that any Reform minyan would count women as equal partners.

As a general rule we are and have been lenient in most ritual matters, and the opinions of Rabbis Mann, Freehof and Jacob reflect this trend. They are in tune with the sentiment of *Pirkei Avot:* "When two sit together and discuss words of Torah the *Sh'chinah* is present with them"—which may be taken to mean that it does not matter how few Jews gather together for services, their sacred intent entitles them to full liturgical expression. Why should they be denied the hearing of Torah and *K'dushah* because others may not feel prompted to come to the synagogue? Why should Jews be dependent on others when they need to say *Kaddish,* whether at home, at a shivah, or when observing *yahrzeit?*

Having stated these questions we must, however, also ask: *If the needs of the individual can be satisfied without others, what then is the difference between public and private worship?*

Whether six, seven or ten constitute the required forum is not the heart of the issue; rather it is the question whether there is an abiding value in the obligation of Jews to join others in worship. The synagogue functions as the *mikdash me'at* (literally, the small sanctuary) which invokes the image of the Sanctuary of old. Moses and Ezra expounded Torah in the presence of the people, and the reading of Torah on Shabbat and other occasions is a recurring enactment of those hallowed moments. The rabbi, as teacher of the community, expounds sacred texts and traditions, and does so before the *tzibbur,* the representatives of the Jewish people who have come to participate in common rites of prayer and learning. The *tzibbur* is indeed the proper context of certain liturgical rubrics, and by tradition these include, in addition to those mentioned, the reading of Torah from a scroll, and the Mourner's *Kaddish.*

It seems to us that the idea of a minyan deserves renewed attention. Reform Judaism has broken much new ground by giving individuals a measure of religious scope they did not previously have. Withal, we may not overlook the needs of the community which, when properly met, benefit all its members. Public worship belongs to these categories of Jewish life, and withholding certain individual prerogatives for the benefit of all has always been the context of Jewish prayer.

Thus, the obligation of *Kaddish* is traditionally fulfilled in community, and therefore the congregation at prayer is the proper locus for it. However, should there be no quorum or should the individual be unable to go to the synagogue, the need for the community does not simply fall away. . . .

We would therefore urge the Reform Practices Committee of the CCAR, together with the Liturgy Committee, to take up the need for devising alternate expressions for those who cannot worship in community, be it because of personal circumstances or because a minyan has not or cannot be brought together.

The maintenance of the requirement of a minyan has also a strong educational force: it reminds all those who are or might be affected by the rule of the importance of public worship. R. Freehof reminds us of the injunction of the *Shulchan Aruch* that it is the duty of the members of the community to exert pressure upon each other so that there should always be a minyan in the synagogue. "The feeling of piety at the time of *yahrzeit* is one of the justifiable motives which urges people to come to public worship." And R. Jacob adds that we should make "a more vigorous effort and assemble a necessary minyan, if it is at all possible, for a service whether public or private."

We heartily endorse these sentiments which reflect the abiding value of a minyan in our liturgical structure, and we urge the inquiring congregation to devise ways and means to maintain and enhance this ancient Jewish institution.

Dissent

Three members differed somewhat from these conclusions. They felt that *Kaddish* deserves an exemption from the rule, and that perhaps in special circumstances the rule of three ought to be invoked (as at the *Birkat HaMazon*). One believes that the few should also not be deprived of reading (or hearing) the words of Torah from the scroll, and would have the leader of the service emphasize that the fewer-than-ten who are assembled do not constitute a proper congregation but rather a *chug*, a small group who have come together for study and edification.

***

Source: "Need for a *Minyan*," in *Teshuvot for the Nineties: Reform Judaism's Answers for Today's Dilemmas,* ed. W. Gunther Plaut and Mark Washofsky (New York: CCAR Press, 1997), 23–27.

The *Kippah* Syndrome (1928)

While in Europe the custom of covering the head remained firmly entrenched, in the United States—where Jews strove to be considered Americans in every respect—bareheadedness spread from the last decades of the nineteenth century and achieved the status of identifying Reform Jews. A hundred years later the original, assimilatory motivation had lost its significance, and with the turn toward tradition, the kippah *(or* yarmulke*), and often with it, the* tallit *(the prayer shawl) returned to the ranks of the movement. At the turn of the millennium, most Reform rabbis and cantors were traditionally accoutered at services, and a few of them at all times (like their traditional colleagues). Congregants, too, increasingly wore* kippot *and* tallitot*, though a large number still clung to the earlier practice of praying bareheaded. Jacob Zvi Lauterbach (1873–1942), for many years Professor of Talmud at Hebrew Union College, authored the definitive responsum on bareheadedness versus wearing the* kippah*. The following is an excerpt from a lecture he gave to a CCAR convention.*

***

In the very early post-Talmudic times, . . . we find that the Babylonian Jews considered it already forbidden to utter the name of God in prayer with uncovered head. It is stated that one of the differences in custom and ritual between the Palestinian and Babylonian Jews was that among the former the priests would recite their benedictions bareheaded while among the latter the priests were not permitted to recite their benedictions with uncovered head.

There was, accordingly, a difference in custom as regards wearing hats between Palestine and Babylon. In the former the people would not cover their heads while praying or when in the synagogue and in general would go bareheaded. In the latter, however, it was the custom of pious people to cover their head.

In France and Germany, following the Palestinian custom, there was no objection to praying or reading from the Torah with uncovered head. Thus R. Isaac b. Moses ... of Vienna (1200–1270) expressly reports that it was the custom of the French rabbis to pray with uncovered head, though he does not favor it.

Beginning, however, with the thirteenth century the Babylonian-Spanish custom began to penetrate into France and Germany. We accordingly find Ashkenasic authorities of the thirteenth century and of the following centuries favoring the Spanish custom and recommending or requiring that one should cover his head when praying or reading from the Torah. But even as late as the sixteenth century it was in German-Polish countries not generally considered as forbidden to read the Torah or to pray bareheaded. R. Solomon Lurya, one of the greatest rabbinical authorities of his time (1510–1573), in his Responsa expressly says: "I do not know of any prohibition against praying with uncovered head."

The famous Gaon of Vilna ... expressly says: "According to Jewish law it is permitted to enter a synagogue and to pray without covering one's head."

And after some discussion in which he cites many proofs for his statement, he closes with the following words: "There is no prohibition whatever against praying with uncovered head, but as a matter of propriety it would seem to be good manners to cover one's head when standing in the presence of great men and also during the religious service."

In the nineteenth century, as a reaction to the first attempts of modern Reform which suggested the removal of the hat by the worshippers in the synagogue, the strict Orthodox Rabbinical authorities became more emphatic in their insistence upon the requirement of covering the head when entering a synagogue, and when praying or performing any religious ceremony.

In summing up the discussion I would say that from the point of view of Jewish law or ritual, there can be no objection to either covering or uncovering the head in the synagogue or when praying and when reading the Torah. The custom of praying bareheaded or with covered head is not at all a question of law. It is merely a matter of social propriety and decorum. As such it cannot, and need not, be the same in all countries and certainly not remain the same for all times. For it depends on the ideas of the people as to what is the proper attire for worshippers in the Temples or what is the proper thing to wear or not to wear at solemn occasions and at public worship. These ideas are, of course, in turn subject to change in different times and in different places. Hence, in countries where the covering of the head is a sign of showing respect and reverence, it certainly would be improper to appear before God in the house of prayer with an uncovered head. And even in countries where it is generally regarded more respectful to remove the hat, if there be congregations who still feel like their grandfathers and consider it disrespectful to pray with uncovered head, they are within their right if they retain the custom of their fathers. We can have no quarrel with them and should rather respect their custom. In visiting them in their synagogues or when participating in some religious service at their homes, we should do as they do. For their motive and their intentions are good, and they observe these practices out of a feeling of respect and a sense of propriety, misguided as they may appear on this point to the occidental and modern mind. On the other hand, no one should find any fault with those people who, living in countries where it is considered to be disrespectful to keep the hat on while visiting in other people's homes or in the presence of elders and superiors, deem it proper to show their respect for the synagogue by removing the hat on entering it. These people also observe their practice with the best intentions and with a respectful spirit. They are not prompted by the desire to imitate non-Jewish practice. Their motive rather is to show their respect for the synagogue and to express their spirit of reverence by praying with uncovered head. And although in the last century this question of "hat on or hat off" was the subject of heated disputes between the Conservative and Liberal groups of Jewry, we should know better now, and be more tolerant and more liberal towards one another. We should realize that this matter is but a detail of custom and should not be made the issue between Orthodox and

Reform. It is a detail that is not worth fighting about. It should not separate Jew from Jew and not be made the cause of breaking the Jewish groups or dividing Jewish congregations.

Source: Jacob Zvi Lauterbach, "Covering the Head in Prayer," in *The Growth of Reform Judaism,* ed. W. Gunther Plaut (New York: World Union for Progressive Judaism, 1965), 307–8.

The Changing Prayer Book

In the 1890s the CCAR began to publish the Union Prayer Book, *which subsequently underwent three revisions. The current version, now called* Gates of Prayer, *is again under review by the Liturgy Committee. In the past, theology was the main issue; today, gender-sensitive language, inclusion of the Matriarchs along with the Patriarchs, increased use of Hebrew texts, healing prayers, and choices of different kinds of services mark the latest attempts.*

---

1. Are We Retired Philanthropists? (1928)

Samuel S. Cohon (1888–1959) was a severe critic of the early prayer books. Professor of Theology at Hebrew Union College, he was instrumental in shaping both the Columbus Platform of 1937 (see chapter 12) and a newly revised edition of the Union Prayer Book *(1940). Cohon represented a growing desire on the part of many Reformers to return to some traditions that had been discarded by an earlier generation and especially to prayer as a true dialogue with God.*

The Union Prayer-book unconsciously reflects the present apathy and scepticism toward prayer. Therein lies its chief distinction from the traditional Book of Prayer. It does not present "the prayer of the afflicted when he fainteth, and poureth out his complaint before the Lord." It expresses for the most part only rhetorically the heart's hunger for God and lacks much of the creative character of the historical *Tefilah*. Like most of the older Reform rituals, it is not designed as a book of *daily* devotion for *private* as well as for congregational use. The few meager prayers for the individual are printed as an afterthought. The weekday public services are in reality arranged for public use on Sundays and for houses of mourning. These as well as the Sabbath and Holy Day services are so arranged as to turn the worshiper into an auditor. They are—with but few exceptions—formal in character. In many synagogs they are consciously used as a mere introduction to the rabbi's discourse.

As if to avoid embarrassment the petitionary prayers have been toned down. This is particularly true of the first volume. God is allowed only as much as the current textbooks of science cannot possibly deny Him. Prayer does not function as an expression of deep felt human needs, as a cry for health, for sustenance and for relief from pain, sorrow and distress, but only as a vague meditation on an ethical theme. An examination of the Union Prayer-book leaves the impression that "the intrusion of the scientific mood" into its fabric has done the mischief against which Dean Sperry warns us. Worship appears as "a means to some good other than itself" and "is justified by its reference to the better control of the world and the better conduct of life." Hence the homiletical nature of most of the additions to the traditional prayers, not only in the opening meditations, but also in the body of the services.

This further explains the persistent and often clumsy appeals to the worshiper. For instance in the special prayer for the evening of the fifth Sabbath of the month, we read:

May we so use this gift (of labor) that day by day we may look back upon our work and declare it good. May the fruit of our labor be a service acceptable unto Thee. May each new Sabbath find us going from strength to strength, so that whatever of good we have done we may do still better; and wherever we have failed, we may by Thy grace be helped to worthier work.

The Union Prayer-book conveys the impression that it was especially written for a people composed of retired philanthropists and amateur social workers. The aged are provided with this prayer on Yom Kippur: "Give me the sweetness of that joy which is reserved for those who serve others through the counsel and guidance learned in the school of life's experience" (Vol. II, p. 184). Compare it with the traditional plea: "*Al tashlichenu l'et ziknah, kichlot kohenu al ta'azvenu*—Cast us not away in old age, when our strength shall be spent do not forsake us." In the grace after meals, we have the sentence: "While we enjoy Thy gifts, may we never forget the needy, nor allow those who want, to be forsaken" (Vol. I, p. 344). How strangely this self-satisfied sentiment appears in the light of the humble petition of the old *Birkat Hamazon*: "We beseech Thee, O Lord our God, cause us not to become dependent upon the bounty of men or of their loans, but only upon Thy hand." . . .

For the religious minded Jew, prayer can be neither a soliloquy nor a dialogue with his own soul. It can have value only if he knows before whom he stands. For him prayer is not a form of auto-suggestion but a communion between finite man and the infinite God, an uplifting of mind and heart on the part of the child of dust toward the heavenly Father.

Source: Samuel S. Cohon, "The Theology of the *Union Prayerbook*," in *Reform Judaism: A Historical Perspective*, ed. Joseph L. Blau (New York: KTAV, 1973), 261–63.

2. Gates of Prayer/Shaarei Tefillah (1975)

This prayer book, published in 1975, is the most recent complete liturgy issued by the CCAR (the volume for the High Holy Days, Gates of Repentance/Shaarei Teshuvah, *followed three years later).* Gates of Prayer *is more than double the size of the* Union Prayer Book; *it contains ten different services for Friday nights, has significantly more Hebrew (even in the English, "Sabbath" has become "Shabbat"), and has replaced the antique "Thee" and "Thou" address to God with "You." Rabbi Chaim Stern (1930–), congregational rabbi, poet, and editor of* Gates of Prayer *and most of the CCAR's liturgical publications during the past three decades, composed many new texts for the book. The following meditation is one example.*

For our ancestors, Shabbat was a sign of God's covenant of peace with the universe. They kept it faithfully; when their lives were torn, Shabbat made them whole; when their lives were bitter, it brought them sweetness; when their lives were peaceful, it deepened their joy.

Our ways are not like theirs. We have many idle days, but few Sabbaths; we speak many words, but few prayers; we make the earth yield to our purpose, but are unsure of the ground beneath us. But here, now, we can begin again. Or, having already begun, we can continue our quest for the wholeness we need.

May the sense of God's presence be with us along our way, helping us to discover the peace and rest some have lost or never known, renewing our covenant of peace with all created things.

And may we become more than we have been, more than we are: reaching for a pefection beyond our grasp, growing and learning one day to make this day's peace a peace for all days, learning one day to do justly, and love mercy, and walk alongside the One who walks with us.

Source: Gates of Prayer (New York: CCAR Press, 1975), 246.

3. The Liturgical Message (1977)

Lawrence A. Hoffman (1942–), Professor of Liturgy at HUC-JIR, has become the prime interpreter of Jewish public worship. He has identified four elements that determine its character: the content of the liturgy (eliminating old concepts, reflecting North American religious consciousness); its structure (English predominates, the book reads from left to right or vice versa, instructions are provided); its choreography (like standing for certain prayers, cantorial and congregational singing); and the architecture of the place of worship.

Jews have . . . prayed in a great many ways, ranging from "davening" to silent meditation, from highly elaborate synchronized dramatics to informal spontaneous worship. Reform choreography of this century stands out merely as one more instance in which the structural score and content-message combine to make a certain type of worship that is consistent with a Jewish community's self-image at a particular time and place.

No doubt the choreography of *Union Prayer Book* worship services did vary from place to place. Nevertheless the spirit of the time exercised its influence over this aspect of the liturgical message no less than over the content and structural coordinates. Thus the self-image of the Jewish community as a religion fully in step with the progress of western society was, not unexpectedly, mirrored by a manner of worship similar to that which prevailed in upper-middle-class American churches. . . .

The description of such services should not, however, be confused with an evaluation of them. Opponents of Reform labeled them cold, boring, and churchlike; advocates saw them as majestic, uplifting and spiritual. Once we realize that such terms are evaluative rather than designative, we can see that both parties to the debate were equally right, their evaluation corresponding not to the service itself but to the extent to which the choreographic message accorded with their own sense of Jewish identity. Those imbued with the western European heritage pictured Judaism as another western religion. Like the Episcopalian or Roman Catholic Mass it would feature highly dramatic ritual, but stripped of any vestige of medieval superstition. Like the Protestant church it would feature magnificent congregational hymns. The Jewish heritage would provide moral preachments befitting the religion which had fostered the monotheistic principle in the first place. The whole would be presented with a sense of staid decorum fully in keeping with an upwardly mobile middle class who had been taught by French *philosophes* and German idealists alike to view detached philosophical speculation as the highest form of human activity. Such decorum was compatible also with the Puritan-American tradition which frowned on excessive display of emotion; and it seemed particularly important now, as immigrants threatened to inundate America with their *shtetl* form of worship which was so heavily laden with Hasidic abandon, medieval symbolism, and, in general, a choreography completely alien to the self-image which German Jews had been developing for an entire century. . . .

Gates of Prayer, like all prayerbooks which preceded it, provides a picture of the Jews who use it. . . . We might conclude simply by drawing a concise picture of the type of Jewish community which *Gates of Prayer* assumes.

It is a community born and bred in America, but committed to membership in the Jewish people. Our Jews are intelligent and informed, though they are still struggling with the Jewish aspect of their education. They are exploring the fullness of the Jewish tradition, giving no necessary priority to any specific aspect of it. In fact they are still in the first stage of discovering many traditional themes of whose existence they have often been completely unaware.

Their Reform heritage is evident by the openness they show to all aspects of the tradition, their refusal to compromise intellectual honesty and ethical imperative, and their candid admission that religion is a commitment to search and to wonder, to affirm and to doubt. The events of the Holocaust and the birth of modern Israel stand foremost in their mind, but the increasing necessity for developing a synthesis of Americanism and Judaism is high on their agenda. As Reform Jews they want to be free to draw nourishment from the totality of the Jewish tradition, be it Hasidic joy, Talmudic wisdom, philosophic wonder, Kabbalistic mystery, prophetic idealism or liberal openness to experimentation and change. And they want to blend this with the best of modern culture: colloquial English, modern poetry, new music, American democracy, and the commitment (both Jewish and American) to an educated constituency.

To the extent that this portrait is correctly drawn and that *Gates of Prayer* reflects it, the Reform movement will have found a liturgy responsive to its constituents' self-image. It will be Reform liturgy come of age—a creative synthesis of Jewish liberalism and American freedom—that will truly be a liturgical rite for American Jews. Our founder, Isaac Mayer Wise, called his prayerbook *Minhag America*, envisioning a ritual appropriate for America; one hundred years later, his vision may be becoming a reality.

Source: Lawrence A. Hoffman, "The Liturgical Message," in *Gates of Understanding*, ed. Lawrence A. Hoffman (New York: CCAR Press, 1977), 147–48, 162–63.

Gender Sensitivity

By the 1980s the influence of the feminist movement began to make itself felt in the realm of Reform Jewish prayer. But the mills of liturgical revision grind slowly, and the first book issued by the CCAR that was gender sensitive appeared only in 1993. By that time, feminist theology had gone far beyond adjustments of selected passages and advocated an entirely new approach to and relationship with the Divine (see chapter 3).

1. Reclaiming the Covenant (1992)

Ellen M. Umansky (1950–), Professor of Judaic Studies at Fairfield University, has been a leading voice for changing old texts that excluded women and depicted God as if of the male gender.

Within the last few years, my own struggle to reclaim the Jewish covenant as a bond between God and *all* of the Jewish people—male and female—has been both challenging and frustrating. At times, I have almost abandoned my struggle. The continued exclusion of women from positions of secular and religious leadership within the Jewish community, the extent to which women's spirituality—past and present—is still ignored, the lack of formal ceremonies celebrating important life-cycle events of women, and the liturgical description of God as "God of our Fathers" (but not our mothers) make me angry and sad. At first, I directed my anger toward Judaism itself, ready to write it off as hopelessly patriarchal. But more recently, I've come to redirect my anger. It's not Judaism itself that angers me but those who seem to have forgotten that Judaism has never been monolithic and that in every period of Jewish history Judaism has developed and grown.

Those who argue that liturgy cannot be changed have lost sight of Judaism as a living religion. How meaningful today are images of God as King, Lord, and Shepherd? And why, if both men and women have been created in God's image, should we not address the Divine as Father *and* Mother, Master and Mistress of Heaven? Martin Buber envisioned Judaism as arising out of a We-Thou dialogue between the Jewish people and God. I'm beginning to suspect, however, that my forefathers did most of the talking. Consequently, Judaism as we now know it was largely fashioned by generations of men who decided what *they* wanted Judaism to be.

Yet even the rabbis of the Talmud admitted that the covenant established at Sinai was given to men *and women*. Perhaps my foremothers were content to live out their membership vicariously, through the rituals and prayers of their fathers, husbands, and sons. Vicarious membership, however, will no longer do. As a feminist, I have begun to reclaim my voice; as a Jew, I am ready to activate my membership within the covenant and to reopen the dialogue with *our* God.

As I think about my spiritual journey, I realize that my search for meaning may never end. What I've learned in the seventeen years since I took my Confirmation vows is that the ground rules are *not* preestablished, that it is my obligation as a Jew to help create a Judaism that is meaningful for my generation. Three thousand years ago, Moses stood at Mt. Sinai and received the Ten Commandments from God. When he came down the mountain and saw the Israelites worshiping a golden calf, he broke the tablets in anger. Perhaps he did so not only to warn us against idolatry but also to make it clear that not even God's words are irrevocably carved in stone.

Source: Ellen M. Umansky, "Reclaiming the Covenant: A Jewish Feminist's Search for Meaning," in *Four Centuries of Jewish Women's Spirituality*, ed. Ellen M. Umansky and Dianne Ashton (Boston: Beacon Press, 1992), 234.

2. Protector of Sarah (1993)

The opening benediction of the Amidah, *the central prayer of the service, has been adjusted by adding the names of the Matriarchs to those of the Patriarchs in both the Hebrew (here in transliteration) and the English.*

———————————————

Ba-ruch a-ta Adonai, Eh-lo-hei-nu vei-lo-hei a-vo-tei-nu v'i-mo-tei-nu: Eh-lo-hei Av-ra-ham, Eh-lo-hei Yitz-chak, vei-lo-hei Ya-a-kov. Eh-lo-hei Sa-rah, Eh-lo-hei Riv-hak, Eh-lo-hei Lei-ah, vei-lo-hei Ra-cheil. Ha-eil ha-ga-dol ha-gi-bor v'ha-no-ra, Eil el-yon. Go-meil cha-sa-dim toh-vim, v'ko-nei ha-kol, v'zo-cheir chas-dei a-voht v'i-ma'hoht, u-mei-vi g'u-la li-v'nei v'nei-hem, l'ma-an sh'mo, b'a-ha-va.

Between Rosh Hashanah and Yom Kippur Add:

Zoch'rei-nu l'cha-yim, meh-lech cha-feitz ba-cha-yim, v'cho-t'vei-nu b'sei-fer ha-cha-yim, l'ma-an-cha Eh-lo-him cha-yim.

Meh-lech o-zeir u-mo-shi-a u-ma-gein.
Ba-ruch a-ta Adonai, ma-gein Av-ra-ham v'ez-rat Sa-rah.

Praised be our God, the God of our fathers and our mothers: God of Abraham, God of Isaac, and God of Jacob; God of Sarah, God of Rebekah, God of Leah and God of Rachel; great, mighty, and awesome God, God supreme.

Ruler of all the living, Your ways are ways of love. You remember the faithfulness of our ancestors, and in love bring redemption to their children's children for the sake of Your name.

Between Rosh Hashanah and Yom Kippur Add:

Remember us unto life, Sovereign who delights in life, and inscribe us in the Book of Life, that Your will may prevail, O God of life.

You are our Sovereign and our Help, our Redeemer and our Shield. We praise You, Eternal One, Shield of Abraham, Protector of Sarah.

———————————————

Source: Gates of Prayer for Weekdays (New York: CCAR Press, 1993), 12.

Prayers for Healing

1. How It Began (1997)

While in Christian circles healing prayers and services have long been established, the first major effort in our environment dates back to only 1991, when five women laid the foundation for an institution devoted to Jewish healing. The Jewish Healing Center was an outgrowth of women's nurturing and caring instincts and quickly spread to the whole Reform movement. Rabbi Nancy A. Flam (1960–) was one of the founders and has remained a leader of this newest spiritual dimension of our faith.

In 1991 a group of five women began to organize what would become the Jewish Healing Center, a service organization dedicated to helping meet the spiritual needs of Jews living with illness. . . .

Among the original organizing group of five women were three rabbis. I believe it not to be coincidental that the organized work of Jewish healing was begun by women, and no accident that female rabbis found a natural home in healing work. . . .

It is refreshing for female rabbis (and, perhaps, for male rabbis, too) to work in an area where there are no binding precedents defined by men. Those who engage in the work of modern Jewish healing surely draw strength and insight from healing prayers in the Bible, healing relationships from the Talmud, and healing principles from the Codes, for example. Nonetheless, as opposed to the model of rabbi as teacher and judge, there is no clear, paradigmatic, two-thousand-year-old model in relation to which rabbis must define themselves as healers. This liberating absence of precedent leaves open to invention such important elements as rabbinic function (more midwife of the spirit than legal authority), language (that is, encouraging God-language based upon personal experience), and communication styles (stressing listening rather than speaking).

Men and women are now equally involved in the work of the Jewish Healing Center (now the National Center of Jewish Healing). Today, male and female rabbis might be equally interested and involved in the work of healing: running healing services, spiritual support groups, and *Bikkur Holim* [visiting the sick] trainings, attending conferences on Jewish healing, and focusing on Jewish means of providing pastoral care. Yet, I agree with Rabbi Neil Gillman that the field of Jewish healing would likely not have arisen without the ordination of women as rabbis. Although pastoral care and counseling have always been part of the rabbinic role, the entrance of women into the rabbinate, with our unique cultural experience as care providers, brings a new dimension to that work. Among our many contributions to a changing rabbinate, our healing work has helped bring to Jewish life a fresh focus on the holiness of human relationship.

Source: Nancy Flam, "Jewish Healing and the Ordination of Women as Rabbis," *CCAR Journal,* summer 1997, 101–2.

2. A Healing Prayer (1988)

Debbie Friedman, composer and popular performer of Jewish music, provided both text and melody for the following prayer now used in many of our synagogues. The first two words, Mi shebeirach *(He who blessed), are the traditional opening for special blessings spoken or chanted from the pulpit.*

Mi she-bei-rach a-vo-tei-nu
M'kor ha-bra-cha l'i-mo-tei-nu
May the source of strength
Who blessed the ones before us
Help us find the courage
To make our lives a blessing
And let us say, Amen

Mi she-bei-rach i-mo-tei-nu
M'kor ha-bra-cha l'a-vo-tei-nu
Bless those in need of healing
With r'fu-a sh'lei-ma
The renewal of body
The renewal of spirit
And let us say, Amen

Source: Debbie Friedman, "Mi Shebeirach" (San Diego: Sounds Write Productions, 1988).

Musical Diversity

In the ancient Temple, a levitical choir embellished public worship; in later centuries, a cantor (chazan) *chanted the entire service, and the congregants joined him by "davvening" individually. In earlier Reform services, a reader would lead the service and a choir supply the music, while congregational participation consisted primarily of joining in responsive English prayers and the singing of English hymns. A Union* Hymnal *for general congregational singing was created; but by the end of the twentieth century it had largely disappeared from the synagogue.*

---

1. Union Hymnal (1932)

The following is taken from the introduction to the third edition of the Union Hymnal, *published in 1932.*

The present edition of the Union Hymnal is the second revision of a work published originally by the Central Conference of American Rabbis in 1892. At that time the need of a Hymn Book that would answer the religious requirements of Reform congregations was apparent. In the discussion of the subject, the founder and first president of the Conference, Isaac M. Wise, said: "It is not the prayer coming from the spirit of Judaism which is fundamental, so much as it is the indestructible element in the psalmody of the people." The late Maurice H. Harris added this significant word to the discussion: "The choir has driven the congregation out as far as worship is concerned. It is time the congregation be given a hearing before God." . . .

One of the main purposes kept constantly in view was to make it as Jewish as possible, and thus meet one of the needs of our modern synagogal life, namely the adaptation of Jewish traditional music to the usage and taste of our own days. This involves a two-fold question: what elements of synagogal melody best express our religious life in music employed by our congregations; and how shall we clothe them in harmony that shall reveal their own peculiar modal character and melodic contours? We would not assert that we have solved these two problems. Not only in this Hymnal, but in our religious-musical life in general, they are still far from a solution. But we have made an earnest effort to proceed in this direction. We have called upon Jewish composers for aid. As noted elsewhere in this Preface, a considerable number of them contributed compositions to this collection. Composers were urged to utilize some of the wealth of synagogal melody. This plea found a ready response. Even a superficial glance through the contents of this volume indicates how many of the hymns are based upon traditional melodies. . . .

It has been our aim to combine Jewish and general musical values. Such a Hymnal as this is not an end, but an advance on the road toward the achievement of a difficult goal. It is our ardent hope that it will help educate our congregations in the beauties of our musical heritage, and lead them God-ward "on the wings of song."

Source: Union Hymnal, 3rd ed. (CCAR, 1932), v–vii.

2. The Cantorate (1999)

In European Liberal congregations, the cantor retained his traditional role of chanting the service, but in North American Reform practice the rabbi led the reading, while a choir dominated the singing with its renditions. For many years, non-Jews sang in such choirs, but in recent years this practice has diminished. Instead, the musical leadership has fallen once again—as it does in traditional synagogues—to cantors, especially after HUC-JIR began to train them in its School of Sacred Music. Female cantors have enjoyed full equality and have been unreservedly accepted by Reform congregations. Here, Howard Stahl, a leading figure in the American Conference of Cantors who currently serves Temple B'nai Jeshurun in Short Hills, New Jersey, discusses changing forms of music in the Reform synagogue.

The American reform synagogue is at a crossroads today. The rabbinic, cantorial, and lay leadership is in the hands of men and women who are products of our movement. We are the true beneficiaries of the legacy of Wise and Sulzer. When cantors lead worship, we create sacred moments in sacred space. Through *chazanut,* the art of the cantor, we link past, present, and future as *klei kodesh.* Though those around us may demand that we sing friendly tunes that create a high comfort level for them, our goal must be to create a sense of *k'dushah,* not *klezmer.* We cannot be afraid to disturb the comfortable. After all, the Hebrew word for worship, *avodah,* is the very same word for work. Wise and Sulzer were not concerned with winning popularity contests. They were committed to instilling reverence for the Divine through worship experiences which were at once artistic, intellectually honest, authentic, and enduring. Wise's paradigm animated my teachers, and they, in turn, transmitted it to their students.

Yet the turbulent sixties shook the rigid and formulaic approach to life. The baby-boomer generation protested the archaic forms of its forebears and sought to tear down the established walls of order and propriety. The synagogue did not escape this modern-day reformation. The classical Reform models of a dignified service read in stentorian tones by a black-robed rabbi, interspersed with a thirty-two bar choral piece with an eight bar solo for an operatic voiced cantor or baritone soloist, no longer found favor in the ears or hearts of the worshiper. Responsive readings and hymn singing in English seemed stilted and arcane. The "king of instruments," the organ, was dethroned—it seemed better suited for cathedrals rather than suburban synagogues that began to spring up in rapid order. With increased Hebrew literacy, fueled by the growing commitment to the state of Israel, congregants wanted to read and sing less and less in the vernacular. Reform's commitment to universalism was replaced by a return to ethnic pride. We were not embarrassed by our unique rituals and customs, and we were no longer concerned with homogenizing worship. The pursuit of freedom and creativity supplanted the quest for dignity and predictability. God was still in His/Her holy Temple, only now sitting beside us in the pew. We needed to re-think and re-tool *Minhag America* to meet contemporary needs. We had come a long way from Albany circa 1846.

And so the pendulum swung radically, plunging us into a swaying, hand-holding, sing-along-with-Mitch, neo-chassidic modality—a kind of Pete Seeger meets Nachman of Bratslav. If liturgical music didn't meet the severely delimited criteria of being singable by all, accessible to all, instantaneously gratifying to all, it was condemned and rejected as being at best off-putting, at worst sacrilegious. We were quick to abandon Wise's plea for "uplifting solemnity." We were equally quick to engage in self-serving, self-gratifying forms which nostalgically reminded us of the good old days—our good old days. But what about the previous generation's good old days? Or for that matter, how *chutzpadik* of us to presume that the *next* generation might relate to what made us feel good. As young adults, my grandparents danced to Rudy Vallee's music. My parents thought he was arcane—they danced to Benny

Goodman. We thought he was square—we danced to a disco beat. My children laugh at the polyester-clad vision and dance to their own drummer. This is as it should be. We need to allow for diversity of form, permitting people of all ages, of all musical tastes, people who seek an immanent God and those who look towards a transcendent one, to feel comfortable and included. We need to look for that rainbow in the sky rather than simply a patch of blue.

Source: Howard Stahl, "A Wise Legacy," *Koleinu B'yachad—Our Voices as One: Envisioning Jewish Music for the 21st Century* (New York: ACC, 1999), 31.

A Revolution in Worship (1999)

At the end of the twentieth century, renewed attention was focused on worship. New initiatives sought ways to make the synagogue more attractive and the service more meaningful, especially to younger people. In his 1999 Biennial Assembly address, excerpted here, the president of the UAHC, Rabbi Eric H. Yoffie, urged nothing less than a revolution.

I propose ... that at this Biennial Assembly we proclaim a new Reform revolution. Like the original Reform revolution, it will be rooted in the conviction that Judaism is a tradition of rebellion, revival, and redefinition; and like the original too, this new initiative will make synagogue worship our Movement's foremost concern.

I further propose that this worship revolution be built upon the premise of partnership: rabbis will be its architects, cantors its artists, and lay people its builders. This has always been the way of our Movement. No other religious movement in Jewish life has ever been as democratic, as open, and as rooted in the collective partnership of rabbi, cantor, and lay person.

And what is generally true is especially important in this case. Because prayer is not a noun but a verb; it is not something that is done to us or for us, but by us; it is not something that you create and give to the congregation, but something that the congregation creates with you. So it is critical that vested interests be put aside and that the laity be admitted into the dialogue, even as we acknowledge that Jewish wisdom is ultimately the rabbis' expertise.

The revolution that I propose will require an accurate understanding of what we mean by "tradition."

The heart of the worship tradition is the order of prayers that has become standardized during the last two millennia. And while Reform Judaism has revised this liturgy to make it fully inclusive, the *Shema,* the *Amidah,* and the Torah service are not very different from what they were in the third century.

Everything else, however—the chanting styles, the music, the aesthetics—has been ever-changing. If we have learned anything at all from Jewish history, it is that there is no one way to worship God. In fact, much of what we now refer to as "tradition" is not tradition at all, but reflects European culture of the eighteenth and nineteenth century.

And we need not be bound by cultural precedents that no longer resonate. Eighteenth century Minsk is not our worship ideal. Neither is Berlin of the 1850s, nor suburban America of the 1950s.

And just as we reject nostalgia disguised as tradition, so too do we reject worship that is purely "contemporary." Communal prayer requires recognizable constants; there is no Jewish worship without age-old prayers and time-honored chants. In short, we need not choose between "traditional" worship and "contemporary" worship. As Reform Jews, we insist on the best of both worlds: continuity with our tradition and constant reformation.

To do this, we need both innovators and conservators: those who push the envelope and those who hold back. But at this moment it is innovators that we need most. We must give our leaders the freedom to experiment, and to develop forms of communal prayer that are both Jewishly authentic and fully indigenous to North America. . . .

Above all else, our success will depend on creating . . . partnership. . . .

We do not want to be rabbis who are spiritual imperialists, insisting that worship is ours alone; we do not want to be cantors who are operatic obstructionists, intent on performance at the expense of prayer; and we do not want to be lay people who are conscientious objectors, objecting to everything that is not as it was.

What we do want is for our members to join together with rabbi and cantor in creating worship that leaves us all uplifted—connected to ancient wisdom and to our deepest selves.

And to join together in creating a synagogue that is a center of Jewish life in all its sweep and scope, but that is first and foremost a center of *avodah*—of worship, reverence, and awe.

And we will do this because we are the most creative movement in Jewish life; because, in the absence of prayer, all our crowded congregational calendars are for naught; and because to live without prayer is to live without God.

And so, together, we will give Reform Jews the meaningful prayer they demand from us—worship rooted in tradition that manages still to seduce the soul and electrify the heart.

Source: Eric H. Yoffie, "Realizing God's Promise: Reform Judaism in the 21st Century" (UAHC Biennial Assembly address, Orlando, FL, December 1999), 2–3, 7.

SHABBAT AND HOLY DAYS

✦ Shabbat was once the central Jewish experience. Week after week, so it seemed, our eyes were focused on the day on which we could have a foretaste of the Garden of Eden. A famous saying had it that as long as Jews would cherish Shabbat, it in turn would protect them. A social critic of our time might conclude that inasmuch as Jews today seem to be so well protected, they must indeed be cherishing the seventh day more faithfully than ever. Yet the very opposite is true. In the Diaspora, in any case, Shabbat as a twenty-four-hour observance has disappeared from the lives of most Jews.

This decline of observance, and even awareness, is not altogether new. It was, in fact, an early result of Emancipation and later, in North America, of changed priorities. The biblical command to rest from work appeared to interfere with making a decent living. Working at one's job or keeping the shop open on Shabbat began to take precedence over religious tradition, and Saturday morning attendance at synagogue services became restricted to women and retired folk. The introduction of Friday evening services at a set time was an attempt to counteract this development, but the awareness of the whole day's holiness is all but gone. It has become merely another day in the week and has been absorbed in popular perception as part of the weekend. Jews see it no longer as Shabbat but as Saturday. Recreation has replaced religion, and leisure has taken the place of rest.

Similar problems have affected the celebration of the holy days, with the seder, Rosh HaShanah, and Yom Kippur remaining the last regular strongholds of religious attention for the majority. But toward the end of the twentieth century, countervailing trends could be seen as increasing numbers of Reform Jews were turning to broader observance.

Saving Shabbat

Early North American Reformers struggled to maintain the two pillars of Shabbat observance: the command to abstain from work and the mitzvah of public worship.

---

1. The Friday Night Experiment (1869)

In the face of public inattention to Shabbat morning worship, Isaac M. Wise in 1869 joined colleagues in Cleveland and Louisville in introducing a late Friday evening service at a fixed time. Probably no other Reform innovation was crowned with such long-lasting success.

What is the meaning of this reform[the late Friday evening service]? Our readers know that innovations for innovation's sake do not suit us. Reforms must have an object. What is the object of this particular one? We will state it, chiefly for the consideration of sister congregations all over the country who might take the matter into fair consideration.

In the first place, evening services are much more impressive and solemn than the day service. Nevertheless this natural point of advantage was almost entirely neglected in the synagogue. The services being held at twilight, as the evening sacrifice was made in Jerusalem, were not attended on account of the improper and ever changing time, and in many congregations given up entirely.

In the second place, during the hottest months of the summer, in this climate at least, the Sabbath morning service also was neglected; still, the cool evening when people love to go out was not used for the purpose, although the advantage is evident.

In the third place, there are a great many in every congregation who can not attend divine service in the morning. We need hardly remind our readers, that there are business men, clerks, book keepers, apprentices, female servants, and even many mothers, who can not leave their houses always in the morning, and attend divine service.

There is no excuse left to anybody. Seven o'clock in the evening, every Israelite in this city, and most likely also in every other city, can attend divine service. Those who do attend their temples on Sabbath morning and those who can not, the old and the young, those who are and those who are not their own masters, can come and spend one hour in higher reflections, in worship and prayer, in divine lessons and solemn contemplations.

It has been objected that many prefer the theater and the opera to the temple, and will go to those places of amusement in preference to the house of worship. Good bye to you, ladies and gentlemen, we will see you again. Persons who have no higher than fictitious ideals, who prefer play to reality, self-deception to self-elevation, fiction to truth, amusement to instruction, the fleet shadows of the moment to the rock of eternity, persons who worship selfishness in lieu of the Eternal God, will go almost anywhere. But we do not suppose we are mistaken in the bulk of our coreligionists, if we maintain that the vast majority of them will visit the temple, when opportunity offers, and go to hear artists some other evenings, if they wish to hear them. Managers of theaters and operas will have to put off their gala evenings from Friday to Saturday evening. We do not suppose to be mistaken, if we predict that our members and our personal friends will be in the temple, young and old, every Friday evening, and will soon convince themselves that there is the proper place to spend an hour or so in devotion, after a week of toil and turmoil. We entertain not the least doubt, it will be same in all other cities, where our brethren reside in large numbers. Try it, and convince yourselves.

On our part, it will be our duty to establish a Friday evening service, which shall be as sublime, as edifying and elevating as God has placed the means within our reach.

Source: Isaac M. Wise, "Friday Night Services," in *The Growth of Reform Judaism,* ed. W. Gunther Plaut (New York: World Union for Progressive Judaism, 1965), 277–78.

2. The "Sunday Sabbath" (1885)

Morning services on the seventh day had run upon the shoals of economic priorities, and a Sunday service seemed to many as a logical, if unhappy, alternative. For a while, the idea caught on, but in time the Reform movement returned to Shabbat. The matter was heatedly argued at the convention that passed the Pittsburgh Platform (1885). The following are excerpts from the debate.

Dr. [*Adolph*] *Moses:* Some years ago I wrote and published in the *Zeitgeist* several articles against Sunday service. Candor compels me to state here, that in the light of later and wider experience, I have come to see that the opinions then held and expressed by me on this question were erroneous. Things have indeed come to such a pass that, unless we boldly advocate and strenuously strive to introduce Sunday service, the future of Judaism in this country looks gloomy in the extreme. Most of us preach twice every Saturday. To whom? On Friday night we usually address about the sixth part of our congregation, at times outnumbered by the Gentiles present. On Saturday morning we preach to women, children, and a few old men. But the great mass of even those Jews that belong to a congregation, goes from year's beginning to year's end without religious and moral instruction. The fact is, Saturday morning is the busiest and, commercially, the most profitable day of the week. . . .

Dr. [Emil] Hirsch: . . . I know . . . that it is but a question of time, when I shall have no audience on Saturday, and I alone and the pews certainly are powerless to keep the almost dead Sabbath alive. Give the people their Sunday services. Give those that cannot come on Saturday an opportunity to derive spiritual benefits from their hours of leisure. Now, they grow up without them! . . .

Dr. [Isaac M.] Wise: I am not opposed to the idea of Sunday service where it is a necessity. It is not contrary to Judaism, it means not falling into Christianity, but I cannot recommend Sunday services; where there is no extraordinary power to attract, there will be no greater attendance than on Saturday. This is an irreligious age. Sunday service has been tried, it has failed in many places. . . .

Dr. [Samson] Falk: I came to this Conference with the intention of helping to tune up the religious sentiment, which in Israel at present, is indeed, more necessary than anything else, and the best method, as it seems to me, would be to work in that direction with combined efforts. It is a serious detriment to Judaism to see the time-honored Sabbath-eve so flagrantly neglected. Let us begin work by restoring the sanctity of the Sabbath, by glorifying the Friday evening in our temples, when the plea of business engagements, if any, has no excuse. I admit, the religious observance of the Sabbath meets with formidable, almost insurmountable obstacles. But let us try it first with the Friday evening, and step by step we would accomplish a return of our people to the observance of the Sabbath, in spirit and in deed. Regarding Sunday services, I draw your attention to the fact, that great majorities in our congregation would at any time prefer having their children duly instructed in the religion of their fathers on Sunday forenoon, to Sunday services themselves to which they cannot warm up. . . .

Dr. E. Hirsch then offered the following which was unanimously adopted as the sense of the Conference on the subject.

Whereas, We recognize the importance of maintaining the historical Sabbath as a bond with our great past and the symbol of the unity of Judaism the world over; and

Whereas, On the other hand, it cannot be denied that there is a vast number of working men and others who, from some cause or other, are not able to attend the services on the sacred day of rest; be it

Resolved, That there is nothing in the spirit of Judaism or its laws to prevent the introduction of Sunday services in localities where the necessity for such services appears, or is felt.

Source: "Authentic Report of the Proceedings of the Rabbinical Conference Held at Pittsburgh, Nov. 16, 17, 18, 1885," in *The Pittsburgh Platform in Retrospect,* ed. Walter Jacob (Pittsburgh: Rodef Shalom Congregation, 1985), 115–19.

3. Recovering Shabbat (1965)

In 1965, the CCAR devoted an entire day of its annual convention to the problem of Shabbat observance. The keynote address was delivered by W. Gunther Plaut (1912–), then senior rabbi of Holy Blossom Temple in Toronto.

I venture to say that a test of free association with the words "Friday night" would produce one overwhelming response amongst rabbis and another amongst our members. When *you* hear "Friday night" you think, quite naturally, of services. The majority of our members, if they think in Jewish terms at all, will probably associate Friday night first and foremost with candles and Kiddush, or more likely, with family, and only then with services. I have tested it often enough to state this with confidence, and I draw an important conclusion from it.

Friday night as a family night, with or without some mitzvot performed, *is still a reality amongst many of our people.* What have we done to give this feeling a meaningful mode of expression? Next to nothing. . . .

The reason for this studied underplay of Friday night observance at home is obvious: We do not want to compete with ourselves. We want our people to light candles, yes; we want them to say Kiddush and a prayer or two, yes; but not too long, not too much, because we also want them to get through with dinner and hurry to Temple. We even put our emaciated ברכת המזון [*prayer after food*] some place else, lest they spend too much time at home. . . .

Even if I would be convinced that a concerted Friday night home service program would be superlatively effective and eventually diminish my Friday night attendance to the vanishing point, even then would I gladly proceed with my efforts, in fact I would redouble them. I would then happily abandon my Friday night services and concentrate on Shabbat morning, as my traditionalist colleagues in Toronto have done. There, all Conservative and Orthodox synagogues have closed down their late services on Friday and instead record increased attendances on Sabbath morning. Their members come from the same neighborhoods as mine and belong to the same occupational and social strata. For them Shabbat morning is a possibility—but only because they no longer have Sabbath Eve services. Meanwhile, for most of us this will not be the immediate problem, although I think that we ought to consider the reascendency of Shabbat morning most seriously.

In any case, our Friday night worship hours are in no danger from a resuscitation of home observance. Of course, there will be no overnight success in this effort. But we must start. Our Brotherhoods are already on record as favoring this enterprise and surely we can enlist our Sisterhoods for a task which is so well fitted to their purposes. What is needed, and I repeat it once more, is for us to cease considering Judaism a Temple activity. None of *us* believes that it is, but by inadvertence and circumstance we have led our members to accept this as תורה למשה מסיני [Torah from Sinai]. In the area of social action we have already magnificently demonstrated our capacity for making Judaism effective beyond the synagogue; now let us do for Jewish observance what we have done for social action. Instead of making our congregants come to us, let us go to them into their homes with our treasures of Jewish life. And if we go to them they will also come to us.

Source: W. Gunther Plaut, "The Sabbath in the Reform Movement," in *Reform Judaism: A Historical Perspective,* ed. Joseph L. Blau (New York: KTAV, 1973), 246–49.

Enhancing Shabbat

1. A Shabbat Manual (Tadrikh l'Shabbat) (1972)

Privately published guides to enhance Shabbat observance had already appeared (e.g., one by Doppelt and Polish; see chapter 7) when the 1965 convention of the CCAR established a Sabbath Committee, which produced A Shabbat Manual *for official adoption by the CCAR. The book spoke of commandments (mitzvot) but left it to a later publication to discuss their compelling source (see chapter 7).*

Purposes of Shabbat Observance

What we do or abstain from doing on Shabbat should be directed toward the fulfillment of five major purposes. These five purposes historically have been identified with Shabbat and represent the core of Jewish existence as expressed in *sh'mirat Shabbat,* Sabbath observance.

1. Awareness of the World.

In our weekday life, we rarely pause to consider the nature of the universe around us; we seldom meditate on the meaning and purpose of our existence in it. The observance of Shabbat affords us a singular opportunity to reflect upon the marvel of the universe which God has created, to rejoice in the glory and beauty of creation, and to consider our part in God's continuing process of creation. This is the core of the Fourth Commandment (in Exodus), and is emphasized in the *Kiddush* which reminds us that the Shabbat is instituted "in remembrance of the work of creation" *(zikaron lema'aseh Bereshit).*

2. Commitment to Freedom.

In our tradition, God is acknowledged not only as a creator and source of life but also as a presence in human history, especially in the history of the Jewish people. The *Kiddush* also speaks of Shabbat as "a memorial of the exodus from Egypt" *(zecher litzi'at Mitzrayim,* reflecting the Fourth Commandment in Deuteronomy). This means that as God delivered us from slavery so must we strive to help all who suffer from every form of bondage and degradation in the world. Shabbat reminds us of our historic commitment to freedom and justice. It shows us the world that can be if we will it.

3. *Identity with the Jewish People.*

On Shabbat, we have a weekly opportunity to remember God's covenant (*b'rit*) with Israel and to reaffirm our identity with, and loyalty to, the house of Israel. Shabbat is "a sign between Me and the children of Israel forever." It summons us to a renewal of our responsibility to promote the welfare and dignity of the Jewish people. It calls upon each Jew to help further the high and noble purposes of the community and to use the precious hours of the Shabbat to deepen the unique historic fellowship of the Jewish people.

4. *Enhancement of the Person.*

The Shabbat tradition provides three modes for the enhancement of personal life: *k'dushah, m'nuchah, oneg.*

K'dushah (holiness) requires that Shabbat be singled out as different from the weekdays. It must be distinguished from the other days of the week so that those who observe it will become transformed by its holiness. One ought, therefore, to do certain things which contribute to an awareness of this day's special nature, and to abstain from doing others which lessen our awareness.

M'nuchah (rest), as expressed through Shabbat, is more than relaxation and abstention from work. It is a condition of the soul, a physical and spiritual release from weekday pressures. If the week is characterized by competition, rush, and turmoil, their absence will contribute to serenity. It is this quality of *m'nuchah* which leads tradition to call Shabbat "a foretaste of the days of the Messiah."

Oneg (joy), as experienced on Shabbat, is more than fun and pleasure. It is the kind of joy that enhances our personal lives and leaves us truly enriched for the week ahead. Shabbat gives us a quantity of "free" time and, thereby, a qualitative potential of freedom—time during which man can be himself and do for himself and for others what he could never accomplish during the other days of the week.

5. *Dedication to Peace.*

More than any other day, Shabbat embodies our yearning for peace. Its traditional greeting, "Shabbat Shalom," as well as the day's all-pervasive mood, attunes us to the value of peace and teaches its centrality in the Jew's hope for the world today and for the future. Each week it calls us to renewed effort and dedication "to make peace between man and man." Shabbat can become a foundation of human reconciliation, for as we observe it and remember its purposes, we—and thereby the world—will have made a turning toward peace.

The rewards of making Shabbat meaningful are many. We cannot afford to spurn them. As Jews, we ought to know that Shabbat is one of the cornerstones of our faith. When we secure this cornerstone for ourselves, we do so for the kingdom of God and for the community of the Eternal People.

Source: A Shabbat Manual, ed. W. Gunther Plaut (New York: CCAR Press, 1972), 5–6.

2. Gates of Shabbat (Shaarei Shabbat) (1991)

A Shabbat Manual *was updated and greatly enlarged a generation later, under the editorship of Mark Dov Shapiro (1950–), rabbi in Springfield, Massachusetts. It addressed Reform Jews in their individual existential condition.*

Questions and Answers

Shabbat sounds wonderful, almost too good to be true. What if it doesn't mean as much to me as it does to some other Jews?

It is quite possible that Shabbat is not as high a priority in your life as it is in the lives of some Jews. Your Shabbat may not even resemble the ideal Shabbat described in many parts of this book. That does not matter at this point. What matters is that you begin to learn. Many options for interpreting and observing Shabbat are offered in these pages so that different people in varying circumstances can all find something of significance. The meaning of Shabbat is not a given. It grows as you begin to encounter Shabbat from wherever you find yourself now as a Jew.

Where do I begin if I'm a novice?

Begin simply. Look over the possibilities described in this book and choose one or two ways to observe Shabbat. Starting with candlelighting on Friday night is one of the easiest ways to enter Shabbat. Whatever you choose, remember you don't need to restructure your entire lifestyle in one weekend! Just give yourself some time to experience Shabbat and the day will begin to take shape.

Even at that, don't be surprised if your "new" Shabbat also changes with time. You should continue to grow as a Jew so that Shabbat takes on greater meaning with the passing years. The process of "making" Shabbat is truly lifelong.

Should all the prayers be recited in Hebrew?

It is not necessary to read Hebrew in order to begin your observance of Shabbat. The blessings in this book are translated so that anyone can have access to them. Hopefully, your enriched experience at home and in the synagogue will at some point lead to your learning to read and understand Hebrew if you cannot yet do so.

Everyone in our home works. How can we find the time to prepare for Shabbat and make the day different?

If your days are already so full that finding time for any new activity, let alone Shabbat, seems unrealistic, you will probably not find time for Shabbat by simply hoping some "open" moments will appear on the weekend calendar. The open moments will only appear if you decide in advance that *you want to make them appear.* In other words, you will need to make time for the time to observe Shabbat.

That might involve starting to think about Shabbat as early as Monday. Early in the week you may need to choose a Friday evening menu or plan a special activity suitable for Shabbat day.

When Friday evening actually arrives, try an experiment to help yourself get started. For a set period of four weeks commit yourself to a particular ritual like the Friday evening *Kiddush.* Promise yourself to do the *Kiddush* under almost all circumstances.

That discipline might be just what you need to begin to make the *Kiddush* a habit. After four weeks, even if you do once again become "too busy" for *Kiddush,* you may discover that your familiarity with the *Kiddush* has made it into something you miss. You will find yourself making time for the *Kiddush* because it has become a natural part of your life.

By the way, the welcoming of Shabbat from candles to challah does not take much time. It can take as little as five minutes to say the blessings, or somewhat more time if you complement the blessings with singing and . . . other possibilities. . . .

I'm a single person. How can I have Shabbat?

You can have Shabbat by not allowing yourself to think about Shabbat or Judaism as solely a family affair. The Shabbat message about sanctifying time and renewing our relationship with prayer and Jewish study is very much directed to individual, adult Jews.

Despite that, those parts of Shabbat that do focus on the home, especially Friday evening's dinner, can be difficult for the single person. Even though the blessings can all be done by an individual of either sex, many people will be more comfortable sharing dinner with others. For that reason it makes sense to plan ahead and arrange to spend Friday evening with friends or family. The essence of Shabbat, however, is still very much yours as a single, Jewish adult.

My spouse is not Jewish. How do we observe Shabbat?

If your spouse is willing to join you in exploring Shabbat, the two of you ought to begin together. Even though a non-Jew might not feel comfortable reciting blessings with such phrases as "who has commanded *us*," Shabbat allows so many possibilities for observance and enjoyment that it can act as a powerful mechanism for giving your home a Jewish ambience.

Source: *Gates of Shabbat,* ed. Mark Dov Shapiro (New York: CCAR Press, 1991), 3–5.

The Holy Days

1. The Aesthetics of Mitzvot (1983)

A guide for observing the special days of the Jewish calendar, Gates of the Seasons *(Shaarei Mo-eid), was published by the CCAR in 1983. A relatively small book, it describes the major and minor occasions of the year and at the same time challenges the individual Jew to observe them to the fullest extent possible. Among its rubrics is hiddur mitzvah, the aesthetics of mitzvot.*

The sources delineate the minimum requirements of the mitzvot. A sukkah must have certain dimensions and must be constructed in a particular manner. The cup for *Kiddush* must be large enough to hold a specified minimum amount of wine. While some may be satisfied with minimum standards, the Jewish tradition recognizes and encourages the addition of an aesthetic dimension. Beauty enhances the mitzvot by appealing to the senses. Beautiful sounds and agreeable fragrances, tastes, textures, colors, and artistry contribute to human enjoyment of religious acts, and beauty itself takes on a religious dimension. The principle of enhancing a mitzvah through aesthetics is called *hiddur mitzvah*.

The concept of *hiddur mitzvah* is derived from Rabbi Ishmael's comment on the verse, "This is my God and I will glorify Him" (Exodus 15:2).

> Is it possible for a human being to add glory to his Creator? What this really means is: I shall glorify Him in the way I perform mitzvot. I shall prepare before Him a beautiful *lulav,* a beautiful sukkah, beautiful fringes *(tzitzit),* and beautiful phylacteries (*tefillin*).

The Talmud adds to this list a beautiful shofar and a beautiful Torah scroll which has been written by a skilled scribe with fine ink and fine pen and wrapped in beautiful silks.

"In keeping with the principle of *hiddur mitzvah,*" Rabbi Zera taught, "one should be willing to pay even one third more [than the normal price]." Jewish folklore is replete with stories about Jews of modest circumstances paying more than they could afford for the most beautiful *etrog* to enhance their observance of Sukkot, or for the most delectable foods to enhance their observance of Shabbat.

The Midrash suggests that not only are mitzvot enhanced by an aesthetic dimension but so is the Jew who observes it: "You are beautiful, my love, you are beautiful, through mitzvot . . . beautiful through mitzvot, beautiful through deeds of loving kindness, . . . through prayer, through reciting the *Shema,* through the mezuzah, through phylacteries, through sukkah and *lulav* and *etrog.* . . ." There seems to be reciprocity of beauty through the agency of mitzvot: the Jew becomes beautiful as he/she performs a mitzvah. "But, conversely, Israel 'beautifies' God by performing the commandments in the most 'beautiful' manner. . . ."

There are many ways to apply the principle of *hiddur mitzvah.* For example, one might choose to observe the mitzvah of kindling Chanukah lights with a cheap, stamped tin *chanukiyah* or one might make an effort to build one by hand or to buy a beautiful one. Some families might prefer an oil-burning *chanukiyah,* rather than one that uses the standard candles, in order to relate their observance of the mitzvah more closely to the times of the Maccabees. Certainly the mitzvah of lighting Chanukah candles is fulfilled with any kind of *chanukiyah,* but by applying the principle of *hiddur mitzvah,* one enriches both the mitzvah and him/herself.

Source: Gates of the Seasons, ed. Peter S. Knobel (New York: CCAR Press, 1983), 162–63.

2. The High Holy Days (1978)

As shown in chapter 4, Reform prayer books for Shabbat and Festivals have undergone significant revisions. The same is true also for the Rosh HaShanah and Yom Kippur liturgies, a CCAR-sponsored gender-sensitive prayer book for the High Holy Days appearing for the first time in 1996. Since for Avinu Malkeinu (literally, "our Father, our King") no gender-sensitive translation could be found, the new edition leaves the two Hebrew words untranslated. The Kol Nidrei prayer, as introduced below in Gates of Repentance (1978), has presented another challenge. That prayer, which gives its name to the eve of Yom Kippur, is a medieval creation. Literally rendered, it prays for cancellation of promises that will be made in the coming year. Since the early Reformers were embarrassed by the text, they eliminated it but kept the familiar music. The latest edition of our prayer book does print the original Aramaic text, though the English freely reinterprets it by speaking not of all promises, but only of those that we meant to keep but could not.

Kol Nidrei is the prayer of people not free to make their own decisions, people forced to say what they do not mean. In repeating this prayer, we identify with the agony of our forebears who had to say 'yes' when they meant 'no.' *Kol Nidrei* is also a confession: we are all transgressors, all exiled from the Highest we know, all in need of the healing of forgiveness and reconciliation. For what we have done, for what we may yet do, we ask pardon; for rash words, broken pledges, insincere assurances, and foolish promises, may we find forgiveness. . . .

Let all our vows and oaths, all the promises we make and the obligations we incur to You, O God, between this Yom Kippur and the next, be null and void should we, after honest effort, find ourselves unable to fulfill them. Then may we be absolved of them.

Source: Gates of Repentance (New York: CCAR Press, 1978), 250–52.

For many years our movement considered fasting a dispensable ritual, but of late it is once more widely observed. Gates of the Seasons (1983) suggests that fasting continues to possess significance for the Reform Jew.

Yom Kippur is a day set apart by the Torah for us to "practice self-denial" (Leviticus 23:27). The "self-denial" which seems to be most expressive of Yom Kippur is fasting, abstaining from food and drink for the entire day.

Fasting is an opportunity for each of us to observe Yom Kippur in a most personal way. It is a day of intense self-searching and earnest communication with the Almighty. This search requires an internal calm which derives from slowing down our biological rhythm. Fasting on Yom Kippur provides the key to our inner awakening.

On Yom Kippur we seek reconciliation with God and humanity. Repentance *(t'shuvah)* involves a critical self-assessment of the past year and the resolve to avoid lapses in sensitivity in the future. *T'shuvah* requires discipline. Our fasting on Yom Kippur demonstrates our willingness to submit to discipline. How can we atone for our excesses toward others unless we can curb appetites which depend on no one but ourselves? To set boundaries for our own conduct in this very private matter is to begin the path toward controlling our public behavior.

The fast of Yom Kippur reaches beyond our inner spiritual awakening and discipline into our ethical behavior. In the haftarah we read on Yom Kippur morning of the prophet Isaiah providing us with the ultimate goal of our fast—to unlock the shackles of injustice, to undo the fetters of bondage, to let the oppressed go free, to share bread with the hungry (Isaiah 58:1–14).

Finally, to fast on the Day of Atonement is an act of solidarity with the suffering of the Jewish people. Through fasting we are drawn closer to all who live lives of deprivation. Our faith demands more of us than twenty-four hours of abstinence from food. It demands that upon the completion of our fast we will turn back to the world prepared to act with love and compassion. In this way fasting touches the biological as well as the spiritual aspects of our being.

Source: Gates of the Seasons, ed. Peter S. Knobel (New York: CCAR Press, 1983), 146–47.

Pesach (1974)

The first Passover Haggadah issued by the CCAR was fairly "classical" (i.e., old-line Reform) in content and appearance. A generation later a much more elaborate volume made its appearance and achieved instantaneous acceptance. The book was not so much a revision of its predecessor as a new attempt to recover large elements of tradition without shrinking from the use of new material. For instance, the recital of the ten plagues that befell the Egyptians had been omitted from the earlier Reform Haggadah as "unworthy of enlightened sensitivities" but was restored in the new version, which "represents a fusion of the particular Jewish experience of deliverance with the universal human longing for redemption." The following selection shows how the new Haggadah integrates contemporary texts with traditional ones.

So they set taskmasters over them with forced labor and they built garrison cities for Pharaoh: Pithom and Raamses. The Egyptians embittered their lives with harsh labor at mortar and brick and in all sorts of work in the fields. But the more they were oppressed, the more they increased and spread out, so that the Egyptians came to despise and dread the Israelites. So Pharaoh charged all his people, saying, "Every boy that is born shall be thrown in the Nile, but let every girl live." We cried unto the Lord, the God of our Fathers, and the Lord heeded our plight, our misery, and our oppression.

"The Egyptians Embittered Their Lives"

We got used to standing in line at seven o'clock in the morning, at twelve noon, and again at seven o'clock in the evening. We stood in a long queue with a plate in our hand into which they ladled a little warmed-up water with a salty or a coffee flavor. Or else they gave us a few potatoes. We got used to sleeping without a bed, to saluting every uniform, not to walk on the sidewalks, and then again to walk on the sidewalks. We got used to undeserved slaps, blows, and executions. We got accustomed to seeing piled-up coffins full of corpses, to seeing the sick amidst dirt and filth, and to seeing the helpless doctors. We got used to the fact that from time to time, one thousand unhappy souls would go away. . . .

From the prose of fifteen-year-old Peter Fischl, who perished in Auschwitz in 1944

"Our Misery"

The "misery" refers, commentators say, to the enforced separation of husbands and wives. Husbands and wives were not allowed to live together. Nevertheless, the women of Israel were a source of strength to their husbands, bringing them food, consoling them when they visited, giving them hope of liberation.

Midrash

"Our Oppression"

We are taught that the Egyptians taunted the Israelites for observing the circumcision of their sons. They mocked the Hebrews for this, since the infants were to be put to death anyway. But the Hebrews answered, "We perform our duty; whatever you do later cannot affect our practice of our faith. As our ancestors were faithful to God's covenant, so shall we be."

Midrash

Source: A Passover Haggadah, ed. Herbert Bronstein, with drawings by Leonard Baskin (New York: CCAR Press, 1974), 40–41.

Old and New Observances

1. Tishah B'Av (1895)

The 1895 Union Prayer Book *balanced the mourning for the destruction of the ancient Temple with the recognition that the dispersion had enabled the Jewish people to bring its mission to the world.*

We commemorate to-day the saddest event in Jewish history: the time when the glory departed from Judah, and Jerusalem was made desolate, when the enemy poured out his wrath upon the holy city, gave over the sanctuary of Zion a prey to the devouring flames. Twice was the crown and pride of Israel, the sacred spot on which patriarchs and prophets taught and where the Levites sang their holy hymns, a spoil to strangers. Bitter was the cup which Israel had to drink. He was driven from his home to lands whose people knew not love and had no compassion on the sufferer. Myriads fell by the enemy's sword or were cast to the wild beasts; but harder still was the fate of those who escaped, for they were sold as slaves and doomed to drag out a miserable existence. But all these hardships and trials were rendered all the harder as our ancestors were led to believe that they were inflicted on them as a punishment for sins their fathers had committed when they dwelt in the land of their inheritance.

And while they hoped and longed to return to their home and to see the temple restored as a sign of God's pardon and favor; alas, the night of the exile grew ever darker and the sufferings and the persecutions increased. Ever louder became their wailing and lamentations and they cried: Why, O

Lord, did Thou cast us off? Tears are our meat day and night, while our enemies continually say unto us: Where is thy God? How long, O God, how long? When will Thy anger cease and Thy tender mercies be shown again unto those who have not forgotten Thee?

But the house of Jacob was not cast off nor forsaken by the God whose name was called upon it. Like the thorn-bush on Sinai which burned, but was not consumed, because God's majesty was manifested in it, so was Israel preserved by the very fire that raged about him. It had pleased the Lord to make His servant the wonder of the nations, and a witness to His own imperishable truth; though a bruised reed, he was not broken. He was put to grief and numbered with the transgressors, yet he bore the sin of the nations, and out of his wounds flowed the balm of healing for mankind. A man of sorrows, smitten of God, despised and rejected of men, he was as a lamb brought to slaughter and would not open his mouth; yet his death did give life, the darkness of his imprisonment brought light to the Gentiles. The One temple in Jerusalem sank, but thousands of the sanctuaries of the God who once hallowed it, rose in its stead all over the globe where the same God was worshiped and the same truth proclaimed. Thus has the Lord comforted Israel and turned his sackcloth into garments of joy. Praise be to Him. Amen.

Source: Union Prayer Book (Cincinnati: Bloch Publishing, 1895), 283–84.

2. Yom HaShoah (1975)

A hundred years later the ancient mourning had been brutally updated by the Shoah, the bitter experience of the Holocaust. Now the two were linked in Reform prayers, for both confronted tragic events. Abraham Shlonsky (1900–1973) was Israel's first modernist poet. His "In the Presence of Eyes" has found a place in the current Reform prayer book.

In the presence of eyes
which witnessed the slaughter,
which saw the oppression
the heart could not bear,
and as witness the heart
that once taught compassion

until the days came to pass
that crushed human feeling,
I have taken an oath: To remember it all,
to remember, not once to forget!
Forget not one thing to the last generation
when degradation shall cease,
to the last, to its ending,
when the rod of instruction
shall have come to conclusion.
An oath: Not in vain passed over
the night of the terror.
An oath: No morning shall see me at flesh-pots again.
An oath: Lest from this we learned nothing.

Source: Avraham Shlonsky, "In the Presence of Eyes," trans. from Hebrew by Herbert Bronstein, in *Gates of Prayer* (New York: CCAR Press, 1975), 573.

3. Yom HaAtzma-ut (1975)

Contrary to Orthodox practice, the Reform movement has recognized Israel Independence Day as an official holy day. This is a dramatic reversal from its earlier opposition to Zionism, a position that was definitively reversed at the Columbus convention of the CCAR in 1937. The special liturgy, which takes up twenty-two pages in the 1975 edition of Gates of Prayer, *contains the following passages near its conclusion.*

You are the hidden God; You are Israel's God; You are the God who redeems. Our people crushed, Zion restored, in a single generation! None has felt such pain as ours, none has known such joy!

And yet, even now, Exile persists, no less real than before: for still our enemies plot to destroy us, still they hack at our roots. Still nations beat plowshares into swords and pruning-hooks into spears. Still earth awaits its true redemption. . . .

A long road, full of torment, from the fall of Jerusalem to its rebuilding. A long road from Jerusalem rebuilt, to the building of God's kingdom. We cannot be silent over our loss. We cannot pretend to understand. And yet, O Lord, we cannot give You up; we will not give the tyrant the final victory.

We stand before You in pain and need, remembering our martyrs and heroes, praising the Source of life, from whom we come, to whom we return.

Source: Gates of Prayer (New York: CCAR Press, 1975), 609–10.

4. The Recovery of Rosh Chodesh

In biblical days, the celebration of sighting the new moon (Rosh Chodesh) was as important as Shabbat. But after the destruction of the Temple by the Romans in 70 C.E. and the scientific calculation of the first day of the month, it became a minor festival. Though, as on Purim, work was permitted, women were to refrain from it—a special gift to them from God, said tradition, for not having worshiped the Golden Calf. In recent decades feminism has given new emphasis to the day as an acknowledgment of a woman's monthly cycle and has created special poetry and prayers to celebrate it.

The new moon, the new moon, slim bright light, pregnant with
   possibilities.
Our lives are like the new moon.
How great are our talents, which God has given us.
How little of them we reveal.
Adonai, our God, in the coming month, help me/us shed light on the
   great gifts You have blessed me/us with, so that next month I/we may
   say, "What God has given me/us, I/we have truly shared with others."

Source: Jo David, untitled, *Covenant of the Heart: Prayers and Meditations from the Women of Reform Judaism* (New York: Women of Reform Judaism, 1993), 89.

Blessed are You, Our God, Monarch over time and space, Who by a word
   created the heavens, and by a whisper, all the ends of the cosmos.
Law and appointed times has God set for all living things.
This ordering allows all things to maintain their character.
They will fulfill the will of their Creator in joy and gladness.
The Source of Truth pursues work that is Truth.
God ordained that the moon be renewed each month as a crown of
   glory to those sustained from the womb until this time, whose life
   will be renewed as that of the moon, to glorify the Creator.

Blessed are You, Our God, Who renews the months.

May it be your will, Our God and God of our Mothers and Fathers, to
bring on the coming of the new month for Good and for Blessing.
Grant us long life, a life of peace, a life of goodness, a life of blessing,
with sustenance, a life of vigor and vitality.
May it be a life with awe of God and fear of sin, a life of riches and
honor, a life in which there shall be among us love of Torah and
God. May it be a life in which the prayers of the heart shall be
fulfilled for Good.
May God who brought miracles for our ancestors, and redeemed them
from slavery to freedom, from darkness to light, redeem us and
gather us from all the ends of the earth.

Source: Karen Fox, untitled, *Covenant of the Heart: Prayers and Meditations from the Women of Reform Judaism* (New York: Women of Reform Judaism, 1993), 89–90.

The following excerpt is taken from a poem by Rabbi Vicki L. Hollander (1952–), who serves the hospice movement. It was composed for the new month of Elul, which precedes Rosh HaShanah.

Elul calls us
to forgive,
to forgive ourselves whom we have wounded
wittingly and unwittingly
by words, and by actions.
She bids us look at ourselves,
which stings like lemon juice in an open wound,
and to ask forgiveness
and to grant forgiveness.

She bids us
to cry the unshed tears,
to loosen jaws which clench,
to open the closed recesses within,
to scour that which has solidified,
like calcium deposits in the inside of a kettle,
staining the inner parts of our being.

She bids us
to wash ourselves clean
that we might be fresh agan,
that we might shine again,
that we might stand restored,
pure as first made.

Harahaman,
support us as we tread this path,
for the way is most arduous.
We lie exposed and open as a freshly cut fig
raw, naked, succulent.

We face choked words, and mottled histories
tortured sculptures of intentions that missed the mark
overgrown gardens of emotions that grew awry
cantankerously
leaving their marks etched without and within

Help us learn Elul's lessons.
Help us wash.
Aid us scrub away the rings.
Enable us to pass through
cleansed,
renewed,
so that we might sing our songs
and bear the flame
higher

Be with us as we walk forward,
as we walk forward
Harahaman.

Source: Vicki Hollander, "Rosh Chodesh Elul," (1990).

SIX

LIFE-CYCLE EVENTS

✦ Judaism, like most religions, distinguishes the major events of a person's life by special rites. Some—like birth and death, or menstruation—depend on the course of nature, while others—like covenantal celebrations after birth, bar/bat mitzvah, confirmation, and marriage—follow human decisions. Reform has, on the whole, maintained the traditional life-cycle observances, albeit with certain changes. It has added rituals for the newly born, such as bringing girls into the covenant, and has abandoned others, like *pidyon haben* (the redemption of the first-born male). It has supported the writing of wedding contracts *(ketubot)* in a modern and egalitarian idiom and has made available a greatly revised version of the traditional divorce certificate *(get)* for those who seek a religious form of closure. In the wake of the prevailing individualism among North Americans, life-cycle events have become so significant for Reform Jews that the personal event is likely to receive close attention, while communal responsibilities, like religious services, are often neglected.

Entering and Affirming the Covenant

God's covenant with Israel included every one of the people, regardless of gender, age, or occupation, and all future generations too were to be bound by it. Yet, while tradition prescribes the method by which a Jewish boy is formally inducted, through the rite of b'rit milah *(the covenant of circumcision), it was Reform Judaism that added a ritual for girls, called* b'rit hachayyim. *The antiquity of circumcision is attested by the biblical record itself and was practiced by many people besides the Jews. Herodotus cites hygienic reasons for the practice, while some fifteen hundred years later Maimonides thought that it was meant to reduce sexual desire to a manageable degree. Most likely, however, it was originally a fertility rite, possibly an offering of human blood to propitiate the gods. The command to Abraham (Genesis 17:9–12) emphasizes the spiritual significance of the rite. In past decades, North American medical practitioners favored circumcision as beneficial for any newborn boy, but lately the former consensus has been breached—and even some Jewish parents abstain from submitting their children to the rite. However, such opposition is rare, and most Jewish boys are still being circumcised. For many years, Reform Jews used either an Orthodox mohel (circumciser who also recites the requisite prayers) or had physicians do the surgery and a rabbi read the ritual. Today Reform Judaism has a Berit Mila Board that trains and certifies Jewish physicians to perform the function of milah.*

---

1. The Mitzvah (1979)

Though in the early days of the movement there was some discussion about the need to maintain the ancient practice, it continued to be observed as a mitzvah incumbent on all Jews.

It is a mitzvah to circumcise a male child on the eighth day, as we read in the Torah: "At the age of eight days every male among you throughout the generations shall be circumcised" (Genesis 17:12). So significant is the mitzvah of circumcision on the *eighth* day that tradition requires the performance of the ceremony on that day even if it falls on Shabbat or Yom Kippur. In cases where this is not possible, the rabbi should be consulted.

Circumcision may be postponed for medical reasons. If postponed, it should be held as soon as possible consistent with the health of the child. In the case of hemophilia or any other medical contraindication, circumcision may be indefinitely postponed. In such cases parents should arrange for appropriate prayers (as in the case of females) initiating their son into the covenant community. Such an uncircumcised Jewish male is considered a full member of the Jewish people and a participant in the *b'rit*. . . .

It is a mitzvah to bring daughters as well as sons into the *b'rit*. Reform Judaism is committed to the equality of the sexes, and in consonance with this principle, parents should arrange a *b'rit* service for girls either at home or in the synagogue.

Gates of Mitzvah, ed. Simeon J. Maslin (New York: CCAR Press, 1979), 14–15.

2. Female Circumcisers (Mohalot) (1999)

Ilana Trachtman here traces the creation of Reform's B'rit Mila Board and the certification of mohalot. Although Maimonides would have permitted female circumcisers, modern Orthodoxy refuses to recognize their legitimacy.

———————

In 1984, under pressure to serve an increasingly diverse community, the Reform movement recognized the need for non-Orthodox mohels. Inspired by Dr. Debra Cohen's request for training (Conservative and Orthodox groups had turned her down), HUC came through. It created the Brit Milah Board, the first training program offered by any liberal Jewish institutions to train medical professionals—men and women alike—to perform ritual circumcision. Gender-blind on principle—women were already ordained as Reform rabbis—the movement didn't meditate on the intense historical chauvinism that surrounds Jewish circumcision. They were not concerned with the psychological question "What does it mean for a woman to preside?" The only question was, "Is there a need?"

When they asked that question, they found parents expressing a desire for their sons' *brit mila* ceremonies to reflect their own Jewish practices. It is reported that Orthodox *mohels* asked to preside over a *brit* have insisted that both parents be Jewish and heterosexual, and often exclude women from the ceremony, making *brit mila* uncomfortable and sometimes impossible for non-traditional couples hoping to raise a Jewish child.

"The opposition"—and there was plenty—"is more psychological and sociological than halachic," wrote the late Solomon Freehof, one of Reform Judaism's preeminent legal authorities, during that first controversial year. "Male functionaries through time have taken unto themselves certain ritual practices. The sociology of the Jewish community has enforced this practice and barred other competent and skilled practitioners from exercising their legal right."

The creation of the Brit Milah Board signified the end of the Orthodox monopoly in the business of the *brit.* It meant that intermarried, unmarried, and gay and lesbian couples could have their sons circumcised in a Jewish ritual. It also meant that women's right to perform a *brit*—for the first time in history since Tzipporah circumcised Moses—was officially recognized. Since the Hebrew Union College's Reform program began in 1984 and the

Jewish Theological Seminary's Conservative program began in 1989, 260 mohels have been trained; 48 are women.

"It's incredibly important for women to have a chance to be *mohalot*—that women can contribute to Jewish culture as men can," says Cohen, the first *mohelet*.

Following the recognition of women as rabbis and cantors, licensing women to be *mohalot* enriches the texture of Jewish ceremonial leadership. But as purveyors of a sacred ceremony, the *mohelet* must grapple with the psychological and social incongruity of performing and perpetuating a ritual that excludes her on both religious and anatomical counts.

Source: Ilana Trachtman, "When the *Mohel* Is a Woman," *Lilith*, spring 1999, 11.

3. The Covenant Ceremony for Newborn Girls (B'rit Hachayyim) (1994)

In 1975 the CCAR reaffirmed its commitment to the religious equality of women and urged the introduction of life-cycle ceremonies for females equivalent to those conducted for males. The latest home prayer book calls the rite b'rit hachayyim (the covenant of life). It is to be distinguished from a naming ceremony and should represent the entrance of a girl into the covenant, equaling in spiritual significance the entrance of a boy through b'rit milah.

This ritual is conducted on the eighth day.

בְּרוּכָה הַבָּאָה.

Blessed be the child whom we now welcome.

Reverence for life has been enjoined on us as a fulfillment of our covenant with God, as it is written, 'And God said to Israel: Choose life, that you and your descendants may live.'

The birth of a daughter brings us joy and hope, and the courage to reaffirm our enduring covenant with life and its Creator.

The mother kindles a light and takes her daughter in her arms:

כִּי נֵר מִצְוָה וְתוֹרָה אוֹר.

The Mitzvah is a lamp; Torah is a light.

בָּרוּךְ אַתָּה יי, הַמֵּאִיר לָעוֹלָם כֻּלּוֹ בִּכְבוֹדוֹ.

We praise You, O God, whose presence gives light to all the world.

Joyfully I bring my daughter into the covenant of our people: a covenant with God, with Torah, and with our people.

Ba-ruch a-ta Adonai,	בָּרוּךְ אַתָּה יי
Eh-lo-hei-nu meh-lech ha-o-lam	אֱלֹהֵינוּ מֶלֶךְ הָעוֹלָם
a-sher ki-d'sha-nu b'mitz-vo-tav	אֲשֶׁר קִדְּשָׁנוּ בְּמִצְוֹתָיו
V'tzi-va-nu l'hach-ni-sah bi-v'rit	וְצִוָּנוּ לְהַכְנִיסָהּ בִּבְרִית
ha-cha-yim	הַחַיִּים.

We praise You, Eternal God, Sovereign of the universe: You hallow us with Your Mitzvot, and command us to bring our daughters into the Covenant of Life.

Source: *On the Doorposts of Your House,* ed. Chaim Stern (New York: CCAR Press, 1994), 116.

4. The Mitzvah of Adoption (1979)

The racial origin of a child is of no significance in Judaism. However, adopting parents are cautioned not to convert a child born of non-Jewish lineage until the adoption becomes valid in civil law.

All the mitzvot and traditions that apply to one's natural children apply equally to adopted children.

An adopted child should be named in the synagogue and entered into the *b'rit* as soon as the initial legal procedures for adoption have been completed. If a male child is not an infant, the rabbi should be consulted about the circumcision.

If the adopted child is not an infant and was born of non-Jewish or undetermined parents, the rabbi should be consulted as to the procedure for formal entry into the Jewish community.

Source: *Gates of Mitzvah,* ed. Simeon J. Maslin (New York: CCAR Press, 1979), 18.

5. Illicit Descent (Mamzerut) (1988)

Jewish tradition affixes a stigma to children of an illicit union, that is, one that cannot be legitimized (such as the child of an adulterous mother or the offspring of unions forbidden in the Torah). Such children are called mamzerim/mamzerot, *and the halachah provides that the only Jews they may marry are those who themselves carry the stigma of* mamzerut. *Reform has taken a different position on this issue.*

Jewish tradition affixes no stigma to children born to unmarried women. The obloquy of *mamzerut* is attached only to a child of an *illicit* union (a union that cannot be legitimized), such as a child born of an adulterous mother or one issuing from a union forbidden by the Torah. But that same tradition has also attempted to downplay the occurrence of *mamzerut* by giving children the benefit of doubt or by its refusal to pursue an inquiry into a person's status when such an inquiry could be avoided.

The question of *mamzerim/mamzerot* has lately been brought to the fore because many women have remarried without first obtaining an halachic *get*. Children of their further marriages would then incur the status of *mamzer/mamzeret* and, in Orthodox tradition, be unmarriageable to any Jews except other *mamzerim/mamzerot*.

Reform Judaism has abandoned the concept of *mamzerut* altogether and considers all Jewish children marriageable with one another.

Source: Maaglei Tzedek—Rabbi's Manual, ed. David Polish, with historical and halachic notes by W. Gunther Plaut (New York: CCAR Press, 1988), 224–25.

6. "No" to Bar Mitzvah (1907)

Early Reformers encouraged the abandonment of bar mitzvah observances and substituted the rite of confirmation in order to celebrate the religious education of both girls and boys. In 1907, Rabbi Kaufmann Kohler, then president of the Hebrew Union College, advanced two arguments for this stance.

Ceremonies which assign to woman an inferior rank according to Oriental notions are out of place with us. Reform Judaism recognizes woman as man's equal and sees in her deeper emotional nature, which is more responsive to the promptings of the spirit, the real inspiring influence for religious life in the household. Accordingly all the ceremonies in the domestic life today should be Occidental rather than Oriental in form and character.

In this connection let me speak of the bar mitzvah ceremony to which many Reform Congregations still adhere. By so doing they ignore the plain fact that the calling up of the thirteen year old lad to read from the Torah is a mere survival of the calling up of all the members of the congregation to the Torah reading. The original significance, which was to indicate thereby the admission of the lad into the membership of the congregation, has been forgotten and consequently the usage today is meaningless. The moment the Oriental notion of the superiority of man over woman in religious life was abandoned, a form of consecration for the young of both sexes was instituted in its place and the beautiful rite of confirmation was adopted.

Source: Kaufmann Kohler, "The Origin and Functions of Ceremonies in Judaism," *CCAR Yearbook* 17 (1907): 226.

7. "Yes" to Bar and Bat Mitzvah (1988)

During the second half of the twentieth century, the spread of bar mitzvah as well as bat mitzvah ceremonies (the latter pioneered by Reconstructionist congregations) caused Reform to admit the practice, which has since become standard in most of its congregations. While confirmation has coexisted with it and stresses the need for Jewish education past the age of thirteen, the number of confirmands has decreased significantly in many places.

Bar and bat mitzvah celebrations have become commonplace in our congregations, and in consequence a considerable body of custom and literature has sprung up

In our educational and religious practices, boys and girls are treated equally, and if a congregation encourages the ceremony all children should be asked to fulfill the educational requirements leading to it.

The customary age for the child for being called to the Torah is thirteen. It is mentioned in Pirkei Avot (5.21) as the age for fulfilling the mitzvot. While this was taken by some, especially among Sefardim, as being an aggadic statement only, and the wearing of *tefillin* was permitted at an earlier age, thirteen remained the customary age for the child's first *aliyah*. Though parents often desire the bar and bat mitzvah celebrations of their child to take place early, rabbis should not accede to such requests except in cases of serious emergency. There is no justification for holding girls' celebrations at an earlier time on the ground that their puberty occurs at the age of twelve or even before. For us, bar and bat mitzvah are way stations in Jewish growth, and not physiologically based *rites de passage*. . . .

The ceremony is firmly linked to occasions when the Torah is read, which, in Reform congregations, frequently includes Friday nights. Sunday mornings should be used for this purpose only when they coincide with Rosh Chodesh or a holy day. "To conduct a Torah reading where no Torah reading belongs, to recite the blessings where none are due *(beracha levatala)*, merely in order to make the religious service convenient to the social celebration, is to consent to an inversion of values and should not be done."

If the celebration is held on Saturday afternoons, the opening portion of the following week's *sidra* is read. . . . Such practice is discouraged when it leads to an emphasis on social rather than religious aspects.

Source: *Maaglei Tzedek—Rabbi's Manual*, ed. David Polish, with historical and halachic notes by W. Gunther Plaut (New York: CCAR Press, 1988), 229–30.

Women's Life-Cycle

Although Mishnah and Talmud devote much space to issues concerning menstruation (niddah), *the onset of menses was not assigned a place among the 100 obligatory benedictions. Intercourse was prohibited during that time and could be resumed only after the woman had visited the* mikveh.

---

1. New Blessings (1994)

Reform has suggested special benedictions for menarche (the first menstruation) and for the onset of subsequent periods.

Menarche blessing

יְהִי רָצוֹן מִלְּפָנֶיךָ, יי אֱלֹהֵינוּ וֵאלֹהֵי אֲבוֹתֵנוּ וְאִמּוֹתֵנוּ,
שֶׁתִּשְׁכּוֹן עִמָּדִי בְּהִכָּנְסִי לְמַעֲגַל הַנָּשִׁים.

Our God and God of our mothers and our fathers, be with me as I begin the cycle of women.

Ba-ruch a-ta Adonai,

Eh-lo-hei-nu meh-lech ha-o-lam,

sheh-heh-cheh-ya-nu, v'ki-y'ma-nu,

v'higi-a-nu la-z'man ha-zeh.

בָּרוּךְ אַתָּה יי

אֱלֹהֵינוּ מֶלֶךְ הָעוֹלָם,

וְקִיְּמָנוּ וְהִגִּיעָנוּ

וְהִגִּיעָנוּ לַזְּמַן הַזֶּה.

I praise You, Eternal God, Sovereign of the universe, for giving me life, for sustaining me, and for enabling me to reach this season of my life.

At the onset of each menstrual period

בָּרוּךְ אַתָּה יי אֱלֹהֵינוּ מֶלֶךְ הָעוֹלָם,

שֶׁעָשַׂנִי אִשָּׁה.

I praise You, Eternal God, Sovereign of the universe, for making me a woman.

Source: On the Doorposts of Your House, ed. Chaim Stern (New York: CCAR Press, 1994), 105.

2. Menstruation and Mikveh (1998)

Elyse Goldstein (1955–), a rabbi in Toronto, here shares her feelings when examining the relevance of a practice that Reform abandoned long ago.

I go to the *mikveh* each month, not so I may be "kosher" for my husband—I'm no chicken product—but as a woman bidding farewell to a regular part of myself. I am a woman who needs some way to existentially experience and then bless special moments. I never feel physically or spiritually dirty during my cycle. I do, however, feel a need to realign myself, to rebalance my emotions and attentions, which have been different during those days. I pay attention to my cycle: its presence has been reassuring and its absence was the first sign—a most welcome and spiritual one—when I wanted to become pregnant.

Because I have learned to count the days and months by my own body, I have never understood why the Jewish tradition—such an essential part of my being—does not have a blessing for this regular monthly event.

Surely a religion which boasts of a positive view of the body, a religion which has a blessing for an activity as mundane as going to the bathroom, would have a way to sacralize such a significant occurrence! The male composers of the liturgy, living in a world where modesty was central and women's bodies were a mystery at best, were not able—or more likely, not willing—to imagine such a blessing. They simply never composed one. If they had, where would it be found—in the back of the prayerbook with other daily blessings? I sometimes wonder if we had such a blessing passed by mother to daughter, which has been lost. Have women always felt ambivalent about menstruation and thus never risen up to bless it, even in private, among themselves? . . .

Each month, at the time I see I have gotten my period, I say, *"Baruch atah Adonai, eloheinu melech ha-olam, she'asani ishah:* Blessed are You, Adonai our God, Ruler of the World, who has made me a woman." It sets the mood for the rest of my month.

Source: Elyse Goldstein, *ReVisions* (Woodstock, Vt.: Jewish Lights, 1998), 105–6.

Marriage (1973)

Already the early Reformers objected to the traditional marriage ritual, which assigned an active role only to the groom. The Orthodox considered mutuality to be contrary to the legal aspects of the marital union and therefore vigorously opposed an exchange of rings. In the course of time, Reform abandoned the use of a chupah *(the wedding canopy), the traditional* ketubah *(the Hebrew/Aramaic marriage contract), and the breaking of the glass at the end of the ceremony. In recent decades these practices have found their way back into many Reform ceremonies, except that the* ketubah *now contains mutual declarations of loyalty and love. Here are two excerpts from a contemporary* ketubah.

On the_____day of the week the_____day of _____Five thousand seven hundred_____since the creation of the world as we reckon time here in_____

The bride_____
daughter of_____
and_____
promised_____the groom
son of_____
and_____
You are my husband according to
the tradition of Moses and Israel. I
shall cherish you and honor you as
is customary among the daughters
of Israel who have cherished and
honored their husbands in
faithfulness and in integrity

The groom_____
son of_____
and_____
promised_____the bride
daughter of_____
and_____
You are my wife according to the
tradition of Moses and Israel. I shall
cherish you and honor you as is
customary among the sons of Israel
who have cherished and honored
their wives in faithfulness and in
integrity

The groom and bride have also promised each other to strive throughout
their lives together to achieve an openness which will enable them to share
their thoughts, their feelings, and their experiences

To be sensitive at all times to each other's needs; to attain mutual intellectual,
emotional, physical, and spiritual fulfillment; to work for the perpetuation
of Judaism and of the Jewish people in their home, in their family life, and
in their communal endeavors

This marriage has been authorized also by the civil authorities
of_____

It is valid and binding

witness_____
bride_____

witness_____
groom_____

rabbi_____

Source: *The Jewish Catalogue,* ed. Richard Siegel et al. (Philadelphia: Jewish Publication Society,
1973), 165.

Divorce (1988)

*Although most Jews have religious weddings, which in all states in the United States
and all provinces in Canada have legal standing, a Jewish divorce is accorded no such*

public recognition. While standard in Orthodox practice, it has been disregarded by most Reform Jews, who do not recognize the sole power of the husband to initiate a divorce and consider a civil decree sufficient. Exceptions are made when a divorced partner needs a get (traditional divorce document) in order to marry a traditional spouse, in which case the husband will be urged to obtain it from the Orthodox rabbinate. Of late, Reform rabbis have conducted a "Ritual of Release" and issued a te-udat pereidah (a document of separation). The following is one version of the ritual.

(It is understood that the following ritual will be conducted only after the rabbi has had the opportunity to counsel with one or, preferably, both of the parties involved, and only after the couple has received a civil divorce decree. The rabbi will explain to the participants that this ceremony and the accompanying document do not constitute a halachic get. The ceremony should take place in the presence of witnesses. Participants might invite their children, family, or close friends to be present.)

RABBI

Since earliest times Judaism has provided for divorce when a woman and a man, who have been joined together in *kiddushin* (sacred matrimony), no longer experience the sacred in their relationship. The decision to separate is painful, not only for the woman and the man (and for their children), but for the entire community. Jewish tradition teaches that when the sacred covenant of marriage is dissolved, "even the altar sheds tears." (Gittin 90b)

W: have you consented to the termination of your marriage?

(W responds.)

M: have you consented to the termination of your marriage?

(M responds.)

W

I, _____, now release my former husband, _____, from the sacred bonds that held us together.

M

I, _____, now release my former wife, _____, from the sacred bonds that held us together.

RABBI

W and M: _____years ago you entered into the covenant of *kiddushin*. Now you have asked us to witness your willingness to release each other from the sacred bond of marriage, and your intention to enter a new phase of life.

What existed between you, both the good and the bad, is ingrained in your memories. We pray that the good that once existed between you may encourage you to treat each other with respect and trust, and to refrain from acts of hostility. (And may the love that you have for your children, and the love that they have for you, increase with years and understanding.)

(Personal words by rabbi.)

This is your Document of Separation, duly signed by you both. It marks the dissolution of your marriage. I separate it now as you have separated, giving each of you a part.

W and M: you are both now free to enter into a new phase of your life. Take with you the assurance that human love and sanctity endure.

יֶצֶף יי בֵּינֵךְ וּבֵינֶךָ. [*Yitzef Adonai beinech uveinecha,*], May God watch over each of you and protect you as you go your separate ways.

And let us say: Amen.

Source: Maaglei Tzedek—Rabbi's Manual, ed. David Polish, with historical and halachic notes by W. Gunther Plaut (New York: CCAR Press, 1988), 97–100.

Dealing with Death

In many, if not most, cultures, mourning the dead is accompanied by formal rituals. Judaism is no exception, and its tradition has provided for specific observances at stipulated times. Thus, burial is obligatory, and cremation is frowned upon. The first seven days after interment (shivah) *are subject to strict rules, which ease as the year passes and the mourners return to the challenges of everyday life. In some respects Reform has favored tradition; in others it has altered or abandoned it.*

---

1. Autopsy (1988)

Orthodoxy, intent on the sanctity of the human body, is generally opposed to postmortem intrusion, while Reform has taken a more permissive position.

We would permit an autopsy when we are assured that it could provide new medical knowledge or relieve the suffering of others, or when the law requires it to establish cause of death. In every case, burial of parts of the body should be arranged.

We consider the offering of tissue for transplanting in order to benefit another person a commendable religious act which increases rather than decreases *kevod hamet*, the honor due to the deceased. The Conservative rabbinate takes a similar position.

Source: *Maaglei Tzedek—Rabbi's Manual*, ed. David Polish, with historical and halachic notes by W. Gunther Plaut (New York: CCAR Press, 1988), 247.

2. Burial (1988)

We generally follow tradition and bury the dead as soon as possible. Questions often arise when the dead is a non-Jewish member of the family.

We permit the burial of a non-Jewish spouse in a Jewish cemetery whether or not the Jewish spouse has already been buried there. "Still greater claim have their children to a regular Jewish burial, whether they have been brought up as Jews or not" (K. Kohler). . . . However, in no case should a non-Jewish service be held at our cemetery.

When the burial takes place in a non-Jewish cemetery, we should not refuse to officiate, provided we use our own Jewish ritual. . . .

We bury in the usual manner persons who died by their own hands, for we consider them to have acted under intolerable stress.

Source: *Maaglei Tzedek—Rabbi's Manual*, ed. David Polish, with historical and halachic notes by W. Gunther Plaut (New York: CCAR Press, 1988), 250–51.

3. Shivah (1988)

A week of mourning, shared with family and friends, begins the process of healing. It is a mitzvah to visit the mourners during this period.

If interment is held on the eve of a holy day, an hour's shivah should be observed; the arrival of the *Yom Tov* then cancels the formal shivah, but it is

Reform practice that it may be taken up informally again after the *Yom Tov*, if the family so desires. Traditional law also stipulates that shivah does not start during the intermediate days of a festival and begins only after the festival days are completed. A drawn-out period during which mourning is delayed may, however, constitute considerable emotional stress, and we may therefore encourage shivah to be held during the intermediate days, to terminate with the arrival of the concluding holy day. Even traditional law prescribes that comforting the mourners is a mitzvah to be observed during a holy day period.

On the Sabbath (which counts as part of the shivah period) formal mourning is suspended and mourners are encouraged to visit the synagogue. Some congregations follow the old custom of welcoming the mourners after the recital of *L'chah Dodi*.

A memorial light is kindled in the home after the return from the cemetery and is kept burning during the shivah. Though the custom is of fairly recent origin, it has become firmly established. . . .

Mourners are encouraged to stay at home during shivah (except on Sabbaths and festivals, when they should join the congregation in prayer), to refrain from their ordinary pursuits and occupations, and to participate in daily services at home. The first three days of the shivah period are considered the most intense. In Reform congregations they are considered the minimum mourning period, and in many places have taken the place of the full shivah (though they do not replace it as the desirable norm).

At the third rabbinic conference of liberal German rabbis (Breslau, 1846) the following resolution was adopted after considerable discussion:

> The assembly declares that the following mourning practices, which have developed from former popular custom, have lost significance and religious value for our time, and, in fact, run contrary to our religious sentiment and are, therefore, to be eliminated:
> The tearing of the clothes, allowing the beard to grow, sitting on the ground, elimination of leather footwear; and also those which custom has almost entirely eliminated, namely, the prohibitions of washing, bathing, and greeting.

Covering or turning the mirrors is based on superstition. The practice is nowadays defended by some because mirrors are a symbol of vanity. The wishes of the family should be followed.

The warning to pregnant women not to attend funeral services or enter the cemetery is based on a superstitious belief in the power of the evil eye.

During the shivah period services should be conducted, if at all possible, at the house of mourning. We would also encourage lay persons to conduct such services; the presence of a rabbi is not required by any religious tradition. . . . We do not require a minyan but would encourage it for the service, and of course make no distinction in this respect between men and women.

In tradition, a small portion of the last day of shivah stands for the whole day. No special ceremonies mark the "rising" from shivah, though it is customary to repeat the formula of consolation at this time. There is also a practice of walking around the block, as a symbolic return to the everyday world.

Source: Maaglei Tzedek—Rabbi's Manual, ed. David Polish, with historical and halachic notes by W. Gunther Plaut (New York: CCAR Press, 1988), 252–53.

4. Kaddish 1988)

Reform has upheld the mitzvah of saying Kaddish *during the year following a loved one's death.*

Originating as a brief *response* to the reader's call to praise God, and assuming—in the Babylonian schools and synagogues—the character of a *doxology* (expressing the Messianic and eschatalogical hopes of Judaism), at the conclusion of a haggadic homily, the *Kaddish* finally acquired its special distinction as the *Orphan's prayer*. In keeping with early notions, it was considered efficacious in rescuing the souls of the dead from Gehenna. As the period of their punishment was supposed to last twelve months, the practice arose about the 12th century in Germany to recite the *Kaddish* throughout the whole year following the day of burial. In order that a man might not consider his own father or mother so sinful as to incur the maximum penalty, the period of reciting the *Kaddish* was reduced to eleven months. It must be observed that the establishment of a year of mourning was at least in part the outgrowth of natural sorrow, as evident from the talmudic saying: "The dead is not forgotten until after twelve months."

Irrespective of its supposedly mediatorial character, the *Kaddish Yatom* [mourner's *Kaddish*] deservedly plays an important part in the religious life of the Jewish people. It expresses faith in the everlasting God in the face of death and resignation to God's will. It also betokens pious regard for the memory of the departed. As such it serves to strengthen both the religious sentiment and the ties of family union. The loved and pleasant in life are not wholly divided even in death. In the words of Israel Abrahams: "Thus is a bridge built over the chasm of the tomb." . . .

Kaddish should be recited by converts for their non-Jewish family, and by members of the family for a deceased apostate as well.

In Jewish tradition, distinctions are made between the death of a parent and that of other relatives. Mourning is more severe in the former case, even after *sh'loshim* [the initial thirty days]. We would encourage the practice of saying *Kaddish* for all close members of the family.

Source: *Maaglei Tzedek—Rabbi's Manual,* ed. David Polish, with historical and halachic notes by W. Gunther Plaut (New York: CCAR Press, 1988), 254–55.

5. Yahrzeit (1988)

The word comes from the German Jahrzeit *(time of the year), denoting the anniversary of someone's death. The custom of remembering the dead every year at this special time is of medieval origin.*

While the practice of fasting on the *yahrzeit* of one's father, mother, and teacher has been generally relaxed in modern times, that of reciting the *Kaddish* has remained a standard obligation. *It should be said by men and women alike,* and in memory of all family members for whom mourning rites are obligatory. The prevailing custom in Reform congregations today is for members of the family to attend the synagogue on the *yahrzeit* date itself or, if the congregation does not conduct daily services, on the Sabbath following the *yahrzeit* date. Although most Reform Jews still observe *yahrzeit* by the secular date, we would encourage the observance to be determined by the Jewish religious calendar, for in this way the *yahrzeit* follows the rhythm of the Jewish year. . . .

It is customary to kindle a memorial light in the house, on the eve of *yahrzeit,* as an act of remembrance. The custom is based on Prov. 20:27: "The human soul is the lamp of Adonai."

At synagogue services mourners stand for *Kaddish;* in most Reform congregations all present stand with them.

Source: Maaglei Tzedek—Rabbi's Manual, ed. David Polish, with historical and halachic notes by W. Gunther Plaut (New York: CCAR Press, 1988), 256.

6. Yizkor (1988)

Yizkor *means "May [God] remember." It is the opening word of a prayer that is traditionally recited on Yom Kippur, Pesach, Shavuot, and Sh'mini Atzeret in remembrance of the dead.*

The Reform liturgy lends the ritual added emphasis by extended prayers, readings, and music. . . .

We do not encourage the custom of keeping those (especially young people) whose parents are still alive away from the service, and neither do the Sefardim. Young people especially should be taught the Jewish way of cherishing the memory of the dead.

Source: Maaglei Tzedek—Rabbi's Manual, ed. David Polish, with historical and halachic notes by W. Gunther Plaut (New York: CCAR Press, 1988), 257.

THE HALACHAH OF REFORM

✦ Reform Judaism began as a movement to reform halachah* and not the religion of Judaism, as is often suggested. The founders did not even aim at remaking halachah itself, but rather at reforming its thrust; they accepted its process and premises. The process of reform consisted of an orderly investigation of precedents, and the premise was, and has remained, to discover how the Jewish people could live in accordance with the Torah tradition. But while in the past it had been the wisdom of earlier scholars that carried the greatest weight, Reform rabbis tended to look less at traditional standards and more at the demands of modernity. By and by, the concept and terminology of halachah disappeared from the vocabulary of Reform. Instead, personal autonomy rather than past practice and precedent had the last word. To be sure, there were learned Reform scholars who wrote responsa on a variety of subjects, but their opinions rarely had an impact on the movement as a whole.

Halachah returned to Reform Jewish life after World War II, sparked by a striving for renewed certainties in a chaotic world and by the timely leadership of Rabbi Solomon B. Freehof (1892–1990), whose halachic studies and responsa, borne by his personal authority, encouraged the Reform rabbinate to look once again to past as well as present for meaningful guidance.

---

* Literally, halachah means "the way to go" and describes the tradition of mitzvot and customs that over the centuries have assumed compelling force for Orthodox Judaism. Obviously, in the Reform context the term has a changed meaning.

New Approaches

1. The Power of Custom (Minhag) (1946)

Author of many books on Jewish practice and responsa, and president of the CCAR, Rabbi Freehof considered the accepted customs of the Reform movement as capable of being elevated into mitzvot.

―――――――――

Without going into the deep and difficult questions involved in the problem of revelation, it is sufficient for our practical purposes to say that those observances which, inspired by the past, are accepted by Israel in the present or become acceptable to Israel, can serve us as a description of the content of Torah. That, in fact, is the way in which the law was creatively developed. *Minhagim* arose all over the world. They were the creative part of Jewish law. It would be a fascinating study to go through the notes of Isserles to the *Shulchan Aruch* and the *Tur* and to list all the instances in which he says: "This is our custom," or "This is not our custom," or "It is our custom to do thus and thus." It would be revealed that a large bulk of Jewish law was derived spontaneously, creatively and anonymously from the life of the people of Israel. This *minhag* was more basic to the development of Jewish law than the law itself has ever acknowledged. . . .

This essentially Jewish procedure is the only practicable one for us and that indeed is what we actually follow. On the basis of material which we find in Jewish literature, we are developing practices which we present before our people. Practices also arise spontaneously. Who, for example, first thought of the late Friday evening service? Who was the first to have the ceremonial lighting of Sabbath candles in the synagog? These things simply arose. We can trace some of them. Some of them are even in our day no longer traceable, as the origin of the bar mitzvah is no longer traceable. Thus is Torah being developed in our day.

This is for us the direction of growth. We are grateful to the founders of Reform Judaism who had the courage of revolutionists to break away from the stifling authority of a legal system once flexible and inspiring and which already in their day had become dogmatic and immovable. Had they left us under the authority of Orthodoxy, Judaism today would have been deprived of its freest creative religious force. Our liberty gives us our opportunity and our obligation. The content of Torah must be built up through *minhag* and we are the ones who are free, creative and confident enough to do it, not only for ourselves but for all of Israel.

Thus Reform Judaism has a special role in Jewish life, a new and creative role. We are the only religious division in Judaism which is completely free from the compulsive power of the now immobile legal system. We are the only ones who can create new *minhagim* freely, try them out without hindrance, and accept or reject according to our experience. We, therefore, are the only branch of Judaism which can best build new ceremonial forms for all of Jewish life. Many of the forms which we have developed in the past are already widely accepted. Many that we will build in the future will provide for Judaism a more stately mansion.

But this task, if we accept it, involves a definite type of self-restraint. We must give up the easy comfort of early codification. We have a great deal of thinking, debating and selection to do before we can presume to say what is God's command and what is mere experiment. We must take a great deal of time to work out general categories as to which observances, which department of observances are of religious moment. Which types of actions are the concern of religion to such an extent that Judaism should regulate them? The ethical life is, of course, first of all and preeminent. Then perhaps the duty of public and private worship must be rebuilt into an intensely felt mitzvah. People have lost that sense of personal obligation and individual responsibility to worship God in the midst of the congregation. The duty to study Jewish law and literature must certainly be rebuilt into a mitzvah. These are just indications of the general task which confronts us.

Source: Solomon B. Freehof, "Slow Growth," in *The Growth of Reform Judaism*, ed. W. Gunther Plaut (New York: World Union for Progressive Judaism, 1965), 239–41.

2. Defining Our Borders (1987)

Rabbi Walter Jacob (1930–) followed Rabbi Freehof not only in his Pittsburgh pulpit, but also as chair of the Responsa Committee of the CCAR. Many responsa of the latter decades of the twentieth century bear his signature. Here he discusses the role of halachah in Reform Judaism.

When we analyze each period of history we discover different strands in the halachah. These appear both in the decisions and underlying philosophy.

Tradition, of course, has chosen a single path and rejected the others, but we recall their existence and the fact that they were suggested and followed by loyal Jews in the past. Diversity has always been the hallmark of our literature and our people. When we find ourselves facing new situations in our age, we are justified in turning to the mainstream of rabbinic thought as well as its divergent paths for halachic guidance. In our view, therefore, the halachah is a vast repository whose old debates are often relevant to new situations.

Sometimes our solutions may parallel those of past generations. On other occasions we may diverge from them. Through this effort we seek solutions for a generation living in lands distant and distinct from those of the ancient Near East or medieval Europe.

Not every question can be resolved by reviewing the rabbinic literature and in some instances totally new legislation is appropriate. That may be buttressed by rabbinic precedent. We must with great care utilize the legislative process alongside responsa.

Our halachic efforts intend to strengthen the role of Judaism in the lives of the million and a quarter American Reform Jews, the largest Jewish community in our land. Our forefathers in Europe and America sought to adapt Judaism to modern times. Their efforts have been justified by history as Judaism languished elsewhere. Our concern in the late twentieth century is less with adaptation and more with the strengthening of Jewish ties in a secular age. This has become especially important as secular Judaism in the form of Zionism has become less influential. Although the enthusiasm for Israel and the desire to help this young country continues, the idealism and fervor associated with early Zionism has disappeared. Modern Jewish philosophy must provide an intellectual basis for our Judaism. Modern halachah and responsa must provide a practical expression for our daily Jewish existence. We are no longer satisfied with guidance but seek governance. It is the duty of liberal Jews to perform mitzvot on a regular basis as a part of their life.

As Reform Judaism has developed halachah, the potential for conflict with traditional Judaism has increased. While our attitude toward halachah was fluid and as long as some radicals rejected halachah entirely, traditional Judaism could ignore us. They can not maintain this attitude in the face of our concern with halachah. Therefore, the next decades will see considerable struggle here and in Israel. That should not trouble us. Our path in

America is clear and our halachic stance is akin to the pluralism of the past, from the days of Hillel and Shammai in the first century through the entire rabbinic period to our own time. It is not our task as liberal Jews to complain about the Orthodox attitude or to be bullied by it, but rather to choose our legitimate path according to the inner logic and development of liberal Judaism.

Responsa are one way in which our rabbinic group, the Central Conference of American Rabbis, has set limits and defined its borders. Those limits may have seemed vague a century ago; as responsa have appeared over several generations, they have become clearer.

Source: *Contemporary American Reform Responsa*, ed. Walter Jacob (New York: CCAR Press, 1987), xx–xxii.

3. A Reform Approach to Halachic Issues (1997)

Rabbi Mark Washofsky (1952–), Associate Professor of Rabbinics at HUC-JIR in Cincinnati, has been chair of the CCAR Responsa Committee since 1997. Here he describes the procedure of the committee: first examining the answer that tradition would likely give and then inquiring whether there are Reform principles that would demand a different response.

Reform responsa are emphatically halachic documents; they speak the language of Jewish law and draw their source material from the texts of the Jewish legal tradition. To this extent, they are much like all the other responsa that have been produced over the course of fifteen centuries and more. Yet there are significant differences. These emerge from our particular experience as a modern expression of Judaism and from a conception of halachah that is very much our own.

A great deal has been written on the general subject of "Reform Judaism and the halachah," and the present setting is too limited to allow us to consider the issue in a systematic way. We think it is essential, though, to point here to certain features of our responsa that testify to the existence of a distinct Reform Jewish approach to Jewish law and that influence our understanding of and relationship to the halachic tradition.

1. Reform responsa do not partake of anything resembling an authoritative halachic process: Our answers are in no way binding upon those who

ask the questions, let alone upon anyone else. Our *t'shuvot* are advisory opinions; they are intended to serve as arguments in favor of a particular approach to a particular issue of observance. Their "authority," whatever we mean by that word, lies in their power to persuade.

2. We wish to know what halachah has to say, but we do not identify the "halachah" with the consensus opinion among today's Orthodox authorities. The "right" halachic opinion is rather the one which best expresses the underlying purposes and values of Jewish religious observance as we conceive them to be. Thus, a minority ruling, or an interpretation abandoned long ago by most rabbis, may offer a superior understanding of the tradition than does the view adopted by the majority. In saying this, we follow the lead of Maimonides and other great theorists of Jewish law who hold that the correct halachic ruling is not determined by the weight of precedent but by the scholar's honest and independent interpretation of the sources. We, too, assert the right of independence in halachic judgment, our right to adopt the minority opinion when that position appears to us to be the correct one.

3. Our decisions are based upon the sources of Jewish tradition. For us, those sources include the tradition of Reform Jewish thought as expressed in our previous responsa, resolutions and publications of the Central Conference of American Rabbis, trends and tendencies in Reform Jewish observance and the like. This reflects our understanding of Reform as a continuation of Jewish tradition and not, as is sometimes asserted, a radical departure from it.

4. As an expression of our identification with the Jewish heritage, we seek to uphold traditional halachic approaches whenever fitting. But we reserve for ourselves the right to judge the degree of "fit." We will modify standards of halachic observance to bring them into accord with the religious, moral, and cultural ideals to which we Reform Jews aspire and which, as we see it, characterize Jewish tradition at its best. And we will depart from the tradition altogether in those cases where even the most liberal interpretation of its sources yield conclusions which are unacceptable to us on religious or moral grounds.

Source: Mark Washofsky, "Introduction: Responsa and the Reform Rabbinate," in *Teshuvot for the Nineties: Reform Judaism's Answers for Today's Dilemmas*, ed. W. Gunther Plaut and Mark Washofsky (New York: CCAR Press, 1997), xxvii–xxix.

Abortion as a Flashpoint

There is hardly a subject engendering greater controversy in American life than abortion. Judaism agrees with pro-life advocates that the fetus has a special status once it has entered the second trimester, but disagrees in that it considers it a person only as it emerges from the womb. Jewish tradition allows the killing of the fetus in order to save the life of the mother, though just what this condition means has been interpreted variously. Reform Judaism has generally held to a broad definition, and its representative bodies have steadfastly battled all attempts to make abortion a legal offense.

1. A Resolution (1975)

At its Biennial General Assembly in 1975, the UAHC adopted the following resolution.

The UAHC reaffirms its strong support for the right of a woman to obtain a legal abortion on the constitutional grounds enunciated by the Supreme Court in its 1973 decision in Roe v. Wade, 410 U.S. 113 and Doe v. Boston, 410 U.S. 179, which prohibit all governmental interference in abortion during the first trimester and permits only those regulations which safeguard the health of the woman during the second trimester. This rule is a sound and enlightened position on this sensitive and difficult issue, and we express our confidence in the ability of the woman to exercise her ethical and religious judgment in making her decision.

The Supreme Court held that the question of when life begins is a matter of religious belief and not medical or legal fact. While recognizing the right of religious groups whose beliefs differ from ours to follow the dictates of their faith in this matter, we vigorously oppose the attempts to legislate the particular beliefs of those groups into the law which governs us all. This is a clear violation of the First Amendment. Furthermore, it may undermine the development of interfaith activities. Mutual respect and tolerance must remain the foundation of interreligious relations.

We oppose those riders and amendments to other bills aimed at halting medicaid, legal counselling and family services in abortion-related activities. These restrictions severely discriminate against and penalize the poor who rely on governmental assistance to obtain the proper medical care to which they are legally entitled, including abortion.

We are opposed to attempts to restrict the right to abortion through constitutional amendments. To establish in the Constitution the view of certain religious groups on the beginning of life has legal implications far beyond the question of abortion. Such amendments would undermine constitutional liberties which protect all Americans.

In keeping with the spirit of this resolution and to actualize its aims, we join with the CCAR in urging Reform Jews and their national and local institutions to cooperate fully with the Religious Coalition for Abortion Rights.

Source: UAHC, *Where We Stand: Social Action Resolutions Adopted by the Union of American Hebrew Congregations* (New York: UAHC, 1980), 115.

2. A Responsum (1985)

In 1985, the CCAR's Responsa Committee responded to the following question: "Assuming that abortion is permitted by halachah, is there a time span in which abortion may take place according to tradition?"

We can see from the recent discussion [among traditional authorities] that there is some hesitancy to permit abortion. A number of authorities readily permit it if the mother's life has been endangered, or if there is potentially serious illness, either physical or psychological. Others are permissive in cases of incest or rape. A lesser number permit it when a seriously impaired fetus is known to exist—not for the sake of the fetus, but due to the anguish felt by the mother.

The Reform Movement has had a long history of liberalism on many social and family matters. We feel that the pattern of tradition, until the most recent generation, has demonstrated a liberal approach to abortion and has definitely permitted it in case of any danger to the life of the mother. That danger may be physical or psychological. When this occurs at any time during the pregnancy, we would not hesitate to permit an abortion. This would also include cases of incest and rape if the mother wishes to have an abortion.

Twentieth century medicine has brought a greater understanding of the fetus, and it is now possible to discover major problems in the fetus quite early in the pregnancy. Some genetic defects can be discovered shortly after conception and more research will make such techniques widely available. It is, of course, equally true that modern medicine has presented ways of keeping babies with very serious problems alive, frequently in a vegetative state, which brings great misery to the family involved. Such problems, as those caused by Tay Sachs and other degenerative or permanent conditions which seriously endanger the life of the child and potentially the mental health of the mother, are indications for permitting an abortion.

We agree with the traditional authorities that abortions should be approached cautiously throughout the life of the fetus. Most authorities would be least hesitant during the first forty days of the fetus' life (Yeb. 69b; Nid. 30b; M. Ker. 1.1; *Shulchan Aruch* Hoshen Mishpat, 210.2; Solomon Skola, *Bet Shelomo*, Hoshen Mishpat 132; Joseph Trani, *Responsa Maharit*, 1.99; Weinberg, *Noam*, 9, pp. 213 ff, etc.). Even the strict Unterman permits non-Jews to perform abortions within the forty day periods (Unterman, *op. cit.,* pp. 8 ff).

From forty days until twenty-seven weeks, the fetus possesses some status, but its future remains doubtful (*goses biydei adam;* San. 78a; Nid. 44b and commentaries) as we are not sure of its viability. We must, therefore, be more certain of our grounds for abortion, but would still permit it.

It is clear from all of this that traditional authorities would be most lenient with abortions within the first forty days. After that time, there is a difference of opinion. Those who are within the broadest range of permissibility permit abortion at any time before birth, if there is a serious danger to the health of the mother or the child. We would be in agreement with that liberal stance. We do not encourage abortion, nor favor it for trivial reasons, or sanction it "on demand."

Source: Contemporary American Reform Responsa, ed. Walter Jacob (New York: CCAR Press, 1987), 26–27.

The Need for a Guide (1957)

For a long time, Reform leaders vigorously rejected any attempt to create a guide for the movement, lest it become a new Shulchan Aruch *("Set Table"—the Orthodox Jew's law code) and smooth the way for a return to Orthodoxy. In 1956, Rabbi Abraham J. Feldman (1893–1977) of West Hartford, Connecticut, published a modest guide—*

"not a code," he averred—that was essentially a description of the then current Reform way of life. To Rabbis Frederic A. Doppelt (1906–1972) of Fort Wayne, Indiana, and David Polish (1910–1995) of Evanston, Illinois, belongs the distinction of having published a Reform guide buttressed by theological and historical considerations. They thereby laid the groundwork for the guides that the movement would adopt in the decades to follow. Here, the authors justify the introduction of a Reform guide.

By its very nature, Reform can tolerate no authoritarian thought-control in the form of a superimposed Code of beliefs and practices. No official body could possibly impose such a Code. But this is altogether different from a Guide which is the work of individuals and is subject to the untrammeled verdict of individuals. Such a Guide would help bring a greater degree of observance, self-disciplining commitment, and spirituality into our religious life, because it is essentially a response to many who have long been seeking guidance.

But will not a Guide of observance end up as a return to Orthodoxy? Here, too, the answer need not be labored. If it is formulated from an Orthodox point of view, it will be Orthodox; if it rises out of a Reform point of view, it will remain Reform. If a Guide simply reconstitutes traditional observances, it is Orthodox in both spirit and content; but if it reconstructs them, revaluating, eliminating and developing, it is a continuation of the living stream of Reform Judaism. For what determines whether a custom, ceremony or symbol is either Orthodox or Reform is not its observance or non-observance; it is rather the right to change it when necessary, to drop it when no longer meaningful, and to innovate when desirable. This is precisely what freedom involves; not to turn order into chaos, but rather to go from one form of order to another form of order. Naturally, if a Guide is permitted to remain static and to become fixed, it will be the Orthodoxy of tomorrow; but if it is revised from time to time to meet changing conditions and rising needs, it will be an expression of Reform Judaism, renewing itself in every age and generation.

Source: *A Guide for Reform Jews*, ed. Frederic Doppelt and David Polish (New York: n.p., 1957), 9–10.

The Ground of Mitzvah

When in 1969 the CCAR did adopt a guide for Shabbat (see chapter 5), the first of several books that reintroduced mitzvot as commandments, it left open the reason why the mitzvot there enumerated should be compelling. Subsequently, the issue was explored in the essays that follow, authored by three presidents of the CCAR. Their perspectives range from theism to religious naturalism to history as a ground for observing mitzvot.

---

1. The Divine Authority of the Mitzvah (1979)

Herman E. Schaalman (1916–) served as a rabbi in Chicago. He was instrumental in having the CCAR adopt a resolution against rabbinical officiation for interfaith couples (1973) and on "patrilineal" descent (1983). He represents the theistic view.

Why do we do mitzvot? Why should we do mitzvot? Because we are the descendants of those ancestors, the children of those parents who said at Sinai: *"Na-aseh venishma*—We shall do and we shall hear" (Exodus 24:7). All authentic Judaism until now has so understood itself, has so acted and so handed it on to hitherto faithful new generations. Thus the Divine Presence waits for us, and we for It. Thus the commandment comes to us in our time, asking to be heard, understood, and done.

Wouldn't we, then, have to do all of them? Why do non-Orthodox Jews not keep all the mitzvot? What entitles anyone to make selections? First off, no one, not even the most meticulous and strictly observant Jew, keeps "all" of the mitzvot as found in the written and oral Torah. Traditional Jewish authority, after the destruction of the Temple and the Diaspora, declared major categories of mitzvot to be inoperative. The scope of commandments, even for the most traditional Jews, has shrunk, for all practical purposes, to mitzvot concerning worship, learning, family life, kashrut, acts of human concern, etc. But even within this shrunken perimeter, there is room for variant interpretations, even disagreement and conflicting opinions. This is one of the characteristics and undoubted virtues of the Jewish life style. . . .

To be commanded—to "listen and do"—must engage me, the doer, as what I am and can do and will do at the moment when the mitzvah confronts me or I seek it. There are times when I cannot or will not do the commandment, and I will know it and bear the consequences, perhaps standing in need of *t'shuvah,* repentance. And there will be mitzvot through which my forebears found themselves capable of responding to the commanding God which are no longer adequate or possible for me, just as there will be new mitzvot through which I or my generation will be able to respond which my ancestors never thought of.

Finally it all depends on whether I am ready to live my life in relationship to God, in response to Him, in my acceptance of His being Commander and of me as His covenant partner, giving life to the *b'rit*—the covenant—by my mitzvah response. And while I have and retain the freedom of choosing my specific means of response at a given moment, the essential fact of my life will be my intention to respond. And once my feet are set on this road, then even what at one time appears opaque and incapable of eliciting my response may do so at another time. The number of mitzvot I thus choose to perform is not nearly as important as is the fullness of my awareness and intention, for it is likely that in time I may hear the authentic "voice of God" in many more mitzvot than at first I could have imagined.

The difficult, the decisive, step is the first one, to place oneself into the covenant with the Commanding God. Thereafter, one's own integrity and the joy of fulfillment will move him along the way. The important step is the first one. Therefore, begin!

Source: Herman E. Schaalman, "The Divine Authority of the *Mitzvah*," in *Gates of Mitzvah*, ed. Simeon J. Maslin (New York: CCAR Press, 1979), 102–3.

2. Mitzvah without Miracles (1979)

Roland B. Gittelsohn (1910–1995), who served for many years as a rabbi in Boston, was active both for social justice and for Zionism. Here he represents the view of a religious naturalist.

What can mitzvah mean to a modern Jew who is a religious naturalist? Perhaps a prior question should be: what is a religious naturalist? Briefly, he or she is a person who believes in God, but asserts that God inheres within nature and operates through natural law. A religious naturalist perceives God to be the Spiritual Energy, Essence, Core, or Thrust of the universe, not a discrete Supernatural Being.

What, then, can mitzvah mean to such in individual? Certainly more than custom or folkway, more than social covenant or mores. Mitzvah, by very definition, must be cosmically grounded; it must possess empyreal signifi-cance. For the religious naturalist, as for all believing, practicing Jews, in order to have mitzvah—that which has been commanded—there must be a *metzaveh,* a commander. That commander, moreover, needs to be more than human ingenuity or convenience.

In the mainstream of Jewish tradition through the centuries, this posed no great problem. The *metzaveh* was God. A mitzvah was God's will. It had to be performed because God wanted it. It may have made sense to the human mind or not; these things were not important. It had to be done, plainly and simply, because God had commanded it.

But how can an Energy or Essence, a Core or a Thrust, command? For the religious naturalist, who is the *metzaveh?* Answer: reality itself. Or, more precisely, the physical and spiritual laws which govern reality. Mitzvot must be observed because only by recognizing and conforming to the nature of their environment can human beings increase the probability of their survival in any meaningful way. Mitzvot are not man-made; they inhere within the universe. Our Jewish mystics suspected this long ago. Mordecai Kaplan has summarized the view of the *Zohar* as holding that "mitzvot are part of the very process whereby the world came into being."

I agree with David Polish that mitzvot are binding upon us "because something happened between God and Israel, and the same something continues to happen in every land and age." What makes me a religious naturalist is interpreting the "something" to be a historic encounter between the Jewish people and the highest Spiritual Reality human beings have ever known or felt. No other people has been so persistent as ours in seeking that Reality and its moral imperatives.

It is easy to illustrate the cosmic nature of mitzvot on the level of physical reality. The universe is so constructed that, if I wish to survive, I must have adequate oxygen, nourishment, and exercise. God "wants" me to breathe fresh air, ingest healthful foods, and regularly move my muscles. These, therefore, are mitzvot.

No less is true in the realm of ethical mitzvot. Honesty is a compelling mitzvah. Human nature (which is, after all, nature at its highest level of development) is such that in the long run the individual or the social group that consistently flaunts the dictates of honesty risks disaster. The struggle for freedom is a compelling mitzvah. . . .

Most of the mitzvot . . . , however, deal with ritual observance rather than physical law or ethics. Are they, too, related to cosmic reality? In a less obvious but equally binding sense than the physical or moral imperatives suggested above, yes. Human nature is such that we need to express our emotions and ideals with our whole bodies, not just our tongues. We need also to be visually and kinetically reminded of our noblest values and stimulated to pursue them. As otherwise lonely and frightened individuals, we need common practices and observances which bind us into meaningful and supportive groups. All of which adds up to the fact that we need ritual as something more than social luxury or convenience. For us as Reform Jews, a particular ritual may not be mitzvah. But the need for a pattern of such rituals, this—because it grows out of and satifies our very basic nature as human beings—is mitzvah. And this we desperately need. . . .

Permeating our theological differences is the common understanding that God, however divergently we interpret Him, is the Core Spiritual Essence of reality. In this sense, God is the *metzaveh* of the religiously naturalistic Jew, who eschews the supernatural not only in theological speculation but also in his approach to mitzvot. He responds naturalistically to his own essence and to that of his universal setting. Mitzvot for him represent the difference between talking or philosophizing about Judaism and *living* it. They bind him firmly, visibly, to his people and his tradition. They speak to him imperatively because he is Jewish and wants to remain so.

Source: Roland B. Gittelsohn, "Mitzvah without Miracles," in *Gates of Mitzvah*, ed. Simeon J. Maslin (New York: CCAR Press, 1979), 108-10.

3. The Backward Look (1979)

Rabbi David Polish, mentioned earlier, finds the compelling source of mitzvot in Jewish history.

The observance of mitzvot reflects a Jewish conception of history. This conception is composed of two elements. The first consists of historical events of which we are reminded by specific practices. The second consists of an outlook upon human events and the world which is embodied in a system of conduct and discipline, individual as well as corporate.

Mitzvot are related to historic experiences in which the Jewish people sought to apprehend God's nature and His will. They are to be observed not because they are divine fiats, but because something happened between God and Israel, and the same something continues to happen in every age and land. Note the words of blessing preceding the performance of a mitzvah: *"asher kid'shanu bemitzvotav, v'tzivanu . . .* who has sanctified us by His mitzvot and has commanded us. . . ."* Mitzvot sanctify the Jewish people because they mark points of encounter by the Jewish people with God. They are enjoined upon us, because through them we perpetuate memories of the encounters and are sustained by those memories. Since they are so indigenous to us, they are incumbent primarily upon us, the Jewish people, and they constitute the singularity of the Jewish religion.

Mitzvot thus emerge from the womb of Jewish history, from a series of sacred encounters between God and Israel. When a Jew performs one of the many life-acts known as mitzvot to remind himself of one of those moments of encounter, what was only episodic becomes epochal, and what was only a moment in Jewish history becomes eternal in Jewish life.

Mitzvot are rooted in the biblical declaration: "It is a sign between Me and the children of Israel forever" (Exodus 31:17). Mitzvot are "signs" of the covenant, affirmed and reaffirmed through the ages at various turning-points in which Jewish existence stood in the balance. Out of these turning-points came hallowed insights, pointing to the pivotal moment and fashioning the mitzvah marking it. Thus, the Chanukah lights, marking Israel's rededication after near-extinction. Thus, *milah* (circumcision), which began with Abraham and which was invoked with special intensity during critical periods in Jewish history. . . .

It cannot be stressed too strongly that the observance of any particular mitzvah is a symbol of, and points to, a higher truth. Some symbols, because of their overpowering hold on us, endure; others change. Some fall into desuetude; new ones come into being. Thus, there is bound to emerge a compelling symbolism and observance which will someday speak to our people of the twin events of twentieth-century Judaism: the Holocaust and the establishment of Israel—catastrophe and rebirth. This new symbolism will capture the essential meaning of those events, a meaning which is fraught with the very elements which informed the Exodus and every one of its counterparts in our history—the presence of God in history, the struggle by Israel to preserve its being, and the confrontation of Israel with the world.

Source: David Polish, "History as the Source of the Mitzvah," in *Gates of Mitzvah,* ed. Simeon J. Maslin (New York: CCAR Press, 1979), 104–6.

ZIONISM AND ISRAEL

✦ Reform Jews in the nineteenth century believed that the Jewish people's dispersion among the nations was providential, that it possessed a mission to bring the essence of Judaism, ethical monotheism, to the nations of the world. They defined themselves as a religious community, not as a present-day or potential nation. Hence, when political Zionism came into being at the end of the century, Reform Jews, along with most of their American coreligionists, rejected it. They not only believed that supporting the World Zionist Organization might cast doubt on their loyalty to America, but more fundamentally that it undermined their cherished belief in the security of their future in the New World and that their presence in North America was a purposeful religious endeavor, not a political exile.

Nonetheless, there were always Zionists within the Reform community, among both rabbis and laypeople. When, in the 1930s, the situation of the Jews in Central Europe grew more perilous and as more ethnic Jews of East European background entered the movement, Reform shifted its position completely, officially endorsing both political and cultural Zionism. The non-Zionists became a diminishing, if sometimes vocal, minority. Among the Reform Zionists, Rabbi Abba Hillel Silver (a Republican) and Rabbi Stephen S. Wise (a Democrat) used their political influence to urge U.S. support for the Zionist enterprise.

The Reform movement welcomed the birth of the State of Israel in 1948. In the wake of the 1967 Six-Day War and the 1973 Yom Kippur War, Israel became central in the consciousness of American Reform Jews. HUC-JIR students began to spend their first year of studies there in 1970. The UAHC created its own Zionist organization, ARZA, and officially encouraged those of its members who desired to fulfill themselves Jewishly and Hebraically to undertake *aliyah*, immigration to Israel.

Official Opposition

The First World Zionist Congress was convened in Basle by Theodor Herzl in August 1897. In anticipation, the CCAR seven weeks earlier unanimously adopted a resolution condemning Zionism as a mischievous misconception of Jewish destiny. A few months after the Congress, the UAHC followed suit, proclaiming, without qualification, that America was the new Zion and that American Jews required no other.

1. The Resolution of the Central Conference of American Rabbis (July 1897)

Resolved, That we totally disapprove of any attempt for the establishment of a Jewish state. Such attempts show a misunderstanding of Israel's mission, which from the narrow political and rational field has been expanded to the promotion among the whole human race of the broad and universalistic religion first proclaimed by the Jewish prophets. Such attempts do not benefit, but infinitely harm our Jewish brethren where they are still persecuted, by confirming the assertion of their enemies that the Jews are foreigners in the countries in which they are at home, and of which they are everywhere the most loyal and patriotic citizens.

We reaffirm that the object of Judaism is not political nor national, but spiritual, and addresses itself to the continuous growth of peace, justice and love in the human race, to a messianic time when all men will recognize that they form "one great brotherhood" for the establishment of God's kingdom on Earth.

Source: "Report of Committee 'B' on President's Annual Message," *CCAR Yearbook* 8 (1898): xli.

2. The Resolution of the Union of American Hebrew Congregations (December 1898)

While we are aware of and deplore the abject conditions to which many of our brethren are subjected in foreign lands, and which have naturally, but unfortunately, aroused in some of them a yearning for a re-establishment in Zion, yet we delegates of the Union of American Hebrew Congregations in convention assembled, in view of the active propaganda being made at present for the so-called Zionistic movement, deem it proper and necessary to put ourselves on record as follows:

We are unalterably opposed to political Zionism. The Jews are not a nation, but a religious community. Zion was a precious possession of the past, the early home of our faith, where our prophets uttered their world-subduing thoughts, and our psalmists sang their world-enchanting hymns. As such it is a holy memory, but it is not our hope of the future. America is our Zion. Here, in the home of religious liberty, we have aided in founding this new Zion, the fruition of the beginning laid in the old. The mission of Judaism is spiritual, not political. Its aim is not to establish a state, but to spread the truths of religion and humanity throughout the world.

Source: *Proceedings of the Union of American Hebrew Congregations* 5 (1898–1903): 4002.

Early Reform Zionists

Until after World War I it was commonly believed that Zionism and Reform Judaism were mutually exclusive. To leave one movement for the other was regarded as a kind of "conversion." To be both Zionist and Reform was to live a contradiction. However, as indicated, from the very beginning there were persons active in both movements who tried to reconcile the two. They included Rabbis Maximilian Heller of New Orleans and Gustav Gottheil of New York. Among Hebrew Union College graduates, early active Zionists were Max Raisin (class of 1903), a prolific author in Hebrew, English, and Yiddish, and Abba Hillel Silver (class of 1915).

1. Max Raisin: Two "Movements of Liberation" (1914)

Logically, if not theologically, these two great Jewish movements have many things in common which makes them not only not adverse to one another, but even brings them into a kinship of spirit and makes them common heritors of certain great Jewish truths which both of them predicate and postulate. When taken together, Reform and Zionism instead of forming an antithesis rather fuse into a synthesis. There is, to begin with, the emancipatory element in each of them. Both Zionism and Reform are movements of liberation. Reform came to emancipate the Jew from the oppressive legalism of the Shulchan Aruch; Zionism from his civil and social disabilities. The one as the other is an attempt to terminate the two thousand-year-old tragedy of the Jew. . . .

Now, Reform proclaims itself as a return to Prophetic Ideals, and as such it implies that to make possible and feasible the ideals taught and propagated by the Hebrew Prophets it is, for the Jew at least, necessary to re-create the very normal atmosphere which alone made those ideals and hopes possible and available. If such an atmosphere is impossible of creation in the Occidental environment where the Jew today lives, it is clear that he must go back to his ancient Oriental moorings. From this point of view Reform in Judaism certainly does stand, if only in its potentialities, upon national ground. From Prophetism to the land where Prophetism was born, and to the conditions which favor the rebirth of Prophetism, is but one short step. . . .

When I say that Reform is a return to Prophetism, I mean that it lays the greatest stress upon social justice as the true and only keynote of all faith. Righteousness and not ritualism, the service of the heart rather than the sheer worship of the lips, justice here and now more than salvation in the hereafter, these are what constitute the genius of Judaism from the Prophetic and the Reform standpoint. Need I tell you my fellow Zionists, that herein we are wholly at one with our Reform brethren? . . .

And right here permit me to indulge in a very fond hope, which some of you will perhaps regard as a chimera, but which I sincerely believe will actually come true, namely, that it is Liberal Judaism which will be the predominant phase of Jewish religious life in the Jew's future home in Palestine. . . .

Such is the declaration of faith of one who is both a Reform Jew and a Zionist, and who feels and believes that, far from antagonizing one another, the two movements are here to complete and to complement each other. Judging from personal experience, I am convinced that Zionism goes a long way towards strengthening and furthering Judaism, and I likewise know that Liberal Judaism will form a not inconsiderable asset in the spiritual economy of the new Jewish life now in the process of creation in Palestine. The Jewish state of the future will, as it must, be more than a mere political entity; its spiritual and moral function in the uplift work of its own people and of the entire world must never be lost sight of. It is towards the fulfillment of this function that Liberal Judaism will exercise the greatest influence.

Source: Max Raisin, "Convention Sermon: Zionism and Liberal Judaism," *The Jewish Exponent,* 3 July 1914.

2. Abba Hillel Silver: A "Total Program of Jewish Life and Destiny" (1935)

The Jewish people produced the Jewish religion, but people and religion are not synonymous terms. The Jewish religion—and I use the term in its customary sense, for I do not believe that a clever neology—the use of a word in a new and unsanctioned sense—is equivalent to a new theology—is a colossal and world-revolutionizing concourse of spiritual ideas unfolding itself in the life of a people of a particular character and temperament, but the Jewish religion does not exhaust the full content of the Jewish people. In relation to its religion, Israel is both immanent and transcendent as is every great artist in relation to the creation of his genius. לולא בני ישראל לא היתה התורה declared Judah Halevi. "If there had been no Jews there would have been no Torah, and the Jews did not derive their high estate from Moses but Moses derived his high estate from the Jews" (Cuzari 11.56).

The Jewish religion is the crowning achievement of our people and our supreme gift to civilization. It possessed such vast reservoirs of spiritual truth that it has been able to sustain and inspire generations upon generations of our people and to retain their sacrificial loyalty under all circumstances and upon all levels of culture. It thus became the strongest factor in the survival of our people, the קשר של קיימא, the enduring tie. It is doubtful whether the Jewish people can long survive in the diaspora without it—unless the other survival factors are reinforced to a degree which will compensate such a major loss. Jewish secular cultural autonomy may be possible in countries where the Jewish groups achieve minority rights. In such countries the Jewish group may survive even if divorced from religious loyalties. This is possible, though not probable. But in countries where minority rights are not possible, where there exists no active anti-Semitism which forces the Jew back upon himself, the task of Jewish survival will become increasingly difficult as religion loses its influence upon Jews and therewith also its power of national conservation. Those religious leaders, therefore, who are, today, teaching the religion of Israel to their people are not only leading them to fountains of living truth which can sweeten and refresh their individual lives, but are also conserving the most potent force which, throughout the ages, has sheltered and preserved the Jewish people.

But such religious leaders should not attempt to substitute a part for the whole—even if it is the major part. Havelock Ellis, in his introduction to J. K. Huysman's *A Rebours* makes the interesting observation that the essential distinction between the classic and the decadent in art and literature is to be found in the fact that in the classic the parts are subordinated to the whole, whereas in the decadent, the whole is subordinated to the parts. "The classic strives after those virtues which the whole may best express; the later manner (the decadent) depreciates the importance of the whole for the benefit of its parts, and strives after the virtue of individualism."

Jewish life also possessed in its great epochs this classic balance, and the aim of religious leaders today should be to restore it. Many tributaries flow into the historic channel of Jewish life. In recent years some zealous and mostly uninformed partisans have attempted to reduce Jewish life to what is only a fraction of itself—to race or nationalism or folkways or theologic abstractions. Quite unconsciously they are all falsifying Jewish life. It is a mark of decadence in the diaspora that so many of our people have lost the sense of the classic harmony in Jewish life and are attempting to substitute a part for the whole.

It is the *total* program of Jewish life and destiny which the religious leaders of our people should stress today—the religious and moral values, the universal concepts, the mandate of mission, as well as the *Jewish people itself,* and all its national aspirations. Thus the strength and security of our life will be retrieved, and, whether in Palestine or in the diaspora, we shall move forward unafraid upon the road of our destiny.

Source: Abba Hillel Silver, "Israel," *CCAR Yearbook* 45 (1935): 341–42.

Official Reversal

The commonly held view that Reform Judaism officially endorsed Zionism only after World War II is refuted by documents from the 1930s. In 1935 the CCAR reversed its stand of 1897 and assumed a neutral position. Two years later, in the Columbus Platform of 1937 (see chapter 12), it explicitly came out in favor of a "Jewish homeland" and a "center of Jewish cultural and spiritual life" in Palestine. A few months before the rabbis adopted their new platform, as the second selection indicates, the UAHC had already taken a similar position.

1. CCAR Neutrality Resolution (1935)

Whereas, At certain foregoing conventions of the Central Conference of American Rabbis, resolutions have been adopted in opposition to Zionism, and

Whereas, We are persuaded that acceptance or rejection of the Zionist program should be left to the determination of the individual members of the Conference themselves, therefore

Be It Resolved, That the Central Conference of American Rabbis takes no official stand on the subject of Zionism; and be it further

Resolved, That in keeping with its oft-announced intentions, the Central Conference of American Rabbis will continue to co-operate in the upbuilding of Palestine, and in the economic, cultural, and particularly spiritual tasks confronting the growing and evolving Jewish community there.

Source: "Report of Committee on Resolutions," *CCAR Yearbook* 45 (1935): 103.

2. UAHC Pro-Zionist Resolution (1937)

RESOLVED that the Union of American Hebrew Congregations, in council assembled, expresses its satisfaction with the progress made by the Jewish Agency in the upbuilding of Palestine. We see the hand of Providence in the opening of the Gates of Palestine for the Jewish people at a time when a large portion of Jewry is so desperately in need of a friendly shelter and a home where a spiritual, cultural center may be developed in accordance with

Jewish ideals. The time has now come for all Jews, irrespective of ideological differences, to unite in the activities leading to the establishment of a Jewish homeland in Palestine, and we urge our constituency to give their financial and moral support to the work of rebuilding Palestine.

Source: UAHC, *Where We Stand: Social Action Resolutions Adopted by the Union of American Hebrew Congregations* (New York: UAHC, 1980), 24–25.

Zionist Activism

Although until after the Six-Day War the American Reform movement's involvement in Israel was peripheral, it assumed centrality in the 1970s. In 1976, the UAHC Board of Trustees came out in favor of aliyah. A year later, the Association of Reform Zionists of America (ARZA) and its Canadian counterpart, Kadima (now combined as ARZA/World Union), were created to represent Reform Jewish ideology and interests in the World Zionist Organization. Finally, in 1997, upon the hundredth anniversary of the First Zionist Congress, the CCAR adopted a comprehensive resolution detailing the Reform commitment to Zionism and to Israel.

1. The Encouragement of Aliyah (1976)

The land of Israel, which is Zion, and the children of Israel who constitute the Jewish people and the God of Israel are all bound together in a triple covenant. As Reform Jews, we perceive the political entity of the State of Israel, together with the Jewish people the world over, as constituting a means for the continued evolution of this convenantal relationship.

Our movement has a unique and critical role to play in shaping Israel's future as a Jewish state. We can do this both by enriching Jewish life in our community and by participating in the fabric of Israeli society. Hence the Israel Commission affirms the value of *aliyah* as a valid option for contemporary liberal Jewish commitment and self-fulfillment. A Reform *aliyah* will expand our role in Israel and further our rightful contribution to the life and religious expression of the State and the Jewish people.

Therefore, be it resolved: We affirm a special duty to encourage and assist those Reform Jews who, individually or in groups, wish to participate more fully in the development of the State of Israel and in the development of Progressive Judaism in Israel by making *aliyah* and settling there.

Source: UAHC, *Where We Stand: Social Action Resolutions Adopted by the Union of American Hebrew Congregations* (New York: UAHC, 1980), 119.

2. The Birth of ARZA (1977)

We Reform Jews—ideologically and programmatically, as individuals, as congregations and as a movement—have manifested our commitment to the State of Israel and its future.

Despite this commitment, Reform Judaism has remained outside the organizational framework of Zionism. The World Zionist Organization is today the one forum in which broad segments of Israeli and Diaspora Jewry have constructive dialogue. Until this day, the only voices in that world-wide Zionist forum affecting programs, funding, quality of Jewish life and education have been those of Orthodoxy and of secularism. The time has come for Reform Judaism to join in this dialogue. The UAHC Board of Trustees has created an opportunity for such dialogue by establishing, subject to ratification by this biennial, national affiliates of the Union to be known in the United States as ARZA (Association of Reform Zionists of America) and in Canada as Kadima. The purpose of these affiliates would be "to seek individual members from amongst our congregations and to seek full voting membership in the World Zionist Organization through its territorial bodies, the American Zionist Federation and the Canadian Zionist Federation."

By giving Reform Judaism a full voice in the councils of the World Zionist Organization, the proposed new affiliates will enable us as Reform Jews to communicate more effectively our concerns regarding Israel and the Jewish future, in particular the status of the Israel Movement for Progressive Judaism. It will also increase potential for a more equitable distribution of funds allocated in Israel and throughout the world for educational and cultural projects. The affiliates would add to the deliberations of world Jewry a flexibility to meet the needs of each generation and the combination of prophetic ideology and relevant action which is the cornerstone of Reform Judaism.

Within our own ranks, ARZA and Kadima will provide the long-awaited vehicles for those who have been frustrated in seeking a channel for their Zionist commitment.

The Board recognized that there are members of our Union who may not wish to seek affiliation with ARZA or Kadima. As is the case with all UAHC affiliates, membership in either is voluntary. Since diversity is an essential strength of Reform Judaism, non-membership in these affiliates will in no way reflect upon any UAHC member's commitment to our Union.

THEREFORE, this Biennial Assembly ratifies the action of the UAHC Board of Trustees, which established ARZA and Kadima. In so doing, we reaffirm the essential freedom of choice of our individual members to join the new affiliates.

Source: UAHC, *Where We Stand: Social Action Resolutions Adopted by the Union of American Hebrew Congregations* (New York: UAHC, 1980), 125.

3. "We stand firm in our love of Zion" — the Reform Zionist Platform (1997)

I. Judaism: A Religion and a People

The restoration of *Am Yisrael* to its ancestral homeland after nearly two thousand years of statelessness and powerlessness represents an historic triumph of the Jewish people, providing a physical refuge, the possibility of religious and cultural renewal on its own soil, and the realization of God's promise to Abraham: "to your offspring I assign this land." From that distant moment until today, the intense love between *Am Yisrael* and *Eretz Yisrael* has not subsided.

We believe that the eternal covenant established at Sinai ordained a unique religious purpose for *Am Yisrael. Medinat Yisrael*, the Jewish state, is therefore unlike all other states. Its obligation is to strive towards the attainment of the Jewish people's highest moral ideals to be a *mamlechet kohanim* [a kingdom of priests], a *goy kadosh* [a holy people], and *l'or goyim* [a light unto the nations].

II. From Degradation to Sovereignty

During two millennia of dispersion and persecution, *Am Yisrael* never abandoned hope for the rebirth of a national home in *Eretz Yisrael.* The *Shoah* [Holocaust] intensified our resolve to affirm life and pursue the Zionist dream of a return to *Eretz Yisrael.* Even as we mourned for the loss of one-third of our people, we witnessed the miraculous rebirth of *Medinat Yisrael,* the Jewish people's supreme creation in our age.

Centuries of Jewish persecution, culminating in the *Shoah,* demonstrated the risks of powerlessness. We, therefore, affirm *Am Yisrael*'s reassertion of national sovereignty, but we urge that it be used to create the kind of society in which full civil, human, and religious rights exist for all its citizens. Ultimately, *Medinat Yisrael* will be judged not on its military might but on its character.

While we view *Eretz Yisrael* as sacred, the sanctity of Jewish life takes precedence over the sanctity of Jewish land.

III. Our Relationship to the State of Israel

Even as *Medinat Yisrael* serves uniquely as the spiritual and cultural focal point of world Jewry, Israeli and Diaspora Jewry are inter-dependent, responsible for one another, and partners in the shaping of Jewish destiny. Each *k'hillah* [Jewish community], though autonomous and self-regulating, shares responsibility for the fate of Jews everywhere. By deepening the social, spiritual, and intellectual relationship among the *k'hillot* worldwide, we can revitalize Judaism both in Israel and the Diaspora.

IV. Our Obligations to Israel

To help promote the security of *Medinat Yisrael* and ensure the welfare of its citizens, we pledge continued political support and financial assistance.

Recognizing that knowledge of Hebrew is indispensable both in the study of Judaism and in fostering solidarity between Israeli and Diaspora Jews, we commit ourselves to intensifying Hebrew instruction in all Reform institutions. Hebrew, the language of our sacred texts and prayers, is a symbol of the revitalization of *Am Yisrael.*

To enhance appreciation of Jewish peoplehood and promote a deeper understanding of Israel, we resolve to implement educational programs and religious practices that reflect and reinforce the bond between Reform Judaism and Zionism.

To deepen awareness of Israel and strengthen Jewish identity, we call upon all Reform Jews, adults and youths, to study in, and make regular visits to, Israel.

While affirming the authenticity and necessity of a creative and vibrant Diaspora Jewry, we encourage *aliyah* [immigration] to Israel in pursuance of the precept of *yishuv Eretz Yisrael* [settling the land of Israel]. While Jews can live Torah-centered lives in the Diaspora, only in *Medinat Yisrael* do they bear the primary responsibility for the governance of society, and thus may realize the full potential of their individual and communal religious strivings.

Confident that Reform Judaism's synthesis of tradition and modernity and its historic commitment to *tikkun olam* [repairing the world], can make a unique and positive contribution to the Jewish state, we resolve to intensify our efforts to inform and educate Israelis about the values of Reform Judaism. We call upon Reform Jews everywhere to dedicate their energies and resources to the strengthening of an indigenous Progressive Judaism in *Medinat Yisrael.*

V. Israel's Obligations to the Diaspora

Medinat Yisrael exists not only for the benefit of its citizens but also to defend the physical security and spiritual integrity of the Jewish people. Realizing that *Am Yisrael* consists of a coalition of different, sometimes conflicting, religious interpretations, the Jewish people will be best served when *Medinat Yisrael* is constituted as a pluralistic, democratic society. Therefore we seek a Jewish state in which no religious interpretation of Judaism takes legal precedence over another.

VI. Redemption

We believe that the renewal and perpetuation of Jewish national life in *Eretz Yisrael* is a necessary condition for the realization of the physical and spiritual redemption of the Jewish people and of all humanity. While that day of redemption remains but a distant yearning, we express the fervent hope that *Medinat Yisrael,* living in peace with its neighbors, will hasten the redemption of *Am Yisrael,* and the fulfillment of our messianic dream of universal peace under the sovereignty of God.

The achievements of modern Zionism in the creation of the State of Israel, in reviving the Hebrew language, in absorbing millions of immigrants, in transforming desolate wastes into blooming forests and fields, in generating a thriving new economy and society, are an unparalleled triumph of the Jewish spirit.

We stand firm in our love of Zion. We resolve to work for the day when waves of Jewish pride and confidence will infuse every Jewish heart, in fulfillment of the promise: When God restores the fortunes of Zion we shall be like dreamers. Our mouths will fill with laughter and our tongues with songs of joy. Then shall they say among the nations God has done great things for them.

Source: "Zionist Platform," *CCAR Yearbook* 107 (1997): 55–57.

SOCIAL JUSTICE

✦ Although the Reform movement in Germany identified strongly with prophetic Judaism, its environment militated against independent activity in the area of social action. Only in America, where it was influenced by Protestant activism, did social justice become an integral part of the Reform program. Before the Civil War, radical Reformer Rabbi David Einhorn spoke out courageously against slavery in Baltimore and had to flee that Southern city. Toward the end of the century, Rabbi Emil G. Hirsch became active as a political and social reformer in Chicago. Other Reform rabbis followed their lead, and the CCAR began to take collective stands on social issues, leading up to the adoption of its first social justice platform in 1918.

During the Great Depression, the Reform rabbinate called for radical measures to curb poverty, while the Reform lay leadership, at that time dominantly conservative, sometimes stood in opposition to the rabbinate. Following World War II, however, it was the laity, represented by the UAHC, that took the initiative. The Union's new president, Rabbi Maurice N. Eisendrath, stressed this aspect of Reform Judaism above all others, and social justice activities became a regular part of the Union's program. It encouraged the formation of social action committees in Reform synagogues, provided educational materials, and issued statements in areas of social concern. The Reform movement became involved in the protection of civil liberties during the heyday of Senator Joseph McCarthy, took strong stands in favor of civil rights, and very early sharply condemned the war in Vietnam. Individual Reform rabbis and laypeople marched in the South against segregation and in Washington against the Vietnam War.

In 1962, thanks largely to the efforts of Reform philanthropist and

NAACP president Kivie Kaplan, the UAHC was able to establish its Religious Action Center in Washington. In recent years, the center has broadened its purview to include matters of specifically Jewish concern such as antisemitism, Israeli issues, and Jewish rights around the world. It has also begun to address issues of personal moral concern such as bioethics, abortion, and sexual orientation.

The First Social Justice Platform of the CCAR (1918)

With the end of World War I in sight, Reform rabbis began to concern themselves about postwar American society. The resolution below, proposed by the CCAR Committee on Synagog and Industrial Relations, contains both general principles and specific desiderata. Some of the latter had recently been written into law, but nearly all remained the subject of controversy.

The next few decades will have as their chief concern the rectification of social and economic evils. The world will busy itself not only with the establishment of political, but also with the achievement of industrial democracy through social justice. The ideal of social justice has always been an integral part of Judaism. It is in accordance with tradition, therefore, that the Central Conference of American Rabbis submits the following declaration of principles as a program for the attainment of which the followers of our faith should strive:

1. A more equitable distribution of the profits of industry.
2. A minimum wage which will insure for all workers a fair standard of living.
3. The legal enactment of an eight hour day as a maximum for all industrial workers.
4. A compulsory one-day-of-rest-in-seven for all workers.
5. Regulation of industrial conditions to give all workers a safe and sanitary working environment, with particular reference to the special needs of women.
6. Abolition of child labor and raising the standard of age wherever the legal age limit is lower than is consistent with moral and physical health.
7. Adequate workmen's compensation for industrial accidents and occupational diseases.

8. Legislative provision for universal workman's health insurance and careful study of social insurance methods for meeting the contingencies of unemployment and old age.

9. An adequate, permanent national system of public employment bureaus to make possible the proper distribution of the labor forces of America.

10. Recognition of the right of labor to organize and to bargain collectively.

11. The application of the principles of mediation, conciliation and arbitration to industrial disputes.

12. Proper housing for working-people, secured through government regulation when necessary.

13. The preservation and integrity of the home by a system of mother's pensions.

14. Constructive care of dependents, defectives and criminals, with the aim of restoring them to normal life wherever possible.

Source: "Report of Committee on Synagog and Industrial Relations," *CCAR Yearbook* 28 (1918): 101–2.

The First UAHC Statement of Basic Principles on the Synagogue and Social Action (1955)

Although the UAHC had adopted resolutions dealing with social issues as early as the first decades of its existence, it did not until 1955 produce a general statement relating the Jewish prophetic heritage to the work of social justice. To a high degree this statement still reflects the movement's motivation for social activism.

We are the heirs of the great Jewish religious tradition which conceives of its ultimate goal as the establishment of the Kingdom of God on earth. The God whom we serve is a God of righteousness who would have us be holy as He is holy. The Torah which we cherish is a guide for spiritual living concerned with every aspect of human experience. The prophets of Israel, dedicated to God and the welfare of their fellow men, bade us pursue justice, seek peace and establish brotherhood among all of God's creatures.

Judaism offers no easy escape from the problems of life. It rejects the device of passing all responsibility for social problems to God. In our tradition, man is called the co-worker or partner of God in the creation of a better world. Judaism insists that we must apply constantly the sharp ethical insights of the prophets to the specific social problems of our generation, as well as to the personal and individual problems of our lives.

It is loyalty to this heritage, and in the furtherance of our ideal of righteousness, that Reform Judaism has developed a program of social action which relates the ethical and spiritual teachings of our faith to the problems of our communities, of our country and of the world, and which strives for a society guided by the principles of divine justice and mercy. . . . A synagogue which isolates itself from the fundamental issues of social justice confronting the community and the nation is false to the deepest traditions and values of the Jewish heritage.

What are these traditions? What are these values? And what are some of their implications for us today?

Judaism gave to the world the concept of the sanctity and dignity of the individual. All men are equal in that they are created in the image of God. "One law and one ordinance shall be both for you, and for the stranger that sojourneth with you." (Numbers 15:16) Respect for the civil rights of all men is each man's duty to God. We Jews are challenged by our religion to support the basic human rights of everyone: "What is hateful unto thee, do not do unto thy neighbor." (Talmud Shabbat 8) As Jews and as Americans, dedicated to the democratic tradition, we are impelled to join with our fellows in overcoming bigotry and prejudice; in seeking through education and legislation the elimination of discrimination and segregation because of race, religion or national origin; in demanding for ourselves and for all other Americans equality of opportunity in work, home, health and education.

Judaism teaches that each man has a right to express or keep private the dictates of his soul, for the soul is the divine element in man and cannot be interfered with by other men or governments of men. "The spirit of man is the light of the Lord." (Proverbs 20:27) The Talmud teaches that where honest differences prevail and agreements are difficult: "These and those are the words of the living God." It was that "flaming fire within" (Jeremiah 25:9) that impelled the prophet to speak out even at grave personal risk. These rights of conscience were enshrined in the Bill of Rights, the cornerstone of the American constitutional system.

We view with deep concern the growing attack upon these principles in American life today. Judaism is fundamentally antagonistic to tyranny—

whether it be totalitarian tyranny manipulated from abroad or a domestic tyranny foisted on the American people in the name of anti-communism. We believe that subversion and espionage can and must be effectively opposed without destroying the tradition of individual freedom on which democracy is based. We have faith in freedom and in democracy. We believe that the religious ideals of justice and security for all men can be fulfilled only in an atmosphere of freedom and security, not in an atmosphere of fearful conformity and suspicion. We pledge ourselves to join with all freedom-loving forces in our community and nation to reverse the alarming trend toward suspicion, recrimination, fear and the equation of dissent with disloyalty. We pledge our unremitting vigilance to the end that neither communist intrigue nor reckless demagoguery shall be allowed to corrode the fundamental liberties which have their origin in religious ideals.

Judaism has always emphasized that our ethical ideals must also be applied to the economic processes of society. Our society must be judged by the extent to which men are enabled to achieve, through their work, a decent standard of living, and to provide for themselves and their families the fullest possible protection of their mental and physical health. We pledge ourselves to the achievement of this ideal not only on the national and world scenes, but most particularly in the conduct of our individual business and professional lives.

Another of the most sacred of our Jewish religious teachings is the vision given us by the prophets of a messianic age of peace, the time when nations shall beat their swords into plowshares and their spears into pruning hooks. Motivated by our belief in world brotherhood, the Jewish community has supported enthusiastically the United Nations as the best available instrumentality for the gradual accomplishment of world peace. We have rejoiced in its constructive achievements in the improvement of health standards in many parts of the world, in the control of narcotics traffic, in child welfare, in technical assistance to underdeveloped nations, in the United Nation's prophetic declarations on human rights, genocide and similar world problems. We have been deeply concerned about the lack of progress recorded within the councils of the United Nations in easing international tensions. Yet we have remained hopeful that our country, committed firmly to international cooperative action and backed strongly by our citizenry, could continue to exercise leadership in the United Nations in the direction of world peace. . . .

Jewish religious bodies—and certainly Reform synagogues—have a deep responsibility to seek to strengthen democracy and the ideals of justice by translating our faith into concrete social action. Such Jewish ideals as reverence for individual freedom, love of peace, concern for the weak, equitable relationships between employer and employee, regard for the stranger and many others are strikingly relevant to the current world scene. . . .

Through an intelligent program of social justice in the synagogue, we help to bridge the gap between confession and commitment, between word and deed, and thus bring a sense of greater reality to our faith. We as Jews fulfil ourselves by working for the establishment of justice and peace, which are fundamental to Judaism as they are to democracy. In the words of our prayerbook: "O may all created in Thine image recognize that they are brethren, so that, one in spirit and one in fellowship, they may be forever united before Thee. Then shall Thy kingdom be established on earth and the word of Thine ancient seer be fulfilled: The Lord will reign forever and ever."

Source: UAHC, *Where We Stand: Social Action Resolutions Adopted by the Union of American Hebrew Congregations* (New York: UAHC, 1980), 43–46.

Vietnam

In the late 1960s the Vietnam War divided Americans as no foreign policy issue had divided them before. The UAHC's resolution in 1967, calling for a halt to the bombing of North Vietnam, represented a minority view in the United States. Rabbi Eisendrath's imaginary letter to President Johnson, written a few months earlier and published in the UAHC's Dimensions in American Judaism, *a precursor to* Reform Judaism Magazine, *was a yet stronger statement and one that aroused anger among some Reform Jews. The "Veterans of Syrian Wars" is a veiled reference to the Jewish War Veterans, who supported the Vietnam War.*

1. The UAHC Position on Vietnam (1967)

We believe that, while men are capable of great evil, they are as children of God also capable of creating those processes by which conflict in a world of dynamic change can be peacefully resolved. Furthermore, we believe that the insights of Jewish tradition, the lessons of Jewish experience, the values of Judaism and our own organizational strength are a precious resource in work for a world without war.

We Jews have ever kept before us the ideal that justice emerges "not by might and not by power but by My spirit."

Along with many millions of our fellow Americans, we are deeply troubled in conscience by the involvement of our nation in Vietnam. The war's continued escalation not only increasingly disturbs a growing number of our citizens, drains urgently needed economic resources and threatens a world war; it also brutalizes and degrades all nations.

We reject the ugly campaign of calumny and vilification which seeks to ascribe to the United States a major responsibility for the creation of the Vietnam problem. Equally do we reject the counsel of those calling for intensified military engagement. We continue to be horrified by the appalling suffering sustained by all subjected to the ravages of this war.

THEREFORE:

1. We commend President Johnson for his offer of November 11, 1967, to meet negotiators from parties to the conflict on a neutral ship and in neutral waters. This offer is consonant with the proposals contained in the UAHC resolution of 1965. In view of reports from many sources that a cessation of bombing is a necessary precondition for peace negotiations, we believe that prospects for a successful outcome to the constructive proposal by the President would be facilitated by an immediate cessation of the bombing of North Vietnam.

2. We urge the government of North Vietnam and the NLF to respond favorably to such United States initiatives.

3. We ask the United States government to announce its support for the free entry into the political life of South Vietnam of all political forces, including the NLF.

4. We support the proposal of the President of the United States that the United Nations establish an international peace corps to aid in the reconstruction and development of Vietnam, inviting all nations to recruit for it, and ask him to designate now the international agencies to which the United States will contribute the billion dollars proposed by him to aid the people of Southeast Asia.

5. We salute the courage and sacrifice of those members of our armed forces now in the service of our country.

Source: UAHC, *Where We Stand: Social Action Resolutions Adopted by the Union of American Hebrew Congregations* (New York: UAHC, 1980), 80.

2. An Imaginary Letter from Rabbi Eisendrath to President Johnson (1966)

Dear President Johnson:

I do not know whether you recall the name of Antiochus Epiphanes. No, he's not a Jewish leader, head of one of those Jewish organizations which have been bothering you so much of late. But it might ring a bell with you and cause you to dig out of your memory a vague recollection of his identity because he too had some trouble with the "stiff-necked" sons of Abraham. (But it's perhaps expecting too much for you actually to know very much about him because in the Christian religious school in which you were reared, the Bible is just about the only textbook used and very little—if any—attention is paid to any post-biblical Jewish history.) Since you might gain some comfort from the knowledge that you have not been alone in being nettled over the disinclination of all the Jews in America to concur in all of your pursuits, it might be well to tell you about Antiochus and some of his obstreperous Jews. This is especially appropriate inasmuch as this is the time of the year when the still obstinate Jews observe a festival called Chanukah which commemorates this very stubborn opposition to that chap Antiochus.

It was in the second century before the Common Era that Antiochus ruled over Syria to which the tiny land of Judea was subject. It was his desire that everyone under his sovereignty should think and act exactly alike. If he wanted to wage a war, no matter how small and weak the opponent might be nor how superior his destructive weapons, he demanded one hundred per cent concensus. And if he set up a pagan idol in the temple—even if it might be that of a swine, so abhorrent to that "peculiar people, the Jews," or, if perchance, it may have been the molten icon of Mars, against the worship of which those selfsame Jews had been solemnly warned by their peace-loving and peace-pursuing rabbis, he expected them to bow down in abject obeisance. But those stubborn mulish Jews refused. How dared they dissent from the national policy of the land! Antiochus would teach them a lesson. And I suppose that he called into consultation the more nationalistically "patriotic" among them, the Veterans of Syrian Wars, to urge them to pass the word around about his extreme displeasure and to warn them that their Temple (read State today) might be jeopardized if they did not toe the line. But it was to no avail. You see, the Veterans of Syrian Wars were but a tiny splinter of the Jewish community and they did not reflect the deep resentments of the masses against this demand for unvarying uniformity of thought and action. So, rallying to the heroic challenge of a few of the troublesome Jewish leaders, they revolted and defeated the conformity-craving Antiochus and that's why around this time of the year, for over two thousand years, we celebrate the Maccabean victory at this Chanukah season.

That's why Chanukah has more than a parochial message for Jews. It speaks to all men. It would warn all Americans, in high places and low, to remember this man Antiochus and the lesson inherent in his downfall. Perhaps, if so we do, we will not become so irate over those who dissent from our dropping those devastating bombs and napalm upon helpless women and children in the rice paddies of Vietnam. Nor will anyone be so naïve as to believe that the opposition of a goodly number of these Jews can be silenced by any suggestion of the possible diminution of aid to our cherished land of Zion. . . .

Remember Antiochus, Mr. President. And inasmuch as your own Christmas season is likewise approaching (since both Chanukah and Christmas have their derivations in far, distant festivals of lights so bravely kindled against the descending darkness of winter), do, Mr. President, remember your Christ's Mass. Remember especially his protest against the encircling gloom of his day and try to envisage whether, at this black hour in the winter of mankind when total world blackout threatens us all, that Jew of Nazareth would have been part of the delegation of Jewish War Veterans or whether he might have joined Bishop Wright and Bishop Lord, distinguished Catholic and Protestant leaders respectively, and Archbishop Iakovos, Greek Orthodox Primate of all the Americas whom you have so consistently refused even to see because they would voice their protest over the un-Christlike, ungodly spectacle of unceasing escalation of the sickening bloodshed in Vietnam. Yes, remember Jesus, Mr. President, and his admonition: "Blessed are the peacemakers!"

Source: Maurice N. Eisendrath, "Letter to the President," *Dimensions in American Judaism,* winter 1966–1967, 25.

Three Specific Issues

There is scarcely a social or moral issue on which the CCAR and/or the UAHC have failed to take a stand. They include the relation of church and state, ecology, population control, corruption in government, immigration, international cooperation, poverty, and many more. Early resolutions tended to be almost completely devoid of references to classical Jewish texts aside from the Prophets, whereas in more recent years such references have come to play a larger role. The UAHC resolutions given below deal with subjects that remain controversial in American society: capital punishment and the rights of gays and lesbians. In Reform congregations, gays and lesbians have been welcomed as spiritual and lay leaders. Although some Reform rabbis continue to believe that the traditional wedding ceremony should be limited to heterosexual couples, the CARR, at its convention in Spring, 2000, passed a resolution legitimating those rabbis who choose, in varying ways, to sanctify gay/lesbian unions.

---

1. Against Capital Punishment (1959)

We believe it to be the task of the Jew to bring our great spiritual and ethical heritage to bear upon the moral problems of contemporary society. One such problem, which challenges all who seek to apply God's will in the affairs of men, is the practice of capital punishment. We believe that in the light of modern scientific knowledge and concepts of humanity, the resort to or continuation of capital punishment either by a state or by the national government is no longer morally justifiable.

We believe there is no crime for which the taking of human life by society is justified, and that it is the obligation of society to evolve other methods in dealing with crime. We pledge ourselves to join with like-minded Americans in trying to prevent crime by removal of its causes, and to foster modern methods of rehabilitation of the wrongdoer in the spirit of the Jewish tradition of *t'shuvah* (repentance).

We believe, further, that the practice of capital punishment serves no practical purpose. Experience in several states and nations has demonstrated that capital punishment is not effective as a deterrent to crime. Moreover, we believe that this practice debases our entire penal system and brutalizes the human spirit.

We appeal to our congregants and to our co-religionists, and to all who cherish God's mercy and love, to join in efforts to eliminate this practice which lies as a stain upon civilization and our religious conscience.

Source: UAHC, *Where We Stand: Social Action Resolutions Adopted by the Union of American Hebrew Congregations* (New York: UAHC, 1980), 54.

2. On the Human Rights of Homosexuals (1977)

WHEREAS the UAHC has consistently supported civil rights and civil liberties for all persons, and

WHEREAS the Constitution guarantees civil rights to all individuals,

BE IT, THEREFORE, RESOLVED that homosexual persons are entitled to equal protection under the law. We oppose discrimination against homosexuals in areas of opportunity, including employment and housing. We call upon our society to see that such protection is provided in actuality.

BE IT FURTHER RESOLVED that we affirm our belief that private sexual acts between consenting adults are not the proper province of government and law enforcement agencies.

BE IT FURTHER RESOLVED that we urge congregations to conduct appropriate educational programming for youth and adults so as to provide greater understanding of the relation of Jewish values to the range of human sexuality.

Source: UAHC, *Where We Stand: Social Action Resolutions Adopted by the Union of American Hebrew Congregations* (New York: UAHC, 1980), 126–27.

3. On Same Gender Officiation (2000)

WHEREAS justice and human dignity are cherished Jewish values, and

WHEREAS, in March of 1999 the Women's Rabbinic Network passed a resolution urging the Central Conference of American Rabbis to bring the issue of honoring ceremonies between two Jews of the same gender to the floor of the convention plenum, and

WHEREAS, the institutions of Reform Judaism have a long history of support for civil and equal rights for gays and lesbians, and

WHEREAS, North American organizations of the Reform Movement have passed resolutions in support of civil marriage for gays and lesbians, therefore

WE DO HEREBY RESOLVE, that the relationship of a Jewish, same gender couple is worthy of affirmation through appropriate Jewish ritual, and

FURTHER RESOLVED, that we recognize the diversity of opinions within our ranks on this issue. We support the decision of those who choose to officiate at rituals of union for same-gender couples, and we support the decision of those who do not, and

FURTHER RESOLVED, that we call upon the CCAR to support all colleagues in their choices in this matter, and

FURTHER RESOLVED, that we also call upon the CCAR to develop both educational and liturgical resources in this area.

Source: "Resolution on Same Gender Officiation," CCAR, 2000.

Jewish Faith and Social Justice (1994)

The question has often arisen whether acts of social justice done by Reform Jews are motivated by their religious faith. Is there a real link between a sense of holiness and helping the homeless? In 1994, Evely Laser Shlensky (1942–), a prominent lay leader in the Reform movement, persuasively addressed this issue.

In recent years, Reform Jews have become increasingly interested in religious experience and religious living. People who are looking for spiritual renewal tend to turn first to prayer, and sometimes to Jewish study as well. My own experience has taught me that righteous *doing* also can result in the experience of awe. . . .

Because my own experience is probably the most valid thing I have to teach, let me begin by telling you of a few times that I felt full of awe.

1. One of my most cherished memories is of the night our Temple board voted to become a Sanctuary congregation, joining the Sanctuary Movement which was protecting refugees fleeing peril in El Salvador and Guatemala in the 1980's. That night we chose to side with the victims of violence, to assert our duty to protect human rights, to call on our Jewish experience with fight and flight. It was a choice that the board knew entailed a willingness to tangle with a government—our own—that was intent on criminalizing the protection of human rights. It was an evening that felt to me to be full of miracles, a time I had yearned for but was not sure I would ever witness.

I felt similarly awed when the UAHC Biennial steered the same course, thoughtfully and religiously. I imagine many activists who have come before Temple boards and Biennial gatherings with bold plans and some trepidation have been similarly moved when those boards and Biennials have decided to do the right thing, overcoming a natural reluctance to take risks, even risking alienating some members of the congregation and some member congregations.

(Of course the vote doesn't always go our way. Perhaps from temporary defeat may come personal growth, if not religious experience.)

2. Another remarkable evening comes to mind. For two years a group of Temple members and unaffiliated gay and lesbian Jews from our city had been meeting and learning together. We wanted our Temple to understand how wonderfully varied the Jewish family is. We decided to present a panel of people to our congregation who live in families unlike those we might imagine are normative. Our group was apprehensive about how the congregation would react. To see and feel the warm and appreciative response by most members of the congregation was for me a religious moment. It was an affirmation that ordinary Jews are willing to perceive humanity and holiness in many of its diverse manifestations.

3. The final awesome encounter I'll relate happened to my daughter, Aviva, when she was about 16. Aviva had just participated in serving lunch in a soup kitchen. On our drive home she said to me, "This may sound strange, Mom, but in that damp kitchen I think I experienced God." I thought of Heschel's representation of a *mitzvah* as a place where God and humans meet.

A precious feature of the work of social justice is that whether or not we experience awe and wonder, if we do the work devotedly, at least we get something done in the world.

Experiencing awe through social justice provides us with an opportunity to think about religious living in some new ways. It may also respond to the compartmentalization of our lives, including our religious lives.

We know that Judaism is built on at least several prongs: prayer, study, and righteous deeds. But because our lives are compartmentalized, sometimes it's hard to see that the prongs are connected at the base. We live in a bureaucratized society. We work through committees. We keep hourly calendars. Our meetings rely on agendas that are not only itemized, but often minitized. How, then, are we to restore integrity, the understanding of wholeness, of holiness? Part of the *tikkun* needs to be the repair of our own compartmentalization.

The fragmentation has been a particular problem for those of us devoted to the prong of Judaism which emphasizes the work of social justice. Why a particular problem? Because much of the work of social justice looks like political activity or human services. So one might miss the fact that when done out of religious commitment, social action is religious action, an inherent, essential prong of Judaism. And the missed perception allows Temple social activists to be marginalized.

So we have on our hands a restoration job: to restore the oneness, the sense of necessity for all the parts in order to create a whole, a holy Jewish life.

How can we set about reclaiming a religious mooring for the work of social justice? My own religious life is nurtured by what I call a sense of enspiritment, by which I mean fullness of spirit. Fullness of spirit is a condition I associate with text study and with social action—and particularly with the interface of these two. When the lessons of the texts lead nowhere but to the streets, to rendering those streets more kind, more just and more peaceful, I feel powerfully and purposefully connected to our tradition.

What I've described as enspiritment seems remarkably different than the more fashionable concept of spirituality, which perhaps the Litvak in me still finds suspect. I am far more drawn to the notion of holiness. I think that holiness is inherently a more Jewish way of understanding what in the world we're doing here.

The difference, as I understand it, between spirituality and holiness is that one is good feeling and the other is good doing. Maybe it's that I've never fully understood the meaning of spirituality, despite the fact that people have tried to explain it to me—it still sounds to me like an emotional rush produced by religious experience. That's appealing: however, we're not commanded to *feel* good, but to *be* good.

Now and then I do experience something that feels like a "*mitzvah*-glow." I described a few such experiences at the beginning of this talk. But the glow seems to be a residual benefit of decent doing, not something we ought to be pursuing as an end. . . .

To reclaim our religious mooring, Jewish tradition needs to find expression through both our individual and collective actions. My hope is that we will find creative ways for social action to permeate Temple life—not just through social action committees, although their role is central and critical, but also through boards of directors, sisterhoods, youth groups, havurot and the membership generally.

I want people to understand that temples are places where Jews gather for prayer, for study, and for formulating plans to bring core Jewish values into the world: justice, mercy and peace. Then the restoration job will be well underway and the synagogue will be more whole and holy.

Source: Evely Shlensky, "Wholeness and Holiness: Social Justice as a Vital Component of Religious Living," *New Menorah,* summer 1994, 5, 11.

Social Justice Dilemmas (1998)

Only recently has the Reform movement attempted to deal in depth with complex moral issues that allow for no easy or clear-cut answers. In introducing the most recent of a series of books produced by the UAHC on issues of social justice, two notable leaders of the movement's social justice initiatives, Albert Vorspan (1924–) and Rabbi David Saperstein (1947–), laid out the difficulties of moral decision making in the twenty-first century.

In the days of the historic civil rights struggle, it seemed so easy to make a clear moral judgment on the big issues in American society. It seemed so easy to tell the good guys from the bad, to stand up and be counted. It did not require great ethical sophistication to distinguish right from wrong when witnessing black children in Birmingham being killed in church bombings and assaulted by police equipped with attack dogs, fire hoses, and electric cattle prods. It was not difficult to salute those fighting to win the elementary right to vote and to condemn those who sought to frustrate that right.

On the international scene, it was easy to shout "Let My People Go" on behalf of Soviet Jewry. And although making an initial judgment on the Vietnam War was less clear-cut than the civil rights issue, most Americans came to see the war as morally wrong.

The clear-cut issues of yesteryear have faded into the complex gray of today's dilemmas. While racial justice is still a high moral goal, through what methods is it to be achieved? Affirmative action? Busing? Quotas? Censorship and limitation of freedom of speech are contrary to American principles. Can the government, however, regulate hate-filled speech or speech on the Internet to protect children from pornography? Do American Nazis have the right to march through a community consisting largely of Holocaust survivors? Do newspapers have the right to refuse to place ads denying the truth of the Holocaust? And what limits, if any, do we set upon a woman's right to have an abortion? We still believe in economic justice, but is that furthered by our welfare system if, while helping the poor, it creates a dependency on government support and perpetuates economic injustice? All tough questions.

The certainties of yesterday have become the ambiguities and conflicts of today, especially when one right collides with another right. This is true for all Americans; for Jews *only more so*. . . .

How do we reconcile our desire to redirect our nation's resources to meet domestic needs with our commitment to maintain strong foreign aid for Israel; the rights of gays and lesbians with the importance of the traditional Jewish family; our commitment to close Black-Jewish relations with our opposition to quotas; our efforts to find peaceful ways for nations to resolve differences with our need to contain Saddam Hussein's Iraq and to intervene in Bosnia and other places where genocidal activity takes place; our joy at the fall of the Communist empire with our concern about the resulting ethnic hatreds, nationalist fervor, and anti-Semitism; our support for the Middle East peace process with our pain at the price Israel must pay because of the increased terrorism that accompanies it; our commitment to the unity of the Jewish people and to *Klal Yisrael* with our determination to stand up for our rights as Reform and Conservative Jews in Israel? How should we balance our Jewish universal ethics and the ethics of our particular self-interest when they collide? . . .

What is the Jewish dimension in each of these issues? What is the Jewish stake? And what do Jewish values teach us about these issues? If Jewish tradition speaks to these conflicts, it does not always do so clearly. No "You shalls" and "You shall nots" were proclaimed at Sinai, no specific answers to our thorny political issues. There are no easy answers as we enter the twenty-first century.

But the complexity of these issues does not exempt us Jews from facing up to our moral challenges. We may have to walk a moral tightrope, yes, but we cannot escape our Jewish mission. With greater modesty and less certainty than in the past, with more tentativeness and greater tolerance for dissenting views, we still bear our historic Jewish burden: to face this world and its pain head-on; to engage in endless study and moral debate; to cherish human life and to pursue justice; to enhance the life of the mind and to struggle to be God's partner in repairing this broken and incomplete world. It was never easy, even in the old days; it is more difficult today and will be even harder tomorrow. But, if the agenda is more nuanced today, our duty to do the right thing, to engage in *tikkun olam,* the "repair of our broken world," is as compelling as ever.

Source: Albert Vorspan and David Saperstein, *Jewish Dimensions of Social Justice* (New York: UAHC Press, 1998), 3–5.

TEN

OUTREACH

✦ Since the days of Ezra and Nehemiah (fifth century B.C.E.), endogamy (in-marriage) rather than exogamy (out-marriage) was and has remained the desirable option for all branches of Judaism, though the second half of the twentieth century has seen an explosive increase in mixed marriages. By the 1990s, in a number of large cities, as well as in some small communities, the rate of mixed marriage between Jews and gentiles had risen to over 50 percent. Because of its more conservative traditions, Canada has been somewhat less affected, but there too the tendency away from traditional endogamy was increasingly in evidence.

Jews in all streams of life have been affected by these changes. While Orthodoxy and Conservatism rejected rabbinical officiation at mixed marriages outright, the Reform rabbinate became deeply divided over the issue. At the same time, Reform was the first movement to wrest positive opportunities from this situation. By reaching out to the gentile partners in the marital union, it increased conversions to Judaism, and it also confronted the need for integrating intermarried families and their children into the congregational fabric. Outreach thus became an important element of Reform's program.

Mixed Marriage

1. The 1973 Resolution on Rabbinical Officiation

Already in 1909, the CCAR had discussed the growing issue of mixed marriage and had resolved "that mixed marriages are contrary to the tradition of the Jewish religion *and should therefore be discouraged by the American Rabbinate." The resolution was reaffirmed in 1947, though an attempt to keep Reform rabbis from officiating at such weddings was turned down. That issue was again debated at the 1973 convention, at which time it was estimated that 40 percent of the rabbis in the CCAR were officiating at mixed marriages because they felt that doing so was an act of important outreach to the intermarrying family. After extensive discussion, the convention adopted a new resolution.*

The Central Conference of American Rabbis, recalling its stand adopted in 1909 "that mixed marriage is contrary to the Jewish tradition and should be discouraged," now declares its opposition to participation by its members in any ceremony which solemnizes a mixed marriage.

The Central Conference of American Rabbis recognizes that historically its members have held and continue to hold divergent interpretations of Jewish tradition.

In order to keep open every channel to Judaism and *K'lal Yisrael* for those who have already entered into mixed marriage, the CCAR calls upon its members:

1. to assist fully in educating children of such mixed marriage as Jews;
2. to provide the opportunity for conversion of the non-Jewish spouse, and
3. to encourage a creative and consistent cultivation of involvement in the Jewish community and the synagogue.

Source: "Resolution of the Committee on Mixed Marriage," *CCAR Yearbook* 83 (1973): 97.

2. Rabbinical Opposition to Officiation (1983)

Subsequently, a group of 100 Reform rabbis who refused to officiate at mixed marriages signed a statement initiated by Rabbi Simeon J. Maslin (who later became president of the CCAR). It was privately published and distributed in pamphlet form. The following are the opening paragraphs.

As rabbis we look at each marriage ceremony as a reaffirmation of the Covenant between God and the Jewish People and as an opportunity to share in the happiness of members of our congregations. During the wedding we invoke God "who sanctifies our people Israel through the covenant of marriage," and the bride and groom consecrate themselves to each other "according to the heritage of Moses and Israel." These words are the essential and traditional heart of the Jewish marriage ceremony, and we recite them with joy.

Every rabbi whose name is appended to this pamphlet has been asked to officiate at mixed marriage ceremonies. It would be easy to say yes, to be accommodating and not add to the pain that is so often felt by couples and their families in such instances. Why, then, must we say no?

When officiating at a marriage ceremony, the rabbi acts as representative of the Jewish people and the Jewish heritage. What the rabbi does or does not do has an effect on the totality of Jewry and on our people's potential for survival in the midst of an overwhelmingly non-Jewish society.

If one of the partners in a marriage is not a member of the Jewish people and is not heir to "the heritage of Moses and Israel," what reasonable purpose is served by using those time-hallowed words? Again, if one of the partners is not Jewish, how can that marriage ceremony "sanctify our people Israel?" Of course, one might suggest that the rabbi omit these traditional statements from a mixed marriage ceremony. But, then, what is the function of the rabbi? The rabbi represents Judaism and the Jewish community.

Our understanding of the essence of Jewish marriage makes it impossible for us to officiate at mixed marriages. Such marriages are, of course, legally valid, and we are willing to meet with and to counsel couples of mixed religious background both before and after marriage. They and their children are welcome to our synagogues—to our worship services, our classes and our programs. But the fact remains that a marriage ceremony involving a person who is not a member of the Jewish people is not a Jewish ceremony.

If we cannot officiate at the marriage ceremonies of Jews and non-Jews, it is not because we reject such couples. They are dear to us, and we shall always seek to meet with them and to extend the hand of friendship.

Source: *Reform Rabbis and Mixed Marriage* (Philadelphia: n.p., 1983), 1–2.

3. Rabbinical Support of Officiation (1985)

Following the adoption of the resolution on rabbinical officiation, a group of Reform rabbis and laity who were more favorably disposed to a rabbinical role at mixed weddings formed an Association for a Progressive Reform Judaism. One of its leaders, Professor Eugene Mihaly (1918–) of HUC-JIR, wrote a series of responsa on the subject of Jewish marriage, from which the following is an excerpt.

Civil marriage, to many of our young people, is not quite being married. For many of our sons and daughters raised in our synagogues and religious schools, a judge or justice of the peace are not even viable, acceptable options. They seek—and often go to endless trouble to arrange—a religious ceremony. They want; they need; they yearn for a Jewish blessing; and if that is denied them by Judaism, they will turn to more sympathetic clergy of other faiths. Will that strengthen the Jewish people and Jewish faith?

One reasonable alternative would be to involve the congregants in addressing this problem. Could not each congregation appoint a committee of competent, dedicated lay persons whose duty it will be to determine whether a marriage meets what the congregation considers to be the legitimate standards set by the congregation, and if the rabbi's conscience will not permit him to officiate, then one of the dedicated members of the committee, after a course of study and licensing by the congregation to satisfy the legal requirements, would solemnize the marriage? The officiant, even according to the most literal interpretation of tradition, need not be an ordained rabbi. Any competent lay person is qualified. Well, let us relieve the rabbi of the burdensome and often painful responsibility and let the congregation and those lay people who are willing to devote themselves to study and serious preparation assume this privilege. The Religious Society of Friends follows a similar procedure. Perhaps we might profit from their experience.

Cantors, whether they were formally invested by an academic institution or not, have been licensed for many decades to officiate at weddings. In Orthodox communities not only *chazzanim,* but other less committed and less qualified functionaries of the synagogue have for generations solemnized marriages. There is a long-standing tradition in Reform Judaism that lay persons in smaller, isolated communities are licensed by the congregation to officiate at weddings and other life-cycle occasions. Can we not with our rich resources devise a syllabus for interested, devoted and competent congregants who, after successful completion of the course, would be authorized by the appropriate authorities to act, with the consent of the congregation, as officiants at marriages and bestow the blessings of Judaism upon the couple?

Whatever alternative we as Reform Jews adopt, however, we cannot, we must not and, with the help of a benign Providence, we will not deny the blessings of Judaism to our children. If we are to speak with the young men and women whom we consecrated and confirmed, we must be prepared to say, as our ancestors heard the good Lord Himself say to His beloved people: "Your pain is My pain *('Immo 'Anochi betzarah)*." "Your joy is our joy; we are with you in your soul struggle, in your travail—open, accepting, loving, understanding. We face this together."

Source: Eugene Mihaly, *Responsa on Jewish Marriage* (Cincinnati: [s.n.], 1985), 81–83.

4. Reaching Out to the Non-Jewish Partner (1978)

In 1978, Rabbi Alexander M. Schindler (1925–), president of the UAHC, made international news when he urged his board of trustees to adopt a national policy of truly welcoming non-Jewish marriage partners into Reform congregations. He also took up a suggestion made by Rabbi Bernard J. Bamberger and others (see below) to undertake an aggressive proselytizing campaign that would win many new adherents for Judaism. The latter proposal bore little fruit, but the former resulted in making Outreach a central and persistent pursuit of the Reform movement.

Not all non-Jewish partners of an intermarriage convert to Judaism as we so well know. The majority, in fact, do not. Statistics are hard to come by, but what we have, suggests these facts: A preponderance of intermarriage involves Jewish husbands and non-Jewish wives and upward to 40% of these women formally accept our faith. In that smaller grouping involving non-Jewish husbands and Jewish wives, the rate of conversion is not much more than 3%. However something extremely interesting has come to light. Social scientists have uncovered a "Jewish drift," the phenomenon of a "turning" to our faith. Their research has established that *"nearly 50% of non-Jewish husbands"* though not formally embracing Judaism, *"by their own description, nonetheless regard themselves as Jews."* (Massarik)

This brings me to my second proposal: I believe that our Reform congregations must do everything possible to draw into Jewish life the non-Jewish spouse of a mixed marriage. The phenomenon of the "Jewish drift" teaches us that we ought to be undertaking more intensive Jewish programs which will build on these already existing ties of identification. If non-Jewish partners can be brought *more actively* into Jewish communal life, perhaps they themselves will initiate the process of conversion or at the very least we will assure that the children issuing from these marriages will, in fact, be reared as Jews.

We can begin by removing those "not wanted" signs from our hearts. I am in substantial agreement with Dr. Fein here: we reject intermarriage—not the intermarried. If Jews-by-choice often feel alienated by our attitudes we can imagine how, unwittingly or not, we make the non-Jewish spouses of our children feel.

We can also remove those impediments to a fuller participation which still obtain in too many of our congregations. Even the most stringent approach to halachah offers more than ample leeway to allow the non-Jewish partner to join in most of our ceremonial and life-cycle events. Thus the halachah permits a non-Jew to be in the temple, to sing in the choir, to recite the blessing over the Sabbath and festival candles, and even to handle the Torah. There is no law which forbids a non-Jew to be buried in a Jewish cemetery.

As for the children born of such a marriage, if the mother is Jewish the child is regarded as fully Jewish. But if she is not, then even Orthodoxy, providing consent of the non-Jewish mother is obtained, permits the circumcision of the boy, his enrollment in religious school and his entitlement to be called to the Torah on the occasion of his bar mitzvah and to be considered a full Jew everlastingly thereafter.

All this is possible under Orthodoxy. How much the more so under Reform! Reform Judaism has never been chained by the halachah, we insist on its creative unfoldment. If we put our best minds to it, we will find many other ways which can bolster our efforts in this realm.

As a case in point, why should a movement which from its very birth-hour insisted on the full equality of men and women in the religious life unquestioningly accept the principle that Jewish lineage is valid through the maternal line alone? Some years ago, I heard a learned paper by Dr. [Ben Zion] Wacholder of our College-Institute, a man most knowledgeable in rabbinic sources and heedful of their integrity who argued that there is substantial support in our tradition for the validity of Jewish lineage through the paternal line. I discussed his paper with one of Israel's foremost rabbinic authorities, who found much weight in Dr. Wacholder's argument.

By way of illustration: a leading member of the United States Senate is not a Jew, although he was born a Jew. His father was Jewish. His mother converted from one of the Christian denominations. He was circumcised, reared as a Jew and attended religious school. When the time of his bar mitzvah approached, the rabbi refused to recognize the validity of his mother's conversion and did not allow the boy to recite the blessings over the Torah. Embarrassed, enraged, the entire family converted to Christianity. This is why a leading United States senator is not a Jew today.

Now I am not about to propose a resolution of this maternal/paternal line issue. I lack sufficient knowledge. I merely insist that there is a possibility of the harmonization of tradition with modern need. And that the Task Force for whose creation I call should include representatives of our Rabbinic Conference's Responsa Committee or enlist its effort in toto as we pursue our delicate tasks.

It may well be that in our collective wisdom and mindful of the needs of a larger Jewish unity we will ultimately determine that certain privileges simply cannot be extended to non-Jews. If we do, then I am certain that the thoughtful non-Jew, who is favorably disposed to Judaism, will recognize that only through conversion can these privileges be won.

It is the inertia which I want to overcome. It is the indifference which I mean to master.

Let no one here misunderstand me to say that I am accepting of intermarriage. I deplore it, I discourage it, I will struggle against it. Rhea and I have five children and we are as ardent as all other Jewish parents in our desire to stem the tide. But if our efforts do not suffice, why then we do not intend to banish our children, we will not say shivah over them. Quite the contrary, we will draw them even closer to our hearts and we will do everything we humanly can to make certain that our grandchildren will be Jews, that they will be a part of our community and share the destiny of this People Israel.

Source: Alexander M. Schindler, "Outreach: The Case for a Missionary Judaism," (address to UAHC Board of Trustees, Houston, TX, December 1978). Another version of this address can be found in *Outreach and the Changing Reform Jewish Community: Creating an Agenda for Our Future* (New York: UAHC, 1989), 86–88.

5. *The UAHC Resolution on Outreach (1978)*

In response to Rabbi Schindler's proposal, the trustees adopted the following resolution.

Rapid demographic change is doing much to affect the future of American Jewry. Among the significant and critical demographic trends are: the growth of mixed-marriage, the decline of the Jewish birth-rate relative to the general population, an increase in the numbers of non-Jews converting to Judaism. These trends require our profound, serious and continuing attention. They call for creative leadership so that we reach out to shape our future and do not become passive products of forces beyond our own control.

Accordingly, the Union of American Hebrew Congregations, at its Board meeting in Houston on December 2, 1978, resolves:

1. To intensify our formal and informal Jewish educational programs within the Reform synagogue and the Reform Jewish movement to stimulate positive and knowledgeable Jewish identification.
2. To develop a sensitive program of welcoming and involving converts to Judaism, recognizing that those who choose Judaism in good faith are as authentic in their Jewish identity as those who are born Jewish.
3. To develop an effective outreach program by which the Reform synagogue can seek out mixed married couples in order to respond to the particular emotional and social stresses in their situations and to make the congregation, the rabbi, and Judaism itself available to them and their families.
4. To plan a special program to bring the message of Judaism to any and all who wish to examine or embrace it. Judaism is not an exclusive club of born Jews; it is a universal faith with an ancient tradition which has deep resonance for people alive today.
5. To implement these principles, we call upon the Chairman of the Board to appoint a special task force, of members of the Board, to examine these recommendations for implementation in all program departments of the UAHC and to report back to the Spring 1979 meeting of the Board.

Source: Resolution from the UAHC Board Meeting in Houston on December 2, 1978. Another version of this resolution can be found in *Outreach and the Changing Reform Jewish Community: Creating an Agenda for Our Future* (New York: UAHC, 1989), p. 91.

6. Outreach Twenty Years Later (1999)

Two decades after Rabbi Schindler had challenged the movement with his demand for an Outreach program and after a special department for this purpose had been established at the UAHC, his successor, Rabbi Eric H. Yoffie (1947–), assessed its impact and needs.

Now that Outreach has been with us for two decades, we are understandably inclined to spend more time discussing its practical dimensions than its theoretical foundations. But it is important for us to review from time to time those theological principles upon which our Outreach efforts are based.

We begin with the premise that Judaism is a rejection of tribalism. Yes, there is a biological dimension to Judaism, but it is only one dimension of many; and yes, Judaism speaks the language of fate, but it speaks as well the language of choice. A tribalistic view of Judaism would be one that exalts the prestige of blood and that roots Judaism solely in race; such a view is utterly contrary to our tradition's most basic teachings.

But it would certainly be wrong to conclude that Outreach rests on some vague, love-the-stranger universalism. Judaism is not a universalistic religion. The opening chapters of Genesis specifically reject universal solutions to the human situation. The Tower of Babel, the eternal symbol of a world of "one people with one language," is portrayed as an act of hubris, destined to remain unfinished, no matter how much violence may be committed in its name.

Instead, the starting point for Jewish Outreach and all Jewish theology is our unique destiny as a religious people, tied to God in a covenant that we trace back to Abraham and Sarah. For 3,500 years, we have been taught to follow Abraham's example and to "keep the way of the Eternal, doing what is right and just." Developing the nuances of meaning and obligation that flow from this covenant is the ongoing task of the Jews: It guides us in a world that is redeemable but not yet redeemed. We have paid a heavy price for our religious destiny, but we have also been eternally blessed by our conviction that this is the reason for our survival. We know that God has established this covenant with us and has sustained us so that we may offer a taste of goodness and compassion to a despairing humanity.

In short, Outreach begins not with an act of inclusion *per se* but rather with an act of self-definition. We begin with an affirmation of our particularism, of our apartness, of our unique destiny. This may seem anomalous, but of course it is not: The first step of Outreach—and the single most important step—is to have a clear sense of who we are and of the boundary that exists between us as Reform Jews and the society around us.

If we have learned anything at all after twenty years, it is this: You do not draw people in by erasing boundaries and eliminating distinctions. If there are no clearly-defined distinctions between our Jewish values and the values of the world around us, then what reason would serious people—Jews or non-Jews—have to cast their fate with ours?

If we have learned anything at all after twenty years, it is this: Intermarried couples are not attracted to us by minimalism or watered-down Judaism. They are attracted by compelling ethical teachings, by ritual experiences rich in meaning, by the mystery of Shabbat, and by the possibility of religious commandment.

If we have learned anything at all after twenty years, it is this: The Jews most successful at the work of Outreach are those who know who they are, who communicate the power and beauty of their heritage, and who model proud and assertive religious behavior. Jews who are confused about who they are and what their movement stands for are utterly incapable of opening for others the door to our Jewish world.

Source: Eric H. Yoffie, "UAHC President's Remarks," in *Twentieth Anniversary Symposium for the William and Lottie Daniel Department of Outreach* (New York: UAHC, 1999), 3.

7. The Status of Children (1988)

In 1983, the CCAR took a radical step in defining the Jewishness of offspring born into a mixed-marriage family. According to the preamble of the highly controversial "patrilineal" resolution, the new definition applied only to America, and in fact, Reform Jewish communities outside that realm have generally stood by the traditional halachic definition. Yet even among Conservative Jews, recognition of patrilineal Jews as Jewish has found widespread support among the laity. The following is a historical account and analysis of Reform opinion on the subject taken from the current Rabbi's Manual (1988).

The previous *Rabbi's Manual* (1961) contained the following statement which reflected the prevailing practice of Reform rabbis (p. 112):

Jewish law recognizes a person as Jewish if his mother was Jewish, even though the father was not a Jew. One born of such mixed parentage may be admitted to membership in the synagogue and enter into a marital relationship with a Jew, provided he has not been reared in or formally admitted into some other faith. The child of a Jewish father and non-Jewish mother, according to traditional law, is a gentile; such a person would have to be formally converted in order to marry a Jew or become a synagogue member.

Reform Judaism, however, accepts such a child as Jewish without a formal conversion, if he attends a Jewish school and follows a course of studies leading to Confirmation. Such procedure is regarded as sufficient evidence that the parents and the child himself intend that he shall live as a Jew.

At the Pittsburgh convention of the CCAR (1980) a special committee was established to review this position. Its report was submitted to the convention held in Los Angeles in 1983 and was accepted in amended form.

It reviewed the halachah pertaining to patrilineal and matrilineal descent, recalling that in all respects save one it is the father who determines the status of the child, as for instance in establishing whether a person is a Kohen. Only in cases of mixed marriage is the mother's identity decisive: the halachah considers the child of a Jewish mother as Jewish, and that of a gentile mother as gentile. A major reason for this exception was the fact that a child of a mixed union (which in Jewish law had no status as a legal marriage) would be brought up in the community of its mother, a community totally separated from that of a father. Besides, mixed unions were relatively rare.

Today's situation has changed dramatically. Mixed marriages abound in the Diaspora and the children of such unions often live in multiple-faith communities. Therefore the exclusive emphasis on the Jewishness of the mother as the determining factor in the Jewishness of the child seems no longer justified.

The CCAR, in reviewing its position, was mindful of the complexity and emotional overtones of any new statement on *ishut.* Nonetheless, it deemed it necessary to frame the prevailing practices of the movement (as described in the 1961 *Rabbi's Manual*) in the form of a resolution that began by stating:

> The purpose of this document is to establish the Jewish status of the children of mixed marriages in the Reform Jewish community of North America.

The operative paragraph (as amended) then went on to state:

> The Central Conference of American Rabbis declares that the child of one Jewish parent is under the presumption of Jewish descent. This presumption of the Jewish status of the offspring of any mixed marriage is to be established through appropriate and timely public and formal acts of identification with the Jewish faith and people. The performance of these mitzvot serves to commit those who participate in them, both parent and child, to Jewish life.
>
> Depending on circumstances, mitzvot leading toward a positive and exclusive Jewish identity will include entry into the Covenant, acquisition of a Hebrew name, Torah study, bar/bat mitzvah and Kabbalat Torah (Confirmation). For those beyond childhood claiming Jewish identify, other public acts or declarations may be added or substituted after consultation with their rabbi.

Two aspects of the statement should be especially noted.

First, *the resolution is advisory* rather than halachic in the traditional sense. It does not establish a new definition of Jewish identity, for its preamble states expressly that it means to be operative only for the Reform community in North America, not for all Jews everywhere.

Second, *the resolution establishes a presumption.* It does not say that any child of a mixed marriage is to be considered ipso facto as Jewish. It does say that such a child may be presumed to be Jewish if certain conditions will subsequently obtain, that is, if certain acts will take place and/or certain declarations will be made. Depending on circumstances, these may range from entry into the Covenant to Jewish education, or from personal identification with the Jewish people to the abjuration of another faith.

Therefore, the CCAR resolution diverges from the traditional halachah in two ways: (a) In the halachah the child of a Jewish mother is *ipso facto Jewish;* in the CCAR position he/she is not, and is to be treated like the child of a Jewish father. (b) In the halachah, the child of a Jewish father and gentile mother is a gentile, to be treated like other gentiles in relation to Judaism and the Jewish people. The CCAR resolution of 1983, on the other hand, considers such a child as *potentially Jewish:* it has, in fact, *a claim to Jewish status.*

In both cases it is up to the child or his/her parents to validate this claim through subsequent and meaningful acts of identification.

The statement does not affect the position of the CCAR that mixed marriages are to be discouraged.

Source: Maaglei Tzedek—Rabbi's Manual, ed. David Polish, with historical and halachic notes by W. Gunther Plaut (New York: CCAR Press, 1988), 225–27.

Conversion to Judaism

1. Seeking Proselytes (1944)

Through most of Jewish history no initiatives were undertaken to win adherents to Judaism, and often those who came to us of their own free will were considered with suspicion. During and after World War II there was a flurry of interest in waging an aggressive missionary campaign, but—like later efforts to this end—the Reform community could not be roused to support this effort vigorously. Rabbi Bernard J. Bamberger (1904–1980) of New York City, a historian, biblical scholar, and president of the CCAR, was an advocate of conversionary efforts.

Anyone who has a deep and abiding faith must want to share it. Otherwise, his faith is either insincere or trivial. If you believe strongly and honestly in vegetarianism, the single tax, the principles of the Republican party, or the doctrines of Karl Marx, you are bound to try to convince others that your views are right. How can you withhold from them the truth as you see it? Above all, this applies to religion. Whenever it rises above the level of tribal cult and becomes a message of significance to man as man, religion takes on a missionary spirit. A faith we do not try to spread is not a conviction—it is just a habit. Every true believer is an apostle.

Many Jews are surprised to learn that this is the case with their religion. We sometimes hear it said—even by some who should know better—that Judaism does not seek converts. Whatever truth this statement contains is the result of historical accident. Judaism was once an aggressively missionary religion. In the centuries immediately before and after the birth of Christianity, we carried on vigorous propaganda throughout the Mediterranean world, and with amazing success. We gave up seeking converts only because Christian and Moslem authority, armed with police power, forced us to stop. We gave up the effort slowly and reluctantly. As late as the eighth century, the royal family of the Chazars (in what is now southeastern Russia) and many of their subjects adopted Judaism. Since then, only scattered individuals have entered the Jewish fold; and the Jewish communities, fearful of persecution, were often hesitant about accepting them. Forced to abandon missionary effort, the Jews gradually lost the urge for it.

When the ghetto walls fell and Jews entered more fully into the life of the world around them, you might have expected a change. Now that they were again in free contact with their fellow men, they could have tried to propagate their faith. Especially, you might think, Reform Judaism, with its stress on the universal message of the religion, should have directed this message to all men!

But things did not happen that way. In Germany, where the Reform movement started, the Jews felt much too insecure to take a step that might irritate the Christian authorities. In America, Jewish life was so chaotic that all our efforts were absorbed in putting our own house in order (though Isaac M. Wise had a missionary zeal that went far beyond the house of Israel—but this is a separate story). We had to make the synagogue effective first for those who were born Jews before we could bring its message to a larger audience.

To many Jews, however, the whole idea of proselytizing was repellent. In many countries of Europe, conversion to the dominant faith was the condition of worldly advancement. The numerous Jews who were baptized, or who had their children baptized, seemed to us hypocritical cowards. We assumed that all who change their religious affiliations are insincere turncoats. Again, we resented the establishment in this country of special missions to convert the Jews, sometimes staffed by "professional" converts of dubious character. And so we did not want to missionize others.

Yet, strange to say, Reform Judaism laid the greatest stress on the *Mission of Israel.* Our preachers constantly proclaimed that the Jewish people had been called by God to proclaim His unity and to spread his law of righteousness and peace. This idea is plainly stated in the Bible; the spokesmen of Reform reemphasized it with great eloquence. Rarely, however, did they suggest how the mission was to be carried out in practice. It remains a somewhat vague, though sublime concept. We are still faced by the problem: If we believe we have a mission, what are we going to do about it?

Source: Bernard J. Bamberger, "A Missionary Religion," *Liberal Judaism,* September 1944, 44–45.

2. A Moral Obligation to Propagate Judaism (1985)

David Belin (1928–1999), a distinguished Iowa lawyer, became the major advocate of making active proselytism a part of Reform Outreach. Here he argues that the subject deserves the attention of every serious Reform Jew.

———————————

"Why should I choose to be Jewish?" It is a question that is being asked with increased frequency throughout the United States and Canada in a variety of circumstances.

When a Jew and a non-Jew fall in love and decide to marry, the Jew may ask his or her intended spouse to choose Judaism. Why? What is there about the Jewish religion that would lead the non-Jew to want to change religious identity?

The parents of a Jew contemplating marriage to a non-Jew usually want the prospective son-in-law or daughter-in-law to consider converting to Judaism. Why should the non-Jew choose Judaism?

If the non-Jew does not convert to Judaism, in what religion will their children be raised? Why should the couple raise their children to be Jewish?

If a child is not raised in the religion of either parent on the rationale of freedom of choice upon reaching adulthood, the young adult may ask: "Why should I choose the religion of my Jewish parent?"

These questions directly relate to what has come to be known as Jewish Outreach—one of the most challenging developments in modern Jewish history

Related to this new development is the increasingly large number of Americans today searching for religious identity. Generally speaking, they have not considered the possibility of choosing Judaism because of the erroneous perception by most non-Jews that Judaism is a closed society or that Judaism does not seek to bring others into the Jewish religion. In fact, Jewish Outreach has historic roots going back to biblical times. But even if those roots did not exist, Jews have a moral obligation to let those searching for religious identity know that they have every opportunity, if they so desire, to choose Judaism.

I believe there is a unique opportunity for thoughtful Jews to enhance the quality of their lives by exploring answers to the questions: "Why should I choose to be Jewish?" and "What is Jewish Outreach and what does Jewish Outreach mean for me?" A similar opportunity exists for non-Jews who may be involved in an interfaith relationship with a Jew or who may have no religious preference but are searching for a personally and philosophically satisfying religious affiliation.

Source: David Belin, *Why Choose Judaism: New Dimensions of Jewish Outreach* (New York: UAHC, 1985), 1–2.

3. Conversion (giyyur) in Classical Reform Judaism (1892)

In 1892, the CCAR decided that religious instruction and a convert's verbal commitment would be sufficient for giyyur *(conversion). Circumcision and immersion in the* mikveh *(ritual bath) were no longer deemed essential—a decision that was in line with the generally low importance the Reformers of that day assigned to ritual.*

Resolved, That the Central Conference of American Rabbis, assembled this day in this city of New York, considers it lawful and proper for any officiating Rabbi, assisted by no less than two associates, and in the name and with the consent of his congregation, to accept into the sacred covenant of Israel and declare fully affiliated to the congregation לכל דבר שבקדושה any honorable and intelligent person, who desires such affiliation, without any initiatory rite, ceremony or observance whatever; provided, such person be sufficiently acquainted with the faith, doctrine and religious usages of Israel; that nothing derogatory to such person's moral and mental character is suspected; that it is his or her free will and choice to embrace the cause of Judaism, and that he or she declare verbally and in a document signed and sealed before such officiating Rabbi and his associates his or her intention and firm resolve:

1. To worship the One, Sole and Eternal God, and none besides Him.
2. To be conscientiously governed in his or her doings and omissions in life by God's laws ordained for the child and image of the Maker and Father of all, the sanctified son or daughter of the divine covenant.
3. To adhere in life and death, actively and faithfully, to the sacred cause and mission of Israel, as marked out in Holy Writ.

Source: "Resolution Relating to 'Initiatory Rites of Proselytes,'" *CCAR Yearbook* 3 (1893): 36.

4. Conversion in Contemporary Reform Judaism (1988)

Though the above resolution has never been changed, increasing numbers of Reform rabbis today suggest or even insist upon the traditional requirements.

———————

We recognize today that there are social, psychological, and religious values associated with the traditional initiatory rites, and therefore recommend that the rabbi acquaint prospective converts with the halachic background and rationale for *b'rit milah, hatafat dam b'rit,* and *t'vilah* and offer them the opportunity to observe these rites. In Israel, Canada, and various communities elsewhere, *giyyur* is performed by our colleagues in accordance with traditional halachic practice.

A rabbinical *beit din* is desirable for *giyyur.* Where it is not available, the rabbi should choose two informed synagogue members as witnesses.

After the conclusion of the ceremony a copy of the *giyyur* certificate should be given to the convert; other copies are for the rabbi and the congregation. It has been suggested that the American Jewish Archives also receive a copy.

It is understood that while the rituals of *giyyur* are important, the preparatory period preceding the ceremony is even more significant and is given a high priority by Reform Judaism. The length of preparation is determined by the rabbi, taking into consideration the time needed by the candidate to obtain the necessary understanding and appreciation of Judaism so that he or she may make an informed decision. The period of study should be reinforced by assisting the prospective convert's active participation in the various celebrations, observances, and worship services of our people. Regular attendance at the synagogue, as well as evidence of concern for Jewish values and causes in the home and community, should be required. This is intended to enable rabbis and their associates to satisfy themselves not only that the candidate has a sufficient knowledge of Judaism but, of even greater importance, that the candidate is a person of sincere and responsible character who is genuinely desirous of making a whole-hearted commitment to the Jewish people, its faith, and its community.

Giving a Hebrew Name

The candidate is invested with a Hebrew name at the time of the ceremony. This name will serve him or her for all those occasions when a Jew is identified by a traditional Jewish name.

The Midrash says: "The father of all converts was Abraham, therefore when a convert is named, he/she is named X, son/daughter of our father Abraham" (*Tanchuma*, Lech Lecha 32). Reform Judaism would expand this statement and end it by saying "... our father Abraham and our mother Sarah."

Benedictions

At the circumcision (or at *hatafat dam*) the benedictions are said by the circumciser or rabbi; after immersion, they are said by the convert because he/she has already entered our gates and is now enabled to recite the *b'rachot*.

Immersion

Tradition requires that the candidate enter the *mikveh* without jewelry or cosmetics of any kind.

Immersion should take place three times, to the accompaniment of the *b'rachot* indicated in the text.

Where *t'vilah* is desired but a *mikveh* is not available, the ceremony might take place in the ocean, or in a lake or river. The Conservative movement has sanctioned the use of a swimming pool when other alternatives fail. This option might be exercised especially when the local *mikveh* is not made available to Reform converts.

Conversion of a Child

When a non-Jewish woman who is pregnant is converted, upon birth her child is automatically Jewish, as the child of a Jewish mother. If, however, the child is born before *giyyur*, other rules apply.

Giyyur must be purposeful and voluntary, but this condition is absent in the case of small children who are converted with their parents. In such a case a child's *giyyur* takes place conditionally, and when the child reaches maturity he/she may annul the conversion. The age of maturity is, according to tradition, 12 years for girls and 13 for boys, and the option must be exercised at once. We, however, do not deem children of such ages as capable of making decisions for life and would therefore extend the period of option until a later time and would not hold young persons to membership in the Jewish people against their will. Once full adulthood is reached (which may be said to coincide with the voting age) and *giyyur* has not been repudiated, the principle obtains that a Jew remains a Jew even if he/she reverts to the former faith.

Source: *Maaglei Tzedek—Rabbi's Manual*, ed. David Polish, with historical and halachic notes by W. Gunther Plaut (New York: CCAR Press, 1988), 232–34.

The Role of the Non-Jew in the Synagogue (1994)

The increase in mixed marriages has had an important impact on Reform congregations. For, although the incidence of such unions is spread across all segments of the community, Reform has been the most open and welcoming of the religious streams in Judaism. Converted gentiles have made their contributions to Reform Jewish life and beyond; they have served as congregational presidents and on the boards of the movement's national bodies. However, the question of how to integrate unconverted gentile members of temple families into the religious life of the congregation has remained a controversial issue. The CCAR Responsa Committee received the following question posed by the Reform Practices Committee: "What are the traditional and Reform positions on the participation of non-Jews in synagogue services?" The following are brief excerpts from the lengthy responsum.

During the last quarter of the twentieth century profound changes have taken place in the demography of North American Judaism. The rate of mixed marriage has increased dramatically, with one marriage partner remaining outside the Jewish faith community. When such couples, often with their children, wish to find a synagogue where they can worship and enroll their offspring for a Jewish education, they will most likely turn to Reform congregations, which are sure to welcome and accommodate them.

Since in most congregations the family is the unit of membership, the status of the non-Jewish partners remains frequently undefined, especially when congregational constitutions do not specifically state that members must be of the Jewish religion. But even where the constitution is unequivocal in this respect (as it probably is in the majority of temples), the fact is that emotionally, physically, and financially such families have a stake in the synagogue. They support it; they attend its services; and their children are enrolled in the religious school, where they prepare for bar/bat mitzvah and confirmation. Especially on the latter occasions, questions of parental participation in the celebratory ritual arise and may become the seed bed of conflict. Rabbis are put under pressure to make the widest possible accommodation to the non-Jewish partners, in order to give them a role in the service.

This scenario is paralleled by other developments. The Responsa Committee has lately been asked questions about various kinds of non-Jewish appearances at services which suggest a worrisome tendency toward increasing syncretism. Our decisions have held that there must be boundaries in order to assure the identity and continued health of our congregations as well as our movement. If we are everything to everyone, we are in the end nothing at all. On this, there is general agreement. . . .

Participation in the Torah reading is one of the most potent symbols of inclusion in the Jewish community. It was precisely for that reason that Jewish women had to fight twenty years ago not only for the right to be called to the Torah and to read from it, but even to carry or even touch the scroll. The same emotional response is behind the new "tradition" of passing the Torah from family member to family member to the bar or bat mitzvah. Access to the Torah symbolizes full inclusion in the Jewish community. That is precisely why bar/bat mitzvah is celebrated in the way it is.

For this reason a non-Jew should not be called to the Torah for an *aliyah*. The reading of the Torah requires the presence of a community, because it is one of the central acts by which the community affirms its reason for existence, i.e., the covenant whose words are contained within the scroll. To be called to the Torah is to take one's position in the chain of privilege and responsibility by which the Jewish community has perpetuated itself. A non-Jew, no matter how supportive, does not share that privilege or that responsibility as long as s/he remains formally outside the Jewish community.

In many congregations the pressure to grant non-Jews *aliyot* comes in connection with the celebration of a bar/bat mitzvah. The reasons for this may be found in the ways our movement has both deliberately and unintentionally given the public Torah reading an altogether different context and meaning than the one just outlined. Relieving this pressure, therefore, is for this Committee not merely a matter of issuing clear guidelines; it is also a matter of reeducating our people to the real significance of what they are doing. . . .

A brief word should also be said on congregational membership. Where the constitution of the synagogue is not specific on the subject, Gentiles have obtained membership as partners in a family unit. Some congregations therefore conclude that all who have the legal status of members must be entitled to all religious privileges as well. We would disagree. Religious membership is not the same as synagogue membership. The latter is the outflow of an institutional arrangement, the former a spiritual and historic category. Therefore, even where non-Jewish spouses of Jews are considered full temple members, their religious privileges and obligations derive from sources other than congregational by-laws and partake of the limitations set out above.

We are aware that there are differing views of the nature of Jewish worship and much that pertains to it. However, in the view of this Committee, there is a clear and present danger that our movement is dissolving at the edges and is surrendering its singularity to a beckoning culture which champions the syncretistic. Jewish identity is being eroded and is in need of clear guide lines which will define it unmistakably. To provide such markers is the task of the Responsa Committee.

Source: "Gentile Participation in Synagogue Ritual," in *Teshuvot for the Nineties: Reform Judaism's Answers for Today's Dilemmas,* ed. W. Gunther Plaut and Mark Washofsky (New York: CCAR Press, 1997), 55ff.

EDUCATION

✦ Traditional Jewish education consisted of formal study of religious texts for boys and informal home-based training in Jewish women's duties for girls. The early Reform movement broke with this pattern when it initiated equal and combined instruction in the essentials of the Jewish faith for girls and boys in preparation for the confirmation ceremony. But Reform Jewish education in that period was not intensive. At the beginning of the twentieth century, religious school instruction was mostly limited to the tenets of Judaism as a religion, often taught via a catechism, and it rarely included any significant instruction in the Hebrew language.

In the interwar period, the curriculum broadened to include Jewishness as well as Judaism: Jewish history, current affairs, and holiday observance. The new goal was to create a sense of Jewish peoplehood and mutual responsibility. Following World War II, this trend continued, with Hebrew assuming ever greater importance due to both the State of Israel and the growing popularity of bar (and later bat) mitzvah ceremonies in Reform Judaism. Class time increased from the typical two hours a week in classical Reform Judaism to a longer Sunday session, supplemented for many students by midweek Hebrew. Camps became popular venues for transmitting Jewish experiences to young people, as did trips to Israel sponsored by the North American Federation of Temple Youth (NFTY). The National Association of Temple Educators (NATE), founded in 1954, gave new status to Reform educators.

In the 1970s, the first Reform Jewish day schools came into existence, providing a more intensive Jewish education than the supplementary religious school could offer. Their number has steadily increased, and they have formed the Progressive Association of Reform Day Schools (PARDeS). By the end of the twentieth century, adult education programs, sponsored by local synagogues and by the major institutions of American Reform Judaism, were becoming more widespread, and family education was emerging as a way to close the continuity gap between the generations.

The Goals of Jewish Education (1952)

Beginning in 1923, Emanuel Gamoran (1895–1962), who served as director of American Reform Judaism's Joint Commission on Jewish Education for more than a generation, transformed the role of education in the movement. Under his guidance, its focus moved from theology to sociology. He published new textbooks, and he encouraged the teaching of Hebrew and the expansion of class time. In the following excerpts from an article he published in 1952, Gamoran summarizes his priorities.

———————

The core of our Jewish education in the future should consist of: (a) The great intrinsic values—especially those which have been referred to as "value concepts"—Israel, Torah, God, Justice, and the like, (b) The Hebrew Language, (c) Jewish customs and traditions which are of cultural esthetic value, (d) Jewish literature, music, and art, (e) Jewish history interpreted as creative living on the part of the Jewish people, (f) Our relation to Israel, (g) Our relation to America and to mankind.

Our traditional love of learning should be encouraged and fostered but it should be made relevant, as it will be if we relate it to our life and to the problems of our day. Perhaps what we need to do is to reconsider our plans of extension education so that we include as a minimum a rich series of Jewish experiences such as holiday celebrations, music, dancing, arts and crafts. Perhaps we can achieve more in Hebrew instruction if we make better use in the future than we have in the past of the entire field of Jewish music.

Such an approach to our problem will necessitate the establishment of foundation schools in which large numbers of children will, during ages four to eight, receive their early socialization into the Jewish community. Later they should continue their education in the public schools and in supplementary Jewish schools not less than three days a week, two hours a day, if possible, supplemented by a planned series of Jewish education camps or

Hebrew-speaking camps for the summer. For the select who wish to prepare themselves for Jewish leadership there must be established enough day schools of a liberal-cultural character that will provide an intensive Jewish education of a high spiritual esthetic quality. These should, in my opinion, serve about 10 to 15 per cent of the Jewish population.

In the light of the above analysis not only our elementary school but youth education and adult education will have to be reconsidered and their objectives re-evaluated. Youth education should concern itself to a greater extent in the future than it has in the past with the problems which confront young people in our day such as the choice of a vocation which, though it is a general problem, raises special problems for Jewish young people, for on the one hand they flock to certain occupations which they overcrowd, and are excluded from others which they wish to get into; the choice of a mate which again is a general problem confronting all young people but which has its Jewish overtones if we recognize the Jewish tradition. This is particularly essential in view of the recent studies which have shown the rate of mixed marriage to increase. Furthermore Jewish youth would be bound more closely to Jewish life if they would feel that the Jewish community is interested in their personal welfare. Above all, Jewish youth education should center its attention more and more on the problem of developing a general point of view on Jewish life which will be meaningful to the youngsters.

Similarly, adult education should concern itself to a great extent with (a) The making of a Jewish home, (b) Participation in the synagogue as a living institution, (c) Participation in local and national Jewish community problems and institutions (not merely philanthropic) and the recognition that these institutions are a link in the chain of Jewish life, (d) The solution of present day Jewish problems, (e) Giving the average adult a bird's-eye-view of Jewish history and Jewish literature, (f) Teaching him enough Hebrew to be able to participate intelligently in Jewish worship; to read choice selections from the Bible and from medieval and modern Jewish literature, and (for the chosen ones) to speak Hebrew as a living language.

Finally we must set certain standards in our communities for Jewish education and culture. At present we have practically no standards for Jewish education. If we set high standards we may achieve some satisfactory results; if we set no standards we are bound to achieve little. . . .

Summarizing our position, Jewish education must in the years to come seek to give our children a sense of security by socializing them into the Jewish home, the Jewish school, the synagogue, and the community. It must lead to satisfaction in Jewish living derived from an appreciation of Jewish spiritual-cultural and esthetic values of the Jewish past and from active participation in Jewish life in the present. It must give our children the joy to be derived from an appreciation of the Hebrew language and literature and from a meaningful understanding of Jewish history and lore, divorced from excessive formalism on the one hand and from supernaturalism or chauvinism on the other. In short, by developing intelligent creative Jewish personalities living in America we can help to mold and give character to American Jewish life in the future.

Source: Emanuel Gamoran, "The Role of Jewish Education in Developing a Creative Jewish Center in America," *Jewish Education,* fall 1952, 15–16.

Reform Jewish Day Schools (1967)

In the mid-nineteenth century Jewish day schools were common, but the gradual improvement of public education led to their demise a few decades later. The question of reinstituting them was not raised in the Reform movement until the late 1960s, when it became a highly controversial issue because of Reform's devotion to the public schools. An early effort to justify day school education in Reform Judaism is the following statement, issued in 1967 by a group of interested rabbis and Reform laypeople from the New England area.

There are many reasons why a liberal Jewish preparatory school is needed and desired. Foremost among them is the desire of Jewish parents to offer their children not only a sound general education but an intensive grounding in Jewish studies. Neither the public school, with its proper avoidance of religious issues, nor a part-time program of Jewish education can achieve this end. Only a school which offers a fully integrated program of Jewish and general studies can produce the kind of leaders which the future of the American Jewish community demands.

The education received will enable the students to be in harmony with the highest traditions of American and world culture and will hopefully, with the spiritual vitality of the Jewish faith, enable them to be future leaders of American Jewry. The school's distinguishing characteristics will be:

1. The highest standards of academic achievement.
2. An emphasis on the spiritual development of the student.
3. A transmission of the highest moral and ethical values through education.
4. The creation of a total environment which is reflective of Judaism's ideals.
5. A faculty whose members possess not only the highest academic qualifications, but who are also exemplars of spiritual, moral, and ethical behavior and thought. . . .

[We] recognize that the high school years are the years of search, years during which our children make those commitments which direct their lives. Their search is not only for factual knowledge and information, but they seek answers in the realm of religion, faith, ethics, and morals. The school will not only prepare the student for a vocation, but also prepare him to be the best possible person. This close attention to moral, spiritual, and religious questions will make the school unique and attempt to infuse in the student body a sensitivity toward ultimate values. . . .

The school will emphasize a full understanding of Judaism as it confronts ancient and contemporary thought. Religious studies will not be departmentalized, but will suffuse every aspect of the curriculum and school life. Hebrew will be one of the foreign language subjects. Emphasis will be placed on biblical, theological, and ethical studies. The Sabbath and Jewish holidays will be observed consonant with the liberal Jewish philosophy of the school. Chapel requirements will enable a student religious council together with a chaplain to create experimental worship programs following the pattern of the National Federation of Temple Youth programs. A chaplain will be available to counsel, guide, and help the students with their Jewish religious maturity.

Source: "Statement of Purposes," cited in Samuel Glasner, "The Case For/Against a Reform Day School," *Dimensions in American Judaism,* summer 1969, 38.

The Influence of NFTY (1989)

The North American Federation of Temple Youth, founded in 1939, proved the value of camping experiences for the formation of Jewish religious identity in young people, prompting the introduction of camping into the religious school curriculum. For many years Rabbi Samuel Cook (1907–1998) served as its director, expanding membership and programs. In the following excerpts from an article marking NFTY's fiftieth anniversary, Rabbi Jeffrey Salkin (1954–) points to the organization's influence in three crucial areas.

The influence of the Reform youth movement has been most visible in three areas: worship, theology, and education.

First, worship.

The *Union Prayer Book* provided us with a particular liturgical style. It was formal in tone. Many of our young people found it difficult to pray from the Victorian verb constructions. It did not seem particularly conducive to worship in the camp atmosphere. Thus, the creative liturgy movement emerged largely out of our Camp Institutes and youth movement as a reaction to the *Union Prayer Book* style of worship.

While there was much to criticize in the execution of such youth services, they grew out of our youth's need to worship according to their own cultural backdrop. NFTY's creative services were greatly informed by the cultural, social, and political values of the 1960s. These services were invariably topical, dealing with the current political and social issues of the day. Guitar was *de rigeur*. Services were in the round. Participants sat on the floor. The services were often leaderless. There was an emphasis on small physical distance between worshipers. It is not surprising, then, that the youth and camping movement would be instrumental in introducing the *Havdalah* service to Reform Judaism. It was a natural: always done in a circle; relatively short, but expandable, according to the needs of the moment; visual; aromatic; mystical.

The cut-and-paste service found its way into the mainstream of synagogue life. These services were both contemporary and temporary. They reflected the ancient dichotomy between *keva* and *kavanah,* between that which is fixed and canonized and that which reflects the sincere upward striving of the Jewish heart. They expanded the canon of acceptable liturgy. Psalms, Buber, Gibran, and Dylan often freely co-mingled on the mimeographed page. . . .

Second, theology.

The youth movement has spawned an increased emphasis on emotion, intimacy, and participation. With it has come a theological shift that undergirds what Lawrence Hoffman calls the community of unlimited liability, "which celebrates the care of God for one and all and the care of each for each other . . . where we are aware not only that God is present but that we are each present to each other. And through each other, we know God." Its most tangible programmatic manifestation is the Caring Community. Therefore, our youth movement may have spawned our movement's new emphasis on spirituality, creating a quiet revolution that moved the Eternal from transcendence to immanence. . . .

Third, there is NFTY's influence on education.

The youth movement had a different way of motivating Jewish youngsters from the synagogue religious schools. The phenomena of such organizations as the Coalition for Alternatives in Jewish Education and publishers such as Alternatives in Religious Education and Torah Aura are an outgrowth of the educational benefits derived from techniques such as values clarification, weekend camping, and strategies based on humanistic education. The mood in Jewish education shifted from formal to informal. The goals moved from cognitive to affective. . . .

But such innovations, uncritically used, have also been problematic. As with any revolution, there was the danger that the pendulum would swing too far. The revolution in Jewish education was one of affect over content. But it is not enough merely to feel. For all of our revolt against an earlier generation's hyper-rationalism, we still have not effectively conveyed the value of substantive *Talmud Torah* as a mitzvah for the committed Jew. One does not have to be a right-wing educator to question the long-term educational efficacy of an exclusive diet of values clarification. Neither does one have to be an unmitigated stuffed-shirt to suggest that if worship and education is to *move* us, then it has to move us to something beyond ourselves and even beyond the group.

NFTY's successes and influence, then, are far from trivial. They are not limited to the ever-changing world of adolescence. In many ways, NFTY helped "green" the Reform movement. We are living with its successes, which despite the caveats are substantial. We are still deciding how to evaluate them.

Source: Jeffrey K. Salkin, "NFTY at Fifty: An Assessment," *Journal of Reform Judaism,* fall 1989, 17–20.

The UAHC Torah Commentary (1982)

The UAHC's publication of The Torah: A Modern Commentary *in 1981 opened the door to regular Torah study sessions in Reform congregations. Mostly the work of Rabbi W. Gunther Plaut, and including essays on ancient Near Eastern literature by Professor William W. Hallo and a commentary on Leviticus by Rabbi Bernard Bamberger, the large volume was widely distributed. Shortly after its appearance, it evoked a thoughtful review from critic Robert Alter, of which the following are excerpts.*

Peoplehood, or even nationhood, not just "group loyalty," is repeatedly and proudly affirmed in the commentary. "The covenant at Sinai," Rabbi Plaut writes, "became the permanent incursion of God into the lives of a nation that pledged its faith to Him. The Children of Israel did it then and, despite lapses of commitment and practice, have continued to acknowledge the binding nature of the compact." All the key terms of this formulation are antithetical to the thinking of classical Reform. God here is not an elevated ethical idea but a dynamic presence that effects an "incursion," and a permanent one, to boot, into the life of Israel. The central idea of covenant, which has had strong appeal for modern Orthodox and Conservative theologians as well, would have caused discomfort in bygone Pittsburgh and Columbus because, as the commentary here goes on to make clear, it implies binding commitment and it implies a nation as the party to the covenant with God. . . .

The Plaut commentary, no longer pretending to the dubious criterion of inspirational value, sees in the covenant at Sinai the compelling logic of a way of life that conforms with Halakhah, Jewish religious law. "For to Israel the Presence of the Word implied specific commands, laws that shaped its society then and thereafter. In biblical and post-biblical history, revelation meant divine command and covenant the existence of law." What it seems to me the new commentary is arguing for here and elsewhere is not so much the Halakhah as "halakhism," the need for Judaism to operate in some way as a legal system and not purely as a voluntary or "inspirational" arrangement. Rabbi Plaut speaks with great respect of the Halakhah, though he also notes that in recent centuries it has lost its resilience as an adaptive process. Reform Judaism, he concedes, generally broke with the Halakhah, but he observes hopefully that "There has also been a turn toward a greater incorporation of halakhic principles within the Reform movement, albeit on a basis that allows for individual decision within the framework of a *mitzvah* system." . . .

The key emphasis on the Torah as a record of the experience of the Jewish people provides a bridge of sorts between believer and nonbeliever. The Torah, as the commentary puts it at one point, is an authentic expression of "internal history"—the account of God's acts and wonders, His promises and commands, as they were seen and understood by the people of Israel, or by the leaders who shaped its consciousness. Until modern times, the overwhelming consensus of the people saw and understood and cherished what the founding generations had seen and understood, through the eyes of belief. Now there are many who believe in far less literal, more ambiguous ways. There are many others still who can no longer honestly affirm any version of the old beliefs. But neither group is obliged by the distance it has moved from the traditional religious outlook to renounce its sense of compelling connection with three millennia of Jewish experience. The commentary continuously assumes that the Torah, as the fountainhead of that experience, remains the special possession of the whole Jewish people, not only of those who believe it is the literal word of God.

There is a consequent double emphasis in the presentation of the Torah text here. It is firmly set in its original historical context as a document that reflects the concrete experience of the Israelite nation some three thousand years ago; and it is repeatedly seen overlaid by the fine laminations of subsequent commentary and practice—with pride of place accorded to the formative views of the early rabbis—because the commentary assumes that the Jewish people possesses the Torah by living in a constant, shifting dialectic relation with it. . . .

It is a long road from the 19th-century ethical meliorism of classical Reform, with its sense that the formative past could be held at arm's length while wheat was separated from chaff, to this notion of the past stubbornly embedded in the present, challenging the present, inviting the present to imagine it in its complex vital density. With the publication of this commentary, American Reform Judaism has come fully of age, maintaining the independence of its own viewpoints but proffering an imagination of sacred text and national existence that invites the participation of all modern Jews.

Source: Robert Alter, "Reform Judaism and the Bible," *Commentary,* February 1982, 33–35.

The Educated Reform Jew (1999)

At the end of the twentieth century, it seemed more imperative that Jewish education focus on what set Judaism apart from other religions. In these excerpts from a 1999 article, Michael A. Meyer suggests a relationship between the particular and the universal in Jewish education.

If at the beginning of the period of Jewish acculturation [Jewish educators] set themselves the task of expanding the non-Jewish sphere in the thought and conduct of Jews, today's objective is clearly the opposite: to expand the Jewish sphere. That requires careful consideration of the boundary lines between the Jewish and the non-Jewish realms. If the boundary remains undefined or vague, then the content of Judaism will lack clear differentiation from its milieu and Judaism will appear simply as a historical tradition that validates the values of the dominant culture. As such, it becomes merely ornamental, if not superfluous.

The determination of boundaries is an anxiety-filled and difficult task for it involves nays as well as yeas, the need to maintain openness while yet establishing and upholding a clear sense of self. American society has never been more accepting of Jews nor American religion of Judaism than they are today. However, in each case the result has been potentially devastating for Jewish survival. The acceptability of mixed marriage with Jews by Christians and the acceptability of Jewish traditions (but not a separate, distinct, and fully self-conscious Judaism) within the American multicultural fabric have resulted in a Jewish identity that is no longer hidden out of shame or fear, but whose borders have been rubbed away. As Judaism has burst its own boundaries and entered American society and culture, the assumption has become widespread that these boundaries should become more permeable, allowing an influx not only of American or Western, but also of Christian, elements. Under these circumstances the dominant thrust of Jewish education must be inward. Once it seemed important to show how Jews were similar to Christians and how Jewish traditions anticipated American values enshrined in the Constitution. Judaism was taught via the catechism as a species subordinated to the genus "religion," which also included Christianity. That integrationist perspective did not harm Jewish continuity as long as Jews lived in social separation. Today it is clear that an educated Jew must know Judaism and Jewish values not only in their relation to Christianity and American culture, but as distinguishable from them. The requisite goal of Jewish education today is the creation not of Jewishly educated Americans but of Jewishly educated Jews. The former would be persons who have enriched their fundamental identity as Americans by selected elements drawn from Judaism; the latter are those whose principal identity lies in being Jews.

On the other hand, a cultural (as opposed to a religious) boundary between the Jewish and the non-Jewish spheres cannot but create an isolationism, which, except in a ghetto setting, forces a decision for one against the other. In the open society of the Diaspora, placing students in the position of having to choose will almost invariably result in choice of the non-Jewish culture, which enjoys all the advantages of media exposure and peer-group pressure. Only a total education, which relates the Jewish heritage to the non-Jewish, can create an awareness of both points of contact and points of dissonance—or even antagonism—between Jewish and non-Jewish values. . . .

Although the first objective of Jewish religious education, a strong sense of the Jewish self securely grounded within the Jewish community and within the Jewish religious tradition, requires emphasis on particularity and separation, it does not therein find completion. Judaism itself, in its messianism, turns toward the world. The Jewishly educated Jew is anchored in Judaism, but that very anchorage enables her or him, without loss of Jewish selfhood, to reach outward to the human community and forward to the universal goal. What sets such outreach apart from Jewish self-dissolution is that it is undertaken from a position within Judaism across a boundary that Jewish education has clearly marked. Jewishly educated Jews, knowledgeable in the past and present of the Jewish people and immersed in its spiritual life, need not fear assimilation. They can participate fully in the open society, confidently as Jews.

Source: Michael A. Meyer, "Reflections on the 'Educated Jew' from the Perspective of Reform Judaism," *CCAR Journal*, spring 1999, 10–12, 20.

Torah at the Center (1998)

With the election of Rabbi Eric H. Yoffie to the presidency of the UAHC in 1996, adult and family education became top priorities. At a convention of Jewish educators in 1998, he laid down his goals.

My goals are simple ones, and they have been frequently stated. They begin with the premise that this enterprise of being Jewish is of transcendent importance; that we want Jews to be in dialogue with their ancestors and to be part of Jewish intellect, Jewish values, and Jewish learning; that Judaism in the final analysis is primarily about God and Jewish books and not about whether the Arabs hate us or the Gentiles hate us.

These goals require a particular model of synagogue life—one that has emerged primarily from the work of the Rhea Hirsch School and the Experiment in Congregational Education (ECE) program and that sees the synagogue in a new way: as an interdependent learning community; as a place where education is not confined to the religious school and a few adult classes; as a place where a variety of models exist for serious study, including *havurah, Shabbaton,* family education, and home study; as a place where each member family meets with the rabbi or educator to plot out an educational plan for the synagogue year; as the home of a sophisticated library, where a variety of educational materials not now available are offered to individuals and groups; and as a place where every committee and program group incorporates into its everyday work the study of appropriate Jewish texts.

In short, we need to see the synagogue as a place with Torah at the center.

But that is not all. We also need to say openly and honestly that Jewish education is not an end unto itself: It is a means to an end. And that is because we Jews do not study Torah as an intellectual exercise but as an act of intimacy—as a vehicle for expressing the deepest yearnings of our soul. Let me put it somewhat differently: We study Torah for the purpose of encouraging a Jewish way of life, which involves not only Jewish literacy but also prayer, ritual observance, and the work of *tikkun olam.*

Still, and without contradiction, I am quick to acknowledge that it is very hard to teach belief and communion with the sacred. We do not know how to do that very well. But we do know how to teach Jewish competence and Jewish literacy, and that can serve as the basis for Jewish faith and belief. Ignorance is a greater calamity than doubt precisely because faith built on ignorance is sure to crumble. On this point, the Mishnah (*Avot* 2:6) is clear: "*Lo am haaretz chasid*—An ignorant person cannot be pious." So our goal is not study, it is Jewish living; but as a movement strategy, study may be the best way to get us there.

And finally this: My goals for our future include an absolute rejection of the fatalism that so often surrounds our discussions about Jewish education.

This fatalism takes two forms. Some Reform leaders will affirm the vision that I have articulated but then say that it cannot be realized until we restructure the family and transform the synagogue and invest massive resources into these efforts. There is truth in each of these claims, of course, but the conclusion often becomes that educational change is virtually impossible in the near term: instead we must be patient and wait for better days. . . .

On this point, let us be clear: Fate is a Greek concept and not a Jewish one. We cannot afford to be passive, accepting, or patient. My view is that there is nothing inevitable about the educational crisis that we face; it results from communal and individual choices that can be studied, evaluated, and changed. As I have said many times, Reform Jews believe in the transforming power of leadership and the transforming power of Torah. And there are steps that each of us can take now that will make a difference. . . .

We find ourselves at a unique moment in Jewish history. There is a broad consensus, at least among our leadership, that Judaism and Jewishness matter; that study is our first duty and greatest joy; and that to be a Jew is to be heir to one of the greatest traditions of faith, morality, community and individual living that the world has ever known. We all need to see it as our duty to proclaim this message and in so doing to set a new agenda for our movement.

Source: Eric H. Yoffie, "Keynote Address to the National Association of Temple Educators Convention," (Clearwater, FL, December 23, 1998), 1–3.

THE PLATFORMS OF AMERICAN
REFORM JUDAISM

✦ On five occasions North American Reform rabbis have adopted a set of general principles to guide the movement: for the first time in 1869 and most recently in 1999. These platforms have defined the boundaries of Reform Judaism, setting it apart from Orthodoxy, Conservative Judaism, and secular movements like Ethical Culture. They have also laid out a basis for unity amidst the diversity that has characterized the movement, and they have provided a convenient and succinct expression of Reform Judaism's beliefs and practices for use in instructing older children, incoming members, and converts to the faith.

The relatively frequent adoption of new platforms is indicative of the movement's dynamic character and its ability to adapt rapidly to the challenges posed by a changing environment. Orthodoxy, lacking these characteristics, has never required a platform; Conservative Judaism did not adopt one until 1988.

Like political platforms, Reform platforms have planks—in recent versions especially those on God, Torah, and Israel. Under the constituent elements of this triad, more specific planks can be found—for example, positions on life after death, Shabbat observance, and *aliyah* to the State of Israel.

Reform platforms may deal with issues of current social concern as well as timeless ones such as the nature of God. They sometimes use vague or equivocal language in order to embrace the widest possible consensus. Generally, the language is descriptive, but occasionally adopts a prescriptive tone, suggesting that certain practices are moral or ritual imperatives. Although all of the platforms were written and initially adopted by rabbis, they are intended to reflect the values of the whole movement. Reading them carefully and in sequence provides a remarkably accurate picture of the changing concerns of American Reform Judaism.

The Philadelphia Principles (1869)

The thirteen rabbis who adopted this first set of principles (originally in the German language) wanted, above all, to show how their Judaism differed from Orthodoxy. Hence the platform is replete with negations. Its principal author was the radical Reformer Rabbi David Einhorn, who wanted to stress, above all, the universal mission of the Jews.

Article 1. The Messianic goal of Israel is not the restoration of the old Jewish state under a son of David, nor the continued separation from other nations, but the union of all men as children of God acknowledging His unity, and the oneness of all rational beings and their call to moral sanctification.

Article 2. We do not consider the fall of the second Jewish commonwealth as a punishment for the sinfulness of Israel, but as a sequence of divine intent first revealed in a promise to Abraham and then increasingly manifest in the course of world history, to send the members of the Jewish nation to all parts of the earth so that they may fulfill their high priestly task to lead the nations in the true knowledge and worship of God.

Article 3. The priestly service of the Aaronites and the Mosaic sacrificial cult were only preparatory steps for the true priestly service of the whole people which in fact began with the dispersion of the Jewish nation. For inner devotion and ethical sanctification are the only pleasing sacrifices to the All-Holy One. These institutions which laid the groundwork for the higher religiosity went out of existence once and for all when the second Temple was destroyed. And only in this sense have they educational value and may they be mentioned in our prayer.

Article 4. Any distinction between Aaronite and non-Aaronite in relation to religious rights and obligations has therefore become inadmissible, both in ritual and in life.

Article 5. The selection of Israel as a people of faith, as a bearer of the highest idea of mankind, is to be emphasized as strongly as it has been in the past, but only to the accompaniment of equal emphasis on Israel's universal mission and of the equal love of God for all His children.

Article 6. The belief in bodily resurrection has no religious foundation, and the teaching of immortality is to be expressed exclusively in relation to continued spiritual existence.

Article 7. The cultivation of the Hebrew language, in which the divine treasures of revelation have been couched and in which the immortal monuments of our literature have been preserved (the commanding influence of which extends to all educated nations), must in our midst be considered as the fulfillment of a sacred obligation. However, the language has in fact become incomprehensible for the overwhelming majority of our present-day co-religionists, and therefore in the act of prayer (which is a body without a soul unless it is understood) Hebrew must take second place behind a language which the worshippers can understand insofar as this appears advisable under prevailing circumstances.

Source: Protokolle der Rabbiner Conferenz abgehalten zu Philadelphia (Nov. 3–6, 1869) (New York, 1870), 7ff., in *The Growth of Reform Judaism: American and European Sources until 1948*, ed. W. Gunther Plaut (New York: World Union for Progressive Judaism, 1965), 30–31.

The Pittsburgh Platform (1885)

It was the combination of a growing Ethical Culture movement that was attracting Reform Jews to a faith beyond particularism and an emerging conservative trend that insisted upon the validity of Jewish law that prompted Kaufmann Kohler (1843– 1926), then a rabbi in New York, to convene fourteen like-minded colleagues. Except for the last principle, insisted upon by his brother-in-law, Rabbi Emil G. Hirsch, the comprehensive platform is mainly the work of Kohler. It is the foremost expression of what became known as classical Reform Judaism, and it remained in place longer than any of its successors.

In view of the wide divergence of opinion, of conflicting ideas in Judaism to-day, we, as representatives of Reform Judaism in America, in continuation of the work begun at Philadelphia, in 1869, unite upon the following principles:

First. We recognize in every religion an attempt to grasp the Infinite, and in every mode, source or book of revelation, held sacred in any religious system, the consciousness of the indwelling of God in man. We hold that Judaism presents the highest conception of the God-idea as taught in our Holy Scriptures and developed and spiritualized by the Jewish teachers, in accordance with the moral and philosophical progress of their respective ages. We maintain that Judaism preserved and defended, midst continual struggles and trials and under enforced isolation, this God-idea as the central religious truth for the human race.

Second. We recognize in the Bible the record of the consecration of the Jewish people to its mission as priest of the one God, and value it as the most potent instrument of religious and moral instruction. We hold that the modern discoveries of scientific researches in the domains of nature and history are not antagonistic to the doctrines of Judaism, the Bible reflecting the primitive ideas of its own age, and at times clothing its conception of Divine Providence and justice dealing with man in miraculous narratives.

Third. We recognize in the Mosaic legislation a system of training the Jewish people for its mission during its national life in Palestine, and to-day we accept as binding only the moral laws, and maintain only such ceremonies as elevate and sanctify our lives, but reject all such as are not adapted to the views and habits of modern civilization.

Fourth. We hold that all such Mosaic and rabbinical laws as regulate diet, priestly purity and dress originated in ages and under the influence of ideas altogether foreign to our present mental and spiritual state. They fail to impress the modern Jew with a spirit of priestly holiness; their observance in our days is apt rather to obstruct than to further modern spiritual elevation.

Fifth. We recognize in the modern era of universal culture of heart and intellect the approaching of the realization of Israel's great Messianic hope for the establishment of the kingdom of truth, justice and peace among all men. We consider ourselves no longer a nation, but a religious community, and, therefore, expect neither a return to Palestine, nor a sacrificial worship under the sons of Aaron, nor the restoration of any of the laws concerning the Jewish state.

Sixth. We recognize in Judaism a progressive religion, ever striving to be in accord with the postulates of reason. We are convinced of the utmost necessity of preserving the historical identity with our great past. Christianity and Islam being daughter religions of Judaism, we appreciate their providential mission to aid in the spreading of monotheistic and moral truth. We acknowledge that the spirit of broad humanity of our age is our ally in the fulfillment of our mission, and, therefore, we extend the hand of fellowship to all who cooperate with us in the establishment of the reign of truth and righteousness among men.

Seventh. We reassert the doctrine of Judaism that the soul of man is immortal, grounding this belief on the divine nature of the human spirit, which forever finds bliss in righteousness and misery in wickedness. We reject, as ideas not rooted in Judaism, the beliefs both in bodily resurrection and in Gehenna and Eden (Hell and Paradise) as abodes for everlasting punishment and reward.

Eighth. In full accordance with the spirit of Mosaic legislation, which strives to regulate the relation between the rich and poor, we deem it our duty to participate in the great task of modern times, to solve, on the basis of justice and righteousness, the problems presented by the contrasts and evils of the present organization of society.

Source: M. A. Meyer, *Response to Modernity* (New York: Oxford University Press, 1988), 387–88.

Guiding Principles of Reform Judaism (1937)

By the mid-1930s the Reform movement was drifting away from the anti-Zionism and anti-ritualism that had characterized it at the beginning of the century. On the occasion of the fiftieth anniversary of the Pittsburgh Platform in 1935, CCAR president Felix Levy (1884–1963) initiated an effort to write a new platform. Adopted two years later in Columbus, Ohio, this document came to be known as the Columbus Platform. Largely the work of Samuel S. Cohon (1888–1959), HUC Professor of Theology, it reflected marked changes in the movement's self-understanding.

In view of the changes that have taken place in the modern world and the consequent need of stating anew the teachings of Reform Judaism, the Central Conference of American Rabbis makes the following declaration of principles. It presents them not as a fixed creed but as a guide for the progressive elements of Jewry.

A. *Judaism and its Foundations*

1. Nature of Judaism. Judaism is the historical religious experience of the Jewish people. Though growing out of Jewish life, its message is universal, aiming at the union and perfection of mankind under the sovereignty of God. Reform Judaism recognizes the principle of progressive development in religion and consciously applies this principle to spiritual as well as to cultural and social life.

Judaism welcomes all truth, whether written in the pages of scripture or deciphered from the records of nature. The new discoveries of science, while replacing the older scientific views underlying our sacred literature, do not conflict with the essential spirit of religion as manifested in the consecration of man's will, heart and mind to the service of God and of humanity.

2. God. The heart of Judaism and its chief contribution to religion is the doctrine of the One, living God, who rules the world through law and love. In Him all existence has its creative source and mankind its ideal of conduct. Though transcending time and space, He is the indwelling Presence of the world. We worship Him as the Lord of the universe and as our merciful Father.

3. Man. Judaism affirms that man is created in the Divine image. His spirit is immortal. He is an active co-worker with God. As a child of God, he is endowed with moral freedom and is charged with the responsibility of overcoming evil and striving after ideal ends.

4. Torah. God reveals Himself not only in the majesty, beauty and orderliness of nature, but also in the vision and moral striving of the human spirit. Revelation is a continuous process, confined to no one group and to no one age. Yet the people of Israel, through its prophets and sages, achieved unique insight in the realm of religious truth. The Torah, both written and oral, enshrines Israel's ever-growing consciousness of God and of the moral law. It preserves the historical precedents, sanctions and norms of Jewish life, and seeks to mould it in the patterns of goodness and of holiness. Being products of historical processes, certain of its laws have lost their binding force with the passing of the conditions that called them forth. But as a depository of permanent spiritual ideals, the Torah remains the dynamic source of the life of Israel. Each age has the obligation to adapt the teachings of the Torah to its basic needs in consonance with the genius of Judaism.

5. *Israel.* Judaism is the soul of which Israel is the body. Living in all parts of the world, Israel has been held together by the ties of a common history, and above all, by the heritage of faith. Though we recognize in the group loyalty of Jews who have become estranged from our religious tradition, a bond which still unites them with us, we maintain that it is by its religion and for its religion that the Jewish people has lived. The non-Jew who accepts our faith is welcomed as a full member of the Jewish community.

In all lands where our people live, they assume and seek to share loyally the full duties and responsibilities of citizenship and to create seats of Jewish knowledge and religion. In the rehabilitation of Palestine, the land hallowed by memories and hopes, we behold the promise of renewed life for many of our brethren. We affirm the obligation of all Jewry to aid in its upbuilding as a Jewish homeland by endeavoring to make it not only a haven of refuge for the oppressed but also a center of Jewish culture and spiritual life.

Throughout the ages it has been Israel's mission to witness to the Divine in the face of every form of paganism and materialism. We regard it as our historic task to cooperate with all men in the establishment of the kingdom of God, of universal brotherhood, justice, truth and peace on earth. This is our Messianic goal.

B. Ethics

6. *Ethics and Religion.* In Judaism religion and morality blend into an indissoluble unity. Seeking God means to strive after holiness, righteousness and goodness. The love of God is incomplete without the love of one's fellowmen. Judaism emphasizes the kinship of the human race, the sanctity and worth of human life and personality and the right of the individual to freedom and to the pursuit of his chosen vocation. Justice to all, irrespective of race, sect or class, is the inalienable right and the inescapable obligation of all. The state and organized government exist in order to further these ends.

7. *Social Justice.* Judaism seeks the attainment of a just society by the application of its teachings to the economic order, to industry and commerce, and to national and international affairs. It aims at the elimination of man-made misery and suffering, of poverty and degradation, of tyranny and slavery, of social inequality and prejudice, of ill-will and strife. It advo-

cates the promotion of harmonious relations between warring classes on the basis of equity and justice, and the creation of conditions under which human personality may flourish. It pleads for the safeguarding of childhood against exploitation. It champions the cause of all who work and of their right to an adequate standard of living, as prior to the rights of property. Judaism emphasizes the duty of charity, and strives for a social order which will protect men against the material disabilities of old age, sickness and unemployment.

8. *Peace.* Judaism, from the days of the prophets, has proclaimed to mankind the ideal of universal peace. The spiritual and physical disarmament of all nations has been one of its essential teachings. It abhors all violence and relies upon moral education, love and sympathy to secure human progress. It regards justice as the foundation of the well-being of nations and the condition of enduring peace. It urges organized international action for disarmament, collective security and world peace.

C. Religious Practice

9. *The Religious Life.* Jewish life is marked by consecration to these ideals of Judaism. It calls for faithful participation in the life of the Jewish community as it finds expression in home, synagog and school and in all other agencies that enrich Jewish life and promote its welfare.

The Home has been and must continue to be a stronghold of Jewish life, hallowed by the spirit of love and reverence, by moral discipline and religious observance and worship.

The Synagog is the oldest and most democratic institution in Jewish life. It is the prime communal agency by which Judaism is fostered and preserved. It links the Jews of each community and unites them with all Israel.

The perpetuation of Judaism as a living force depends upon religious knowledge and upon the Education of each new generation in our rich cultural and spiritual heritage.

Prayer is the voice of religion, the language of faith and aspiration. It directs man's heart and mind Godward, voices the needs and hopes of the community, and reaches out after goals which invest life with supreme value. To deepen the spiritual life of our people, we must cultivate the traditional habit of communion with God through prayer in both home and synagog.

Judaism as a way of life requires in addition to its moral and spiritual demands, the preservation of the Sabbath, festivals and Holy Days, the retention and development of such customs, symbols and ceremonies as possess inspirational value, the cultivation of distinctive forms of religious art and music and the use of Hebrew, together with the vernacular, in our worship and instruction.

These timeless aims and ideals of our faith we present anew to a confused and troubled world. We call upon our fellow Jews to rededicate themselves to them, and, in harmony with all men, hopefully and courageously to continue Israel's eternal quest after God and His kingdom.

Source: M. A. Meyer, *Response to Modernity* (New York: Oxford University Press, 1988), 388–91.

Reform Judaism—A Centenary Perspective (1976)

With the approach of the centenary of the UAHC in 1973 and HUC in 1975, and in the wake of the immense upheavals in Jewish life caused by the tragedy of the Holocaust and the promising birth of the State of Israel, it seemed time for a new platform that would reflect backward on the history of the movement itself and take cognizance of new Jewish realities. It was Professor Eugene Borowitz of HUC-JIR in New York who put together a lengthy text that stressed the importance of Jewish survival. It was easily adopted by the CCAR at its San Francisco convention.

The Central Conference of American Rabbis has on special occasions described the spiritual state of Reform Judaism. The centenaries of the founding of the Union of American Hebrew Congregations and the Hebrew Union College–Jewish Institute of Religion seem an appropriate time for another such effort. We therefore record our sense of the unity of our movement today.

One Hundred Years: What We Have Taught
We celebrate the role of Reform Judaism in North America, the growth of our movement on this free ground, the great contributions of our membership to the dreams and achievements of this society. We also feel great satisfaction at how much of our pioneering conception of Judaism has been accepted by the Household of Israel. It now seems self-evident to most Jews: that our tradition should interact with modern culture; that its forms ought to reflect a contemporary esthetic; that its scholarship needs to be conducted

by modern, critical methods; and that change has been and must continue to be a fundamental reality in Jewish life. Moreover, though some still disagree, substantial numbers have also accepted our teachings: that the ethics of universalism implicit in traditional Judaism must be an explicit part of our Jewish duty; that women should have full rights to practice Judaism; and that Jewish obligation begins with the informed will of every individual. Most modern Jews, within their various religious movements, are embracing Reform Jewish perspectives. We see this past century as having confirmed the essential wisdom of our movement.

One Hundred Years: What We Have Learned

Obviously, much else has changed in the past century. We continue to probe the extraordinary events of the past generation, seeking to understand their meaning and to incorporate their significance in our lives. The Holocaust shattered our easy optimism about humanity and its inevitable progress. The State of Israel, through its many accomplishments, raised our sense of the Jews as a people to new heights of aspiration and devotion. The widespread threats to freedom, the problems inherent in the explosion of new knowledge and of ever more powerful technologies, and the spiritual emptiness of much of Western culture, have taught us to be less dependent on the values of our society and to reassert what remains perennially valid in Judaism's teaching. We have learned again that the survival of the Jewish people is of highest priority and that in carrying out our Jewish responsibilities we help move humanity toward its messianic fulfillment.

Diversity within Unity, the Hallmark of Reform

Reform Jews respond to change in various ways according to the Reform principle of the autonomy of the individual. However, Reform Judaism does more than tolerate diversity; it engenders it. In our uncertain historical situation we must expect to have far greater diversity than previous generations knew. How we shall live with diversity without stifling dissent and without paralyzing our ability to take positive action will test our character and our principles. We stand open to any position thoughtfully and conscientiously advocated in the spirit of Reform Jewish beliefs. While we may differ in our interpretation and application of the ideas enunciated here, we accept such differences as precious and see in them Judaism's best hope for confronting whatever the future holds for us. Yet in all our diversity we perceive a certain unity and we shall not allow our differences in some particulars to obscure what binds us together.

I. God

The affirmation of God has always been essential to our people's will to survive. In our struggle through the centuries to preserve our faith we have experienced and conceived of God in many ways. The trials of our own time and the challenges of modern culture have made steady belief and clear understanding difficult for some. Nevertheless, we ground our lives, personally and communally, on God's reality and remain open to new experiences and conceptions of the Divine. Amid the mystery we call life, we affirm that human beings, created in God's image, share in God's eternality despite the mystery we call death.

II. The People Israel

The Jewish people and Judaism defy precise definition because both are in the process of becoming. Jews, by birth or conversion, constitute an uncommon union of faith and peoplehood. Born as Hebrews in the ancient Near East, we are bound together like all ethnic groups by language, land, history, culture and institutions. But the people of Israel is unique because of its involvement with God and its resulting perception of the human condition. Throughout our long history our people has been inseparable from its religion with its messianic hope that humanity will be redeemed.

III. Torah

Torah results from the relationship between God and the Jewish people. The records of our earliest confrontations are uniquely important to us. Lawgivers and prophets, historians and poets gave us a heritage whose study is a religious imperative and whose practice is our chief means to holiness. Rabbis and teachers, philosophers and mystics, gifted Jews in every age amplified the Torah tradition. For millennia, the creation of Torah has not ceased and Jewish creativity in our time is adding to the chain of tradition.

IV. Our Obligations: Religious Practice

Judaism emphasizes action rather than creed as the primary expression of a religious life, the means by which we strive to achieve universal justice and peace. Reform Judaism shares this emphasis on duty and obligation.

Our founders stressed that the Jew's ethical responsibilities, personal and social, are enjoined by God. The past century has taught us that the claims made upon us may begin with our ethical obligations but they extend to many other aspects of Jewish living, including: creating a Jewish home centered on family devotion; life-long study; private prayer and public worship; daily religious observance; keeping the Sabbath and the holy days; celebrating the major events of life; involvement with the synagogue and community; and other activities which promote the survival of the Jewish people and enhance its existence. Within each area of Jewish observance Reform Jews are called upon to confront the claims of Jewish tradition, however differently perceived, and to exercise their individual autonomy, choosing and creating on the basis of commitment and knowledge.

V. Our Obligations: The State of Israel and the Diaspora

We are privileged to live in an extraordinary time, one in which a third Jewish commonwealth has been established in our people's ancient home-land. We are bound to that land and to the newly reborn State of Israel by innumerable religious and ethnic ties. We have been enriched by its culture and ennobled by its indomitable spirit. We see it providing unique opportunities for Jewish self-expression. We have both a stake and a responsibility in building the State of Israel, assuring its security and defining its Jewish character. We encourage *aliyah* for those who wish to find maximum personal fulfillment in the cause of Zion. We demand that Reform Judaism be unconditionally legitimized in the State of Israel.

At the same time we consider the State of Israel vital to the welfare of Judaism everywhere, we reaffirm the mandate of our tradition to create strong Jewish communities wherever we live. A genuine Jewish life is possible in any land, each community developing its own particular character and determining its Jewish responsibilities. The foundation of Jewish community life is the synagogue. It leads us beyond itself to cooperate with other Jews, to share their concerns, and to assume leadership in communal affairs. We are therefore committed to the full democratization of the Jewish community and to its hallowing in terms of Jewish values.

The State of Israel and the diaspora, in fruitful dialogue, can show how a people transcends nationalism even as it affirms it, thereby setting an example for humanity which remains largely concerned with dangerously parochial goals.

VI. Our Obligations: Survival and Service

Early Reform Jews, newly admitted to general society and seeing in this the evidence of a growing universalism, regularly spoke of Jewish purpose in terms of Jewry's service to humanity. In recent years we have become freshly conscious of the virtues of pluralism and the values of particularism. The Jewish people in its unique way of life validates its own worth while working toward the fulfillment of its messianic expectations.

Until the recent past our obligations to the Jewish people and to all humanity seemed congruent. At times now these two imperatives appear to conflict. We know of no simple way to resolve such tensions. We must, however, confront them without abandoning either of our commitments. A universal concern for humanity unaccompanied by a devotion to our particular people is self-destructive; a passion for our people without involvement in humankind contradicts what the prophets have meant to us. Judaism calls us simultaneously to universal and particular obligations.

VII. Hope: Our Jewish Obligation

Previous generations of Reform Jews had unbounded confidence in humanity's potential for good. We have lived through terrible tragedy and been compelled to reappropriate our tradition's realism about the human capacity for evil. Yet our people has always refused to despair. The survivors of the Holocaust, on being granted life, seized it, nurtured it, and, rising above catastrophe, showed humankind that the human spirit is indomitable. The State of Israel, established and maintained by the Jewish will to live, demonstrates what a united people can accomplish in history. The existence of the Jew is an argument against despair; Jewish survival is warrant for human hope.

We remain God's witness that history is not meaningless. We affirm that with God's help people are not powerless to affect their destiny. We dedicate ourselves, as did the generations of Jews who went before us, to work and wait for that day when "They shall not hurt or destroy in all My holy mountain for the earth shall be full of the knowledge of the Lord as the waters cover the sea."

Source: M. A. Meyer, *Response to Modernity* (New York: Oxford University Press, 1988), 391–94.

A Statement of Principles for Reform Judaism (1999)

As the century drew to a close, the Reform Movement was undergoing changes not fully apparent in 1976. Its social composition was becoming more diverse, and it was focusing more on religious than on ethnic issues. Following a long discussion initiated by CCAR president Rabbi Richard Levy (1937–), during which some rabbis and laypeople expressed their objection to the traditional tenor of the document, the CCAR adopted a new platform, once again in Pittsburgh, Pennsylvania.

Preamble

On three occasions during the last century and a half, the Reform rabbinate has adopted comprehensive statements to help guide the thought and practice of our movement. In 1885, fifteen rabbis issued the Pittsburgh Platform, a set of guidelines that defined Reform Judaism for the next fifty years. A revised statement of principles, the Columbus Platform, was adopted by the Central Conference of American Rabbis in 1937. A third set of rabbinic guidelines, the Centenary Perspective, appeared in 1976 on the occasion of the centenary of the Union of American Hebrew Congregations and the Hebrew Union College–Jewish Institute of Religion. Today, when so many individuals are striving for religious meaning, moral purpose and a sense of community, we believe it is our obligation as rabbis once again to state a set of principles that define Reform Judaism in our own time.

Throughout our history, we Jews have remained firmly rooted in Jewish tradition, even as we have learned much from our encounters with other cultures. The great contribution of Reform Judaism is that it has enabled the Jewish people to introduce innovation while preserving tradition, to embrace diversity while asserting commonality, to affirm beliefs without rejecting those who doubt, and to bring faith to sacred texts without sacrificing critical scholarship.

This "Statement of Principles" affirms the central tenets of Judaism—God, Torah and Israel—even as it acknowledges the diversity of Reform Jewish beliefs and practices. It also invites all Reform Jews to engage in a dialogue with the sources of our tradition, responding out of our knowledge, our experience and our faith. Thus we hope to transform our lives through קְדֻשָׁה (kedushah), holiness.

God

We affirm the reality and oneness of God, even as we may differ in our understanding of the Divine presence.

We affirm that the Jewish people is bound to God by an eternal בְּרִית *(b'rit)*, covenant, as reflected in our varied understandings of Creation, Revelation and Redemption.

We affirm that every human being is created בְּצֶלֶם אֱלֹהִים *(b'tzelem Elohim)*, in the image of God, and that therefore every human life is sacred.

We regard with reverence all of God's creation and recognize our human responsibility for its preservation and protection.

We encounter God's presence in moments of awe and wonder, in acts of justice and compassion, in loving relationships and in the experiences of everyday life.

We respond to God daily: through public and private prayer, through study and through the performance of other מִצְוֹת *(mitzvot)*, sacred obligations—בֵּין אָדָם לַמָּקוֹם *(bein adam la Makom)*, to God, and בֵּין אָדָם לַחֲבֵרוֹ *(bein adam lachaveiro)*, to other human beings.

We strive for a faith that fortifies us through the vicissitudes of our lives—illness and healing, transgression and repentance, bereavement and consolation, despair and hope.

We continue to have faith that, in spite of the unspeakable evils committed against our people and the sufferings endured by others, the partnership of God and humanity will ultimately prevail.

We trust in our tradition's promise that, although God created us as finite beings, the spirit within us is eternal.

In all these ways and more, God gives meaning and purpose to our lives.

Torah

We affirm that Torah is the foundation of Jewish life.

We cherish the truths revealed in Torah, God's ongoing revelation to our people and the record of our people's ongoing relationship with God.

We affirm that Torah is a manifestation of אַהֲבַת עוֹלָם *(ahavat olam)*, God's eternal love for the Jewish people and for all humanity.

We affirm the importance of studying Hebrew, the language of Torah and Jewish liturgy, that we may draw closer to our people's sacred texts.

We are called by Torah to lifelong study in the home, in the synagogue and in every place where Jews gather to learn and teach. Through Torah study we are called to מִצְוֹת *(mitzvot)*, the means by which we make our lives holy.

We are committed to the ongoing study of the whole array of מִצְוֹת *(mitzvot)* and to the fulfillment of those that address us as individuals and as a community. Some of these מִצְוֹת *(mitzvot)*, sacred obligations, have long been observed by Reform Jews; others, both ancient and modern, demand renewed attention as the result of the unique context of our own times.

We bring Torah into the world when we seek to sanctify the times and places of our lives through regular home and congregational observance. Shabbat calls us to bring the highest moral values to our daily labor and to culminate the workweek with קְדֻשָּׁה *(kedushah)*, holiness, מְנוּחָה *(menuchah)*, rest, and עֹנֶג *(oneg)*, joy. The High Holy Days call us to account for our deeds. The Festivals enable us to celebrate with joy our people's religious journey in the context of the changing seasons. The days of remembrance remind us of the tragedies and the triumphs that have shaped our people's historical experience both in ancient and modern times. And we mark the milestones of our personal journeys with traditional and creative rites that reveal the holiness in each stage of life.

We bring Torah into the world when we strive to fulfill the highest ethical mandates in our relationships with others and with all of God's creation. Partners with God in תִּקּוּן עוֹלָם *(tikkun olam)*, repairing the world, we are called to help bring nearer the messianic age. We seek dialogue and joint action with people of other faiths in the hope that together we can bring peace, freedom and justice to our world. We are obligated to pursue צֶדֶק *(tzedek)*, justice and righteousness, and to narrow the gap between the affluent and the poor, to act against discrimination and oppression, to pursue peace, to welcome the stranger, to protect the earth's biodiversity and natural resources, and to redeem those in physical, economic and spiritual bondage. In so doing, we reaffirm social action and social justice as a central prophetic focus of traditional Reform Jewish belief and practice. We affirm the מִצְוָה *(mitzvah)* of צְדָקָה *(tzedakah),* setting aside portions of our earnings and our time to provide for those in need. These acts bring us closer to fulfilling the prophetic call to translate the words of Torah into the works of our hands.

In all these ways and more, Torah gives meaning and purpose to our lives.

Israel

We are Israel, a people aspiring to holiness, singled out through our ancient covenant and our unique history among the nations to be witnesses to God's presence. We are linked by that covenant and that history to all Jews in every age and place.

We are committed to the מִצְוָה *(mitzvah)* of אַהֲבַת יִשְׂרָאֵל *(ahavat Yisrael),* love for the Jewish people, and to כְּלָל יִשְׂרָאֵל *(k'lal Yisrael),* the entirety of the community of Israel. Recognizing that כֹּל יִשְׂרָאֵל עֲרֵבִים זֶה בָּזֶה *(kol Yisrael arevim zeh ba-zeh),* all Jews are responsible for one another, we reach out to all Jews across ideological and geographical boundaries.

We embrace religious and cultural pluralism as an expression of the vitality of Jewish communal life in Israel and the Diaspora.

We pledge to fulfill Reform Judaism's historic commitment to the complete equality of women and men in Jewish life.

We are an inclusive community, opening doors to Jewish life to people of all ages, to varied kinds of families, to all regardless of their sexual orientation, to גֵּרִים *(gerim),* those who have converted to Judaism, and to all individuals and families, including the intermarried, who strive to create a Jewish home.

We believe that we must not only open doors for those ready to enter our faith, but also to actively encourage those who are seeking a spiritual home to find it in Judaism.

We are committed to strengthening the people Israel by supporting individuals and families in the creation of homes rich in Jewish learning and observance.

We are committed to strengthening the people Israel by making the synagogue central to Jewish communal life, so that it may elevate the spiritual, intellectual and cultural quality of our lives.

We are committed to מְדִינַת יִשְׂרָאֵל *(Medinat Yisrael)*, the State of Israel, and rejoice in its accomplishments. We affirm the unique qualities of living in אֶרֶץ יִשְׂרָאֵל *(Eretz Yisrael)*, the land of Israel, and encourage עֲלִיָּה *(aliyah)*, immigration to Israel.

We are committed to a vision of the State of Israel that promotes full civil, human and religious rights for all its inhabitants and that strives for a lasting peace between Israel and its neighbors.

We are committed to promoting and strengthening Progressive Judaism in Israel, which will enrich the spiritual life of the Jewish state and its people.

We affirm that both Israeli and Diaspora Jewry should remain vibrant and interdependent communities. As we urge Jews who reside outside Israel to learn Hebrew as a living language and to make periodic visits to Israel in order to study and to deepen their relationship to the Land and its people, so do we affirm that Israeli Jews have much to learn from the religious life of Diaspora Jewish communities.

We are committed to furthering Progressive Judaism throughout the world as a meaningful religious way of life for the Jewish people

**In all these ways and more, Israel gives meaning
and purpose to our lives.**

בָּרוּךְ שֶׁאָמַר וְהָיָה הָעוֹלָם

(Baruch she-amar ve-hayah ha-olam).
Praised be the One through whose word all things came to be.
May our words find expression in holy actions.
May they raise us up to a life of meaning devoted to God's service
And to the redemption of our world.

Source: "A Statement of Principles for Reform Judaism, Adopted by the Central Conference of American Rabbis at the 1999 Pittsburgh Convention May 1999—Sivan 5759" (New York: CCAR, 1999), 2-6.

Epilogue

At the end of the twentieth century, the Reform movement in North America looked very different from what it was a hundred years ago. With starry-eyed optimism and unlimited self-confidence, earlier Reformers saw themselves as forerunners of the messianic age. In the United States they dominated the Jewish landscape with their spiritual certainty, buttressed by a significant measure of economic well-being. Jews had a mission to propagate Judaism in the world, and Reform was leading the way. Conservatism was just emerging, and Orthodox Jews, though their numbers were growing rapidly, had yet to make their way in the New World.

Contrary to all expectations, the new century proved to be the bloodiest in history, with six million Jews becoming the victims of old and new forms of hatred. Yet the century also saw the emergence of the State of Israel. Together, the Holocaust and the birth of the Jewish state became the defining experiences for many, if not most, Diaspora Jews during the last fifty years.

Not surprisingly, Reform Judaism, as a movement that responds to changing times, has been deeply affected by the turmoil of the twentieth century. The certainties of yesteryear have disappeared, leaving a large part of humanity with deep religious doubts or all too often seeking refuge in fundamentalist doctrines and promises. Liberalism thus faces a new challenge, for it eschews certainty as a response to most problems and instead encourages questions, making the search rather than the answer the core of the religious enterprise. This openness is its strength, but at the same time also its weakness. By not providing a system of simple answers and structured, obligatory practices, it appears to accept non-observance as a legitimate option.

Nonetheless, Reform has managed to strengthen its roots and has met the great variety of religious challenges with significant success. A hundred years ago women provided the mere background of Reform; today they are its backbone. The ordination of Sally J. Priesand in 1972 was a milestone in the development of Reform, and in the decades since, women have provided the rabbinate, the cantorate, the institutions of the movement, and its congregations and their governance with a new reservoir of lay and professional leaders, bringing with them a new sense of religious intensity and sensitivity.

Reform's Outreach program has opened new doors and has turned the fears of ethnic dilution into avenues of increased involvement. Many newcomers are found in study groups and have joined thousands of older members in searching out the sources of Judaism and opening themselves up to a richer spiritual experience. In the wake of such changes, Reform is growing in adherents, and in the United States more Jews identify themselves with it than with any other Jewish movement.

At the same time, the individualism that permeates all of North American society has left its mark on the Reform constituency. Many of its members consider personal autonomy the cornerstone of their religion and therefore do not respond readily to the demand of mitzvot, while many others believe mitzvot to be the very hinge of Jewish survival. But despite these differences, it seems clear that in the absence of a volatile antisemitism, neither Jewish ethnicity nor the remembrance of the Holocaust, nor even the presence of Israel, can assure the continuity of Judaism. Religion is its ultimate guarantee, and a strong and vibrant Reform movement that is aware of its religious roots, obligations, and potential can provide ever new opportunities for leading a rich and meaningful Jewish life.

Suggestions for Further Reading

General Literature

The most recent compehensive history of the Reform movement throughout the world is Michael A. Meyer, *Response to Modernity: A History of the Reform Movement in Judaism* (Oxford, 1988; reprint, Wayne State University Press, 1995). A much more extensive collection of sources for American Reform Judaism up to 1948 than is contained in the present volume is W. Gunther Plaut, *The Growth of Reform Judaism* (WUPJ, 1965). The current volume is, in a sense, an extension of that work. Joseph L. Blau, ed., *Reform Judaism: A Historical Perspective* (KTAV, 1973) consists of selected speeches from CCAR conventions. Eugene B. Borowitz and Naomi Patz, *Explaining Reform Judaism* (Behrman House, 1985) is a popular presentation of the subject. Still of interest is David Philipson, *The Reform Movement in Judaism*, originally published in 1907 (rev. ed., KTAV, 1967). A helpful reference source is Kerry M. Olitzky, Lance J. Sussman, and Malcolm H. Stern, eds., *Reform Judaism in America: A Biographical Dictionary and Sourcebook* (Greenwood Press, 1993). On women in Reform Judaism, see Karla Goldman, *Beyond the Synagogue Gallery: Finding a Place for Women in American Judaism* (Harvard, 2000); and Gary P. Zola, ed., *Women Rabbis: Exploration & Celebration* (HUC-JIR Rabbinic Alumni Association, 1996).

Chapter 1. The Heritage of German Progressive Judaism

W. Gunther Plaut, ed., *The Rise of Reform Judaism* (WUPJ, 1963) contains the most important sources in English translation. Jakob J. Petuchowski, in his *Prayerbook Reform in Europe* (WUPJ, 1968), explains and illustrates the liturgical changes introduced by European Liberal and Reform liturgists.

Chapter 2. The Major Institutions of Reform Judaism

Sefton D. Temkin, "A Century of Reform Judaism in America," *American Jewish Year Book* 74 (1973): 3–75, focuses mainly on the history of the UAHC. On HUC-JIR, see Michael A. Meyer, *Hebrew Union College–Jewish Institute of Religion: A Centennial History 1875–1975* (reprint, Hebrew Union College Press, 1976). As yet there are no published histories of the CCAR or the WUPJ.

Chapter 3. Theology

Kaufmann Kohler's classic, *Jewish Theology* (Macmillan, 1918, republished 1968) sets out the way Jews have comprehended God's impact on our people. Since then, Emil L. Fackenheim wrote *To Mend the World: Essays in Jewish Theology* (Beacon Press, 1968), and Eugene B. Borowitz dealt with the subject in a number of books, most importantly *Renewing the Covenant* (Jewish Publication Society, 1991). See also Dow Marmur, *The Star of Return* (Greenwood, 1991). Rachel Adler's *Engendering Judaism* (JPS, 1996) presents a theology based on feminist apperception.

Chapter 4. The Realm of Public Prayer

The two volumes of *Gates of Understanding* (*Shaarei Binah*, CCAR, 1977 and 1984) are treasure troves of information on Jewish prayer in general as well as on *Gates of Prayer* and *Gates of Repentance*. Edited by Lawrence A. Hoffman, with Chaim Stern and A. Stanley Dreyfus, they contain essays on liturgy and give the sources for our prayers. *On the Doorposts of Your House* (*Al Mezuzot Beitecha*, CCAR, 1994) is an elaborate compendium on private worship, edited by Chaim Stern, with Donna Berman, Edward Graham, and H. Leonard Poller. Readers who wish to study the history of Jewish prayer in all its forms will find it in Jacob Milgram's *Jewish Worship* (JPS, 1971).

Chapter 5. Shabbat and Holy Days

Gates of Shabbat, ed. Mark Dov Shapiro (CCAR, 1991), and *Gates of the Seasons*, ed. Peter S. Knobel (CCAR, 1983), are the main guides to Reform observance of our festive days. *A Shabbat Reader: Universe of Cosmic Joy*, ed. Dov Peretz Elkins (UAHC Press, 1998), is a rich collection of brief essays on all aspects and opportunities of celebrating Shabbat.

Chapter 6. Life-Cycle Events

The Reform movement's guide to the life cycle is *Gates of Mitzvah*, ed. Simeon J. Maslin (CCAR, 1979). Lawrence Hoffman's *Covenant of Blood* (University of Chicago Press, 1996) traces the importance of circumcision in Jewish tradition to the fact that the ritual is a blood offering and therefore an offering of life itself. Similarly, Elyse Goldstein's *ReVisions: Seeing Torah through a Feminist Lens* (Jewish Lights, 1998) compares male circumcision to female menstruation and to the blood of the birthing process itself. An imaginative description of life-cycle events across the whole spectrum of Jewish practice can be found in *The Jewish Catalogue*, ed. Richard Siegel and others (JPS, 1973).

Chapter 7. Halachah of Reform

The Responsa Literature (JPS, 1955) is a valuable introduction to the subject of halachah, written by Solomon B. Freehof, who reintroduced halachah to twentieth-century Reform. *American Reform Responsa*, ed. Walter Jacob (CCAR, 1983), is a valuable collection of the most important responsa from 1889 to 1983. See *Teshuvot for the Nineties*, ed. W. Gunther Plaut and Mark Washofsky (CCAR, 1997), for more recent issues.

Chapter 8. Zionism and Israel

Two volumes address this subject: David Polish, *Renew Our Days: The Zionist Issue in Reform Judaism* (World Zionist Organization, 1976); and Howard R. Greenstein, *Turning Point: Zionism and Reform Judaism* (Scholars Press, 1981). See also Roland B. Gittelsohn, *ARZA—From Birth to Bar/Bat Mitzvah* (UAHC Pamphlet, 1990).

Chapter 9. Social Justice

For the resolutions of the UAHC in the area of social justice, see *Where We Stand: Social Action Resolutions Adopted by the UAHC* (Commission on Social Action of Reform Judaism, 1980). See also the major books produced by the commission, especially the first: Albert Vorspan and Eugene J. Lipman, *Justice and Judaism* (UAHC Press, 1956); also Albert Vorspan and David Saperstein, *Jewish Dimensions of Social Justice: Tough Moral Choices in Our Time* (UAHC Press, 1999).

Chapter 10. Outreach

A classic source is Lydia Kukoff's *Choosing Judaism* (UAHC Press, 1981). The author, a convert to Judaism, brings her own valuable perspective to the subject. See also *Why Choose Judaism: New Dimensions of Jewish Outreach* (UAHC Press, 1985) by David Belin, who for many years was chair of the UAHC Outreach program; also *Defining the Role of the Non-Jew in the Synagogue* (UAHC Press, 1990).

Chapter 11. Education

Regrettably, there is no comprehensive history of Reform Jewish education. Samuel Grand and Mamie Gamoran, eds., *Emanuel Gamoran: His Life and Work* (Gamoran Memorial Fund, 1979) provides the best access to this central figure. For an enlightening survey of the present state of Reform education, see Samuel K. Joseph, *Portraits of Schooling: A Survey and Analysis of Supplementary Schooling in Congregations* (UAHC Press, 1997); and the broader analysis by Jack Wertheimer, "Jewish Education in the United States: Recent Trends and Issues," *American Jewish Year Book* 99 (1999): 3–115.

Chapter 12. The Platforms of American Reform Judaism

For the history of the 1869 Philadelphia Principles, see Sefton D. Temkin, ed., *The New World of Reform* (Hartmore House, 1974); for the Pittsburgh Platform, Walter Jacob, ed., *The Changing World of Reform Judaism: The Pittsburgh Platform in Retrospect* (Rodef Shalom Congregation, Pittsburgh, 1985); and for the Centenary Perspective, Eugene B. Borowitz, *Reform Judaism Today*, 3 vols. (Behrman House, 1977). A commentary on the 1999 Principles is in the planning stage.

INDEX

Abortion, 123, 124, 125, 146, 159
Abraham, 40, 100, 131, 141, 178
Adler, Morris, 41
Adler, Rachel, 45, 45
Adoption, 103
Adult education, 183, 184, 192, 193
Adultery, 103
Affirmative action, 159
Afterlife, 19, 37, 195, 197, 199
Ahavat Yisrael. See Jewish nationhood/peoplehood
Ahavat Tzion. See Zionism
Aliyah to Israel
  in Centenary Perspective, 206
  Reform support for, 133, 139, 142–143, 195
  in Statement of Principles, 212
Aliyah to Torah, 105
Alter, Robert, 189
Alternatives in Religious Education, 188
American Conference of Cantors, 73
Americanism, 65–66
American Jewish Archives, 177
American Nazi movement, 159
American Reform Judaism
  American as new Zion, 134
  Americanism and Judaism synthesized, 65–55
  Centenary Perspective, 203–204
  Christian influences on, 66, 81, 145
  coming of age, 190
  commitment to freedom and justice, 84
  current challenges, 191, 213
  defining function of platforms, 195, 208. *See also names of platforms*
  democratically organized, 75
  diversity as value, 25, 27, 120, 141, 195, 204, 208

dynamic spirit, 195, 208, 213
  early years, viii, 1, 213
  East European influences, ix–x, 66, 132
  emergence as denomination, vii
  growth of, xi, 120, 214
  feminist influences, 55, 67. *See also* Feminist theology and German Reform Judaism, viii, 1
  gender blindness of, 101
  "greening" of, 182
  innovativeness, 208
  liturgy, 67. *See also* Liturgical innovations
  number of adherents, 120, 214
  openness to change, 213
  organizations and institutions, 21. *See also names of organizations and institutions*
  personal autonomy, 22, 214
  personal spirituality. *See* Home observances; Prayer
  pluralism, 121, 211
  self-confidence of, 213
  and State of Israel, 132, 141
  trend of increasing observance, 78
  unity amid diversity, 25, 27, 120, 141, 195, 204, 208
  worship services. *See* Friday night service; Public worship; Sabbath
  and Zionism, 132, 143, 144
American Zionist Federation, 140
Amidah, 69, 76
Am Yisrael and *Medinat Yisrael,* 142
Anthropomorphism, 14, 46, 47
Anti-communism, 149
Antiochus Epiphanes, 152
Antisemitism, 146, 160, 214
Apostasy, 115, 174

ARZA. *See* Association of Religious Zionists of America
ARZA/World Union, 139
Assimilation, 42
Association for a Progressive Reform Judaism, 164
Association of Reform Zionists of America, 132, 139–141
Autonomy, personal, 22, 117, 126, 214
Autopsy, 111, 112
Avinu Malkeinu, 90
Avodah, 73

Baeck, Leo, 15–18, 40
Bamberger, Bernard J., 165, 173, 189
Bar/bat mitzvah, 99
  age of, 105–106
  and Jewish identity, 172
  preparatory education, 30, 182
  mixed-marriage child, 166, 172, 179, 180
  origin, 118
  rabbinic role, 30
  Torah reading, 106
  views pro and con, 104–105
Beit din, 177
Belin, David, 175
Berit Milah Board, 100, 101
Bible. *See* Torah
Bigotry, 148, 155, 210. *See also* Gays/lesbians; Race relations
Bikkur Holim, 70
Biodiversity, 210
Bioethics, 146
Birkat HaMazon. See Grace after meals
Birth, 99
Birth rate, Jewish, 168
Black Power, 53. *See also* Race relations
Borowitz, Eugene, 41, 42, 203
Bosnia, 160
Breaking of glass, 108

Breslau Conference, 113
B'rit hachayyim. See Covenant
  ceremony for girls
B'rit milah. See Circumcision
Brothers Karamazov
  (Dostoevski), 41
Buber, Martin, 15, 68, 187
Burial. *See* Death and burial
Busing, 159

Camping. *See* Summer camps
Canadian Zionist Federation,
  140
Candlelighting, 86, 118, 166
Cantorial music. *See* Synagogue
  music
Cantors, 55, 65, 72, 73, 75, 164
Capital punishment, 154
Catechisms, 182, 191
CCAR. *See* Central Conference
  of American Rabbis
Censorship, 159
Centenary Perspective, 203, 208
Central Conference of American Rabbis
  on abortion, 124
  Centenary Perspective, 203,
    208
  committees
    Synagog and Industrial Re-
      lations, 146
    Liturgy, 58, 62
    Reform Practices, 58, 179
    Responsa, 56, 119, 121,
      124, 167, 179-181
    Sabbath, 84
  conventions, 29, 82, 84, 171
  and halachah, 121, 122
  liturgical publications, 62,
    64, 72, 84, 88, 90, 91
  number of members, xi
  and conversion, 176
  on patrilineal descent, 170,
    172
  on proselytizing, 173
  on personal/professional
    needs of rabbis, 30–31
  Pittsburgh convention
    (1980), 171
  on mixed marriages, 127,
    161–162
  role and goal, 29, 30
  Shabbat Manual, 126
  on Sabbath observance, 82,
    126
  on social activism, 145, 146,
    154
  Statement of Principles for
    Reform Judaism, 208
  on Zionism, 133, 138, 139
  and Wise, ix, 22, 29, 37, 72
  on women's religious equal-
    ity, 102
  presidents
    Bamberger, 173
    F. Levy, 199

Stern, 29
Maslin, 162
Olan, 40
R. Levy, 208
Wise, 29, 72
Chanukah, 89, 131, 152, 153
Chazars, 173
Child labor, 146, 202
Child welfare, 149
Choirs, 72. *See also* Synagogue
  music
Christianity
  and modern science, 36
  influence on Reform Juda-
    ism, 14, 66, 145
  in Pittsburgh Platform, 199
Christmas, 153
Chupah, 108
Church-state relations, 153
Circumcisers, 100, 101-102
Circumcision
  and Abraham, 131
  of adopted child, 103
  of convert, 176, 177, 178
  and covenant, 93, 99, 131
  Egyptian mockery of, 93
  of mixed-marriage child,
    102, 166
  of non-traditional-family
    child, 101-102
  spiritual significance, 100
  See also Circumcisers
Civil divorce, 110
Civil liberties, 145, 148, 149,
  155
Civil marriage, 164
Civil rights movement, 34, 53,
  145, 159. *See also* Race relations
Civil War, 145
Classical Reform Judaism
  America as new Zion, 134
  American and Jewish values
    equated, ix
  attitude toward ritual, 176
  congregational participation,
    72
  covenant, 189
  early history, ix. *See also* Wise,
    Isaac Mayer
  emergence as denomination,
    vii
  ethical emphasis, 190
  fasting on Yom Kippur, 90
  gender blindness of, 101
  German influence on, viii
  halachah, ix, 118, 120
  head covering, 59-61
  Hebrew, 182
  Jewish peoplehood, 189
  Jewish education, 182
  Kol Nidrei, 90
  liberation from legalism, 135
  marriage ritual, 108
  Mission of Israel, ix, 132
  philosophic emphasis, 53

Pittsburgh Platform, 197
  and Prophetism, 135. *See also*
    Prophetic Judaism
  religion-not-nation self-defi-
    nition, 132, 134
  ritual practices, x, 59, 108
  sacrificial system, 54, 198
  sexual equality, 182
  Sunday Sabbath, 80, 82
  universalism vs. particular-
    ism, ix
  worship service, 72, 74
  Zionism, ix, 95, 133, 134
  See also American Reform Ju-
    daism; German Reform
    Judaism
Classic vs. decadent, balance be-
  tween, 137
Coalition for Alternatives in
  Jewish Education, 188
Cohen, Debra, 101
Cohen, Hermann, 15, 38, 52
Cohen, William, 167
Cohon, Samuel S., 62, 199
Cold War, 160
Collective bargaining, 147
Collective security, 202
Columbus Platform, x, 62, 95,
  138, 189, 199-200, 208
Commandments. *See* Halachah;
  Mitzvot
Communism, fall of, 160
Confessional prayers, 54, 90
Confirmation, 99, 104-105,
  172, 179
Congregational singing. *See*
  Synagogue music
Congregation B'nai Israel (Cin-
  cinnati), 26
Congregation B'nai Yeshurun
  (Cincinnati), 26
Conservative Judaism, 101,
  195, 213
  covenant theology, 41, 189
  Frankel, 5
  Friday evening services, 83
  in Israel, 160
  mixed marriages, 161
  organ/tissue transplants, 112
  origin of, ix
  patrilineal descent, 170
  swimming pool as *mikveh,* 178
Constitution, U.S., 124
Conversion to Judaism
  of adopted child, 103
  Centenary Perspective, 205
  of child, 178
  Columbus Platform, 201
  of gentile spouse, 162, 165
  halachic practices, 177
  Hebrew name of convert,
    177–178
  intermarriage, 175
  Kaddish for parent of con-
    vert, 115
  of mixed-marriage child, 171

of pregnant woman, 178
procedure, 176–179, 195
Reform view of, 168, 170
Statement of Principles, 211
See also Outreach
Conversion to other religions.
See Apostasy
Cook, Samuel, 187
Corruption in government, 153
Covenant
centrality of, 42
defines divine/human relations, 42, 43, 128, 209
entrance into, 99, 102. *See also* Circumcision
and halachah, 189
included both sexes, 68, 99
and Jewish identity, 42
and Jewish peoplehood, 42, 141, 189
and moral freedom, 41
and outreach, 169
Plaut on, 189
reaffirmed in Jewish marriage, 163
recalled on Shabbat, 85
Covenant ceremony for girls, 99, 100, 102
Covenant theology, x, 41
Creation, 1, 14, 48
Cremation, 111
Culinary Judaism, 53
Customs and folkways, vii, 49, 118, 119, 183. *See also names of customs and folkways*

Darwinism, 36
Davening, 65. *See also* Prayer; Public worship
Day schools, 182, 184, 185, 186
Death and burial, 99, 111-112. *See also* Mourning practices
Death-of-God theology, 36
Decadence, literary, 137
Decision-making, moral, 159
Decorum. *See* Public worship
Democracy
in Israel, 34
in Jewish tradition, 148, 149
Deutsch, Gotthard, 26
Diaspora
Centenary Perspective, 206
Classical view, 132
Jewish life in, 142-143, 211
mixed marriages in, 171
Philadelphia Principles, 196
and State of Israel, 143
Statement of Principles, 212
theological implications, ix, 127, 132
See also Mission of Israel
Dietary laws, 51, 52, 198
Dignity of individual, 148
Dimensions in American Judaism, 150
Disarmament, 202

Discrimination. *See* Bigotry
Dispersion. *See* Diaspora
Divine Revelation. *See* Revelation
Divorce, 99, 109, 110, 111
Divorce certificate, 99
Doe v. Boston, 123
Doppelt, Frederic A., 84, 126
Dostoevski, Fyodor, 41
Doubt, religious, 213
Dual loyalty, 133
Dylan, Bob, 187

Early-childhood education, 183
East European immigrants, x, 66, 132
Ecology, 153, 210
Economic injustice, 159
Eight hour day, 146
Einhorn, David, viii, ix, 145, 196
Eisendrath, Maurice N., 145, 150, 152
Elbogen, Ismar, 18-19
Ellis, Havelock, 137
El Salvador, 156
Elul, 97
Emancipation, viii, 78
Emotion, religious, 6, 20. *See also* Religious experience
Endogamy, 161
Engendering Judaism (Adler), 45
Enlightenment, vii, 2
Equality of priests and non-priests, 196
Equality of sexes, 100, 104, 115, 166, 211
Equitable distribution of profits, 146
The Essence of Judaism (Baeck), 15
Ethical Culture, 195, 197
Ethical monotheism, ix, 40, 132, 149, 190
Ethiopian Jewry, 34
Ethnicity, Jewish, 42, 74, 205, 214. *See also* Jewish nationhood/peoplehood
Etrog, 89
Exodus from Egypt, 84, 91, 92, 93
Experiment in Congregational Education, 193
Ezra, 161

Fackenheim, Emil L., 41, 47
Fairfield University, 67
Faith. *See* Religious experience
Falk, Marcia, 46
Falk, Samson, 81
Family education, 192, 193
Family services. *See* Home observances
Fasting, 54, 90, 91, 115. *See also* Yom Kippur

Fate, 194
Feldman, Abraham J., 125
Feminism, 45, 55, 67. *See also* Women
Feminist theology, 45, 45, 67, 96. *See also* Liturgical innovation
Festivals, 202. *See also names of festivals*
Columbus Platform, 202
Fetus, viability of, 125. *See also* Abortion
First Amendment, 123
First Zionist Congress, 133, 139
Fischl, Peter, 92
Flam, Nancy A., 70
Foreign aid, 160
Foundation schools, 183
Frankel, Zacharias, 4, 5
Freedom, and ethical monotheism, 40
Freedom of speech, 159
Freehof, Solomon B., 56–58, 101, 117–119
Friday night service
bar/bat mitzvah, 106
origin of, 78, 79, 118
Plaut on, 83
Torah reading, 106
vs. home observance, 83
Wise on, 79, 80
Friedman, Debbie, 71
Fundamentalism, religious, 213
Funerals during pregnancy, 114

Gamoran, Emanuel, 183
Gates of Prayer, 62, 64, 65–67, 95
Gates of Prayer for Weekdays
Gates of Repentance, 64, 90
Gates of the Seasons, 88, 90
Gays/lesbians
circumcision of children of, 101
as congregational leaders, 154
human rights of, 155
marriage ceremonies, 154, 155, 160
non-traditional families, 101, 157
outreach to, 157
and traditional family, 160
Same gender officiation, 155–156
Statement of Principles, 211
Gehenna, 114, 199
Geiger, Abraham, 6, 8, 11
Genetic defects, 125
Genocide, 149
German rabbinical conferences, 12, 13, 15, 113
German Reform Judaism
and acculturation, vii
bareheaded worship, 60
Berlin liberal seminary, 6, 18
Bogen on, 19

brotherhood, 4
Christian influences on, 14
and Enlightenment values,
    vii, 2
and halachah, 2, 117–118
and Hebrew, 4
influence on American Re-
    form Judaism, 1
insecurity of, 174
messianic views, 19, 213
moderate wing, 5
in Nazi period, 2, 15
and diaspora, ix, 132. *See also*
    Mission of Israel
and Zionism, 95
origins, vii–viii, 1–2, 5
and Orthodox Judaism, 2,
    13, 117
and prophetic Judaism, 145.
    See also Prophetic Juda-
    ism
radical wing, 12
rationalism, 2
Sabbath, 14. *See also* Sabbath
secularism, 2
sermons in German, viii, 2,
    6, 19
theology of, 1, 5–6, 8, 11, 12,
    36. *See also* German rab-
    binical conferences
universalism, 2. *See also* Uni-
    versalism
See also American Reform Ju-
    daism; Classical Reform
    Judaism
Get, 104, 110
Gibran, Kahlil, 187
Gillman, Neil, 70
Gittelsohn, Roland B., 128
Giyyur. See Conversion
God
    absence of, 44
    acceptability of diverse ideas
        of, 43
    Baeck's view, 15, 17
    Centenary Perspective, 205
    Columbus Platform, 200–201
    as Commander, 18, 54, 128,
        129, 130
    covenant with, 40, 209. *See*
        also Covenant
    as Creator, 14, 15, 40
    evolving with humankind,
        38, 39
    feminist views, 45–46, 68, 90
    Geiger's view, 11
    gendered language/imagery,
        45–46, 68, 90
    and Holocaust, 44
    human relationship with, 43
    Jewish and Christian concep-
        tions compared, 39
    and Jewish people, 68
    and justice, 40
    love of, 201

man as partner of, 38, 39, 40,
    46, 148, 209
man created in image of, 200
metaphors of power and au-
    thority, 45, 90
and mitzvot, 126, 127–128,
    129, 130. *See also* Mitzvot
oneness and reality of, 209
Reform Platforms on, 195.
    See also names of Platforms
religious naturalist view, 128
Slonimsky's view, 38
as source of spiritual energy,
    128
Statement of Principles, 208
traditional concepts of, 38
as transcendent ground of
    value, 44
as Universal Spirit, 11
Wise's view, 37
Golden calf, 68, 96
Goldstein, Elyse, 107
Good and evil, 41, 43
Gottheil, Gustav, 134
Goy kadosh (holy people), 141
Grace after meals, 59, 63–64, 83
Great Depression, x, 145
Greek genius vs. Jewish, 11
"Greening" of Reform move-
    ment, 188
Guatemala, 156
Guilt, personal, 54

Halachah
    on abortion, 124, 125
    classical view of, ix
    on conversion, 177
    on covenant, 189
    defined, 117
    Freehof on, 118
    as guidance for new situa-
        tions, 120, 122
    as human response to revela-
        tion, 49
    individual adoption/adapta-
        tion of, 50, 54, 117
    innovation and flexibility of,
        x
    Jacob on, 119–120
    and Jewishness, 49
    on matrilineal/patrilineal de-
        scent, 171
    as means of approaching
        God, 50
    on mixed marriage, 166, 172
    and moral law, 49
    origin and development of,
        118
    in Orthodox Judaism, 121
    and personal autonomy, 50,
        54, 117, 126
    and personal religious fulfill-
        ment, 52
    in Pittsburgh Platform, 198
    Plaut's view of, 189–190
    pluralistic approach to, 121

in Reform Judaism, 2, 36,
    117–122 passim, 166,
    189-190
    See also Mitzvot
Halevi, Judah, 36, 136
Hallo, William W., 189
Hamburg Temple, 19
Harris, Maurice H., 72
Hatafat dam b'rit, 177–178
Havdalah, 187
Havurot, 193
Head covering, 59–61
Healing services, 55, 70
Health insurance, 202
Hebrew language
    in Columbus Platform, 203
    in early Reform, 4, 19, 197
    importance of, 142, 182
    and Israel, 142, 143, 212
    in Jewish education, 182–
        184, 210, 212
    lack of neuter gender, 46
    in Philadelphia Principles,
        197
    in summer camps, 184
    in Statement of Principles,
        212
    in worship, 74, 87, 184
Hebrew name, 172, 177–178
Hebrew Union College-Jewish
    Institute of Religion
    campuses and facilities, xi
    catalogues, 25, 26, 38
    Centenary, 208
    during Holocaust, 27
    faculty, 26
        Adler, 45
        Borowitz, 42, 203
        Cohon, 62, 199
        Hoffman, 65
        Lauterbach, 59
        Petuchowski, 50
        Washofsky, 121
    first year in Israel program,
        132
    founding and early history,
        ix, 26, 28
    Library, 26
    mohel program, 101
    presidents, 25
        Deutsch, 26
        Kohler, 26, 104
        Mielziner, 26
        Wise, 26
        Zimmerman, 25
    refugee scholars, 27
    School of Sacred Music, 73
    and Wise, ix, 22, 26
Heller, Maximillian, 134
Hemophilia, 100
Herodotus, 99
Herzfeld, Levi, 12, 13
Herzl, Theodor, 133
Heschel, Abraham Joshua, 157
Hiddur mitzvah, 88
High Holy Days, 90, 210. *See*

also Rosh HaShanah; Yom Kippur
Hillel and Shammai, 121
Hirsch, Emil G., 81, 82, 145, 197
Hirsch, Richard, 33
Hoffman, Lawrence A., 65, 188
Holdheim, Samuel, 12–15
Holiness, 85, 141, 201, 208, 210
Hollander, Vicki L., 97
Holocaust
in American Jewish mind, 65–66
Baeck on, 15
in Centenary Perspective, 204, 207
commemoration of, 92, 94
customs/symbols related to, 131
as defining experience of 20th cent., 131, 213, 214
deniers of, 159
and German Reform, 2
and Israel, 141–142, 207
in new Haggadah, 92
theological implications, 36, 43, 44, 52, 204
and Zionism, 138
See also Covenant theology
Home observances
importance of, 184, 202
mourning services, 63, 111, 113, 114
prayer books and guides, 55, 102, 125, 126
Sabbath, 82, 83, 86, 87
study, 210
Honesty, 129
Hospice movement, 97
Human rights, 145, 148, 149, 155
Human worth
sanctity and dignity of individual, 148
Huysmans, J.K., 137
Hymns, 2, 74. *See also* Synagogue music

Iakovos, Archbishop, 153
Illicit descent, 103–104
Immersion of convert, 176–178
Immortality. *See* Afterlife
Incest, 124
Individualism, 99, 137, 214
Individual worth and dignity, 148
Industrial disputes, 147
Ingathering and return to Zion, 19. *See also* Zionism
Interfaith activities
and abortion, 123
in German Reform, 2, 3
Jacobson on, 2, 3
in Pittsburgh Platform, 199
and Vatican II, x
Intermarriage. *See* Mixed marriage

Internet, 159
"In the Presence of Eyes" (Shlonsky), 94
Iraq, 160
Isaac b. Moses of Vienna, 60
Islam, 199
Israel, State of
aliyah to, 195, 206
in Centenary Perspective, 204, 206, 207
democracy in , 34
foreign aid to, 160
high moral ideals regarding, 141
and Holocaust, 141–142, 207
immigrant absorption, 143
importance for Diaspora Jewry, x, 65–66, 74, 142, 206, 214
Jewish governance in, 143
and Jewish education, 74, 182–183
as *Medinat Yisrael*, 141, 143
peace process/terrorism, 160
Progressive Judaism in, 32, 34, 132, 139, 140, 143, 160, 203, 206
Six-Day War, 44
special Reform obligations to, 142
in Statement of Principles, 212
theological implications of, 44, 131
uniqueness among states, 141
in UAHC Mission Statement, 23
visits to, 142, 182
World Union for Progressive Judaism, 22
Israel Independence Day, 95
Israelite Consistory of Westphalia, 3
Israel Movement for Progressive Judaism, 140

Jacob, Walter, 57, 58, 119
Jacobson, Israel, 2
Jesus, 39, 52
Jewish Agency, 34, 138
Jewish cemeteries. *See* Death and burial
Jewish continuity, 214
Jewish education
affect over content, 188
and bar/bat mitzvah, 30, 182
beyond age thirteen, 105
in camps and youth groups, 182, 188
catechisms, 182, 191
in Columbus Platform, 202
of converts, 30, 168, 176–177
core value concepts, 183
fatalism regarding, 194
focusing on what sets Judaism apart, 191

formal to informal, 188
Gamoran on, 183–185
goals and trends, 183, 192, 193
and Hebrew, 142, 182–184, 210, 212
and intermarriage, 162, 184
and Israel, 74, 182–183
Jacobson on, 2
and Jewish identity, 168
as means to end, 193
Meyer on, 191–192
and mixed-marriage children, 162, 179
new forms in free society, 191
and Reform platforms, 195
relation between particular and universal, 191
traditional, 182
in UAHC Mission Statement, 23
Yoffie on, 192
and Zionism, 34, 74, 182–183
See also Study
Jewish Federations, x
Jewish Healing Center, 70
Jewish history, 183, 205, 207
Jewish home, 211. *See also* Home observances
Jewish identity, 44
erosion of, 181
education programs, 168
mixed-marriage children, 171
mixed-marriage partners, 166
pride in, 191
and Sabbath, 85
and secularism, 120
and summer camping experience, 186
Jewish Institute of Religion, 22, 25, 27, 38. *See also* Hebrew Union College-Jewish Institute of Religion
Jewish law. *See* Halachah
Jewish music. *See* Synagogue music
Jewish nation-hood/peoplehood
Ahavat Yisrael, 24
in Centenary Perspective, 205
in Columbus Platform, 201
and covenant, 189
Geiger on, 6, 8
and Judaism, 136–137
love of the Jewish people, 24
and outreach, 169
in Pittsburgh Platform, 198
and Sabbath, 85
spiritual aspect of, 8
in Statement of Principles, 211
See also Ethnicity
Jewish state, restoration of. *See* Zionism
Jewish study. *See* Study

Jewish Theological Seminary, 102
Jewish unity, 8, 91, 160. *See also* Ethnicity; Jewish nationhood/peoplehood
Jewish War Veterans, 150, 153
Job, 39
Johnson, Lyndon B., 150, 151, 152
Joint Commission on Jewish Education, 183
Judaism
    and monotheism, 41
    and moral freedom, 41
    ongoing reform trend, vii
    as universal religion, 29, 38, 200. *See also* Mission of Israel; Universalism
    See also American Reform Judaism; Classical Reform Judaism; Conservative Judaism; German Reform Judaism; Orthodox Judaism
Justice, universal, 201

Kaddish. See Mourner's *Kaddish*
Kadima, 139, 140, 141
Kant, Immanuel, 52
Kaplan, Kivie, 146
Kaplan, Mordecai, 129
Kashrut. See Dietary laws
K'dushah. See Holiness
Ketubah. See Marriage contract
Kiddush cup, 88
Kiddushin. See Marriage
Kippah. See Head covering
Kohler, Kaufmann, 26, 104, 112, 197
Kol Nidrei, 90
Labor unions, 147
Lay marriage officiants, 164
Lauterbach, Jacob Zvi, 59
L'chah Dodi, 113
Legalism, 135
Levites, 72
Levy, Felix, 199
Levy, Richard, 208
Liberal Judaism, viii
Liberal Rabbinical Seminary (Berlin), 6, 18
Life after death. *See* Afterlife
Life-cycle events, 55, 99, 68, 99. *See also names of life-cycle events*
Liturgical innovations
    Amidah, 69
    Avinu Malkeinu, 90
    Christian influences on, 66
    Elbogen on, 20
    eliminating archaic concepts, 65
    use of English, 65
    gender-sensitive language, 55, 62, 90

German Reform, 1
    healing prayers, 71
    use of Hebrew, 62
    for inclusiveness, 76
    Kol Nidrei, 90
    Matriarchs, 62, 69
    and menstrual cycle, 99, 106–108
    return to Zion, viii
    Rosh HaShanah and Yom Kippur, 90
    Rosh Chodesh, 96
    sacrificial service, viii
    shortening service, 19, 55
    women's life-cycle events, 96, 99, 106–108
    Yizkor, 116
    by youth and camp groups, 187
    See also names of prayer books
Lord, John Wesley, 153
Loth, Moritz, 22
Love of learning. *See* Study
Lulav, 89
Lurya, Solomon, 60

McCarthy era, 145
Maimonides, Moses, 36, 99, 101, 122
Mamlechet kohanim, 141
Mamzerut, 103–104
Mann, Jacob, 56, 57
Manuals and guides on Reform practice, 88, 125, 126
Marriage, 99
    gays and lesbians, 154. *See also* Gays/lesbians
    ketubah. See Marriage contract
    mutuality of bride and groom, 108
    officiants, 164
    rabbinic role, 30, 31
    reaffirmation of Covenant, 162
    traditional ceremonies, 108, 154
Marriage contract, 99, 108–109
Martin, Bernard, 41
Maslin, Simeon J., 162
Massarik, 165
Matriarchs and Patriarchs, 62, 69
Matrilineal descent, 166, 171
Maturity, age of, 178
Medicaid, 123
Medinat Yisrael. See Israel, State of
Memorial lights, 113, 115. *See also Yahrzeit*
Menarche, 106
Men's clubs, x
Menstruation, 99, 106–108
Menuchah, 210
Messianic beliefs, 192
    in Centenary Perspective, 204, 205
    in Columbus Platform, 201

in early Reform, 19, 213
    and *Kaddish*, 114
    on personal messiah, 19
    in Philadelphia Principles, 196
    in Pittsburgh Platform, 198
    and social action, 149
Meyer, Michael A., 191
Mezuzah, 89
Middle East peace process, 160
Mielziner, Moses, 26
Mihaly, Eugene, 164
Mikveh, 106, 107, 176, 178
Minhag America (Wise), 67, 74
Minhagim. See Folkways and customs
Minimum wage, 146
Minyan
    for home service, 57, 114
    and Mourner's *Kaddish*, 56
    for public worship, 56, 58
    and Torah reading, 56
    women in, 57
Mirrors, turning or covering, 113
"Mi shebeirach" (Friedman), 71
Mission of Israel
    in Classical Reform, ix, 94, 132, 134, 196–197, 213
    in Columbus Platform, 201
    and *Medinat Yisrael*, 141
    in Philadelphia Principles, 196–197
    and proselytizing, 174
    Wise on, 38
    in WUPJ constitution, 32
Mitzvot
    adoption of, 103
    aesthetic enhancement of, 88, 89
    and science/modernism, 36
    and personal autonomy, 210, 214
    and repentance, 127
    as place where God and humans meet, 157
    as commandments, 126
    benefits of observing, 50, 89, 129
    circumcision, 100
    ethical vs. ritual, 52
    Gittelsohn on, 129, 130
    God as *metzaveh* of, 18, 54, 128–130
    grounds for observing, 127
    Heschel on, 157
    historicist view, 130–131
    and individual choice, 210, 214
    leading to positive Jewish identity, 172
    Polish on, 130, 131
    religious naturalist view, 128–130
    Schaalman on, 127–128

in Statement of Principles, 210
study and observance of, 210
theistic view, 127–128
visiting mourners, 112
See also Halachah
Mixed marriages
and burial in Jewish cemetery, 112
children of, 101, 166, 170
circumcision of offspring, 101
and conversion to Judaism, 175. *See also* Outreach
increase in, 161, 165, 168, 171, 179, 191
and Jewish education, 184
officiating at, 127, 161–164
and Sabbath observance, 88
in Statement of Principles, 211
and synagogue participation, 179–181. *See also* Outreach
Mixed seating, 55
M'nuchah, 85
Moral determinism, 41
Moses, 40, 101
Moses, Adolph, 80
Mother's pensions, 147
Mourner's *Kaddish*, 114, 116
for apostate, 115
by convert for non-Jewish parents, 115
in house of mourning, 56
and *minyan*, 56–59
on *yahrzeit*, 115
rule-of-three exemption, 59
Mourning practices, 57, 111–115. *See also* Mourner's *Kaddish*
NATE. *See* National Association of Temple Educators
NFTY. *See* North American Federation of Temple Youth
Narcotics traffic, 149
National Association of Temple Educators, 182
National Center of Jewish Healing, 70
National Federation of Temple Brotherhoods, xi
Nazism, x, 2, 25, 132
Nehemiah, 161
Neo-Kantianism, 38
Non-traditional families, 101, 157, 160
North American Federation of Temple Youth, xi, 182, 186, 187
Nostalgia, 76

Olan, Levi A., 40, 40
Old-age pensions, 147, 202
One-day-of-rest-in-seven for workers, 146
Oneg, 85

Organs, viii, 2, 74. *See also* Synagogue music
Organ/tissue transplants, 112
Orthodox Judaism, 213
authoritarian approach of, 51, 126
on autopsy, 111
circumcisers, 100, 101
and covenant theology, 41
and covenant, 189
as deviation from Jewish tradition, vii
and Friday night service, 83
and German Reform, vii, 2, 13, 117
and halachah, 118, 121, 122
headcovering at worship, 60, 61
and Israel Independence Day, 95
lay marriage officiants, 164
and *mamzerut*, 103–104
marriage ceremony, 108
menstrual rules, 106
and mixed marriages, 161, 166
necessity of *get* in divorce, 110
in Reform platforms, 195, 196
and Sabbath, 83
Shulchan Aruch, 125
Outreach, 166–169, 170, 175, 214

Palestine, restoration of, 201. *See also* Zionism
PARDeS. *See* Progressive Association of Reform Day Schools, 183
Particularism, 191, 207
Passover
as existential ethical possibility, 53
Haggadah, 91
misrepresentations of holiday, 53
seder, 55, 78
Yizkor, 116
Pastoral care, 70
Patriarchs, 62, 69
Patrilineal descent, 166, 170, 171, 172
Pesach. *See* Passover
Petitionary prayers, 63
Petuchowski, Jakob J., 41, 50
Philadelphia Principles, 196
Phylacteries, 89, 105
Pidyon Haben, 99
Pinchas of Koretz, 41
Pittsburgh Platform, ix, 80, 189, 197, 208
Plaut, W. Gunther, 41, 82(83, 189
Pluralism, 121, 207, 211
Polish, David, 41, 84, 126, 129–130

Political emancipation, viii, 78
Popular will, as force for reform, 5
Population control, 153
Pornography, 159
Poverty, 153
Prayer
anthropomorphism, 46, 47
centrality of, 24, 77, 157
in Columbus Platform, 202
as communion with God, 24, 64
confessional, 54, 90
davening, 65
as expression of deep human need, 63
in Hebrew, 87, 197
at home, 55, 83. *See also* Home observances
in Jewish education, 193
modes of, 65
neglect of, 55
not a noun but a verb, 75
on Sabbath, 88. *See also* Sabbath
Slonimsky on, 38
in Statement of Principles, 209
true prayer, 38
unsuitability of *Union Prayer Book*, 62–63
in vernacular, 197
Yoffie on, 75
See also Prayer books; Public worship
Prayer books, x, 55, 62, 102. *See also names of prayer books*
Prayer shawl, 59
Priesand, Sally J., 214
Priestly purity laws, 198
Priests and non-priests, 196
Progressive Association of Reform Day Schools, 183
"Progressive" defined, 33
Progressive Judaism, 1
in former Soviet Union, 32
in Israel, 32, 34, 139, 143
in Statement of Principles, 212
Prometheus, 39
Property rights, 202
Prophetic Judaism
attacked inequalities, vii
in Centenary Perspective, 207
in Classical Reform, 134
and ethical monotheism, 40
Geiger on, 6, 11
in German Reform, 145
and social action, 147, 148, 149, 154
and world peace, 202
and WUPJ constitution, 32
in Zionism, 135
Proselytizing, by Jews, 173, 174, 175. *See also*

Outreach
Public employment bureaus,
147
Public housing, 147
Public worship
"choreography" of 65
as *avodah*, 73
cantorial role, 72. *See also* Synagogue music
changing features of, 76
choirs, 72. *See also* Synagogue music
Christian influences on, 66
Cohon's critique of, 63
in Classical Reform, 74
congregational participation, 63, 72
constant features of, 76
decorum, viii, 2, 14, 66
excessive formality, 65
in German/Classical Reform, 4, 60, 66
Hebrew in, 74
key elements of, 65
liturgy of, 65. *See also* Liturgical innovations; Prayer books
minyan for, 57-58
in 1960s, 74
place of worship, 65. *See also* Synagogue
rabbinic role, 73, 75. *See also* Rabbis
Sabbath, 63, 81. *See also* Friday night service; Sabbath
shortening of, viii
solemnity of, 74
summer-camp style, 187
Wise on, 74
Yoffie on, 75
See also Prayer
Purim, 96

Quotas, 159

Rabbis
female, xi, 70, 71, 214
healing function of, 70, 71
leading services, 73, 75
as marriage officiants, 164
pastoral functions of, 31, 71
personal crises of, 30, 31
and prayer revolution, 75, 76
professional needs of, 30–31
as teacher and judge, 70
See also Central Council of American Rabbis
Rabbi's Manual (1988), 170–171
Race relations, 34, 53, 103, 159. *See also* Civil rights movement
Radical left, 53
Raisin, Max, 134
Rape, 124
A Rebours (Huysmans), 137

Reconstructionist Judaism, 105
Reformed Society of Israelites, viii
Reform Judaism. *See* American Reform Judaism; Classical *Reform Judaism Magazine*, 150
Refugees, from Central America, 156
Rehabilitation of criminals, 147, 154
Religious Action Center, x, 146
Religious Coalition for Abortion Rights, 124
Religious education. *See* Jewish education
Religious naturalism, 127, 128
Religious rationalism, x, 40
Remission of sins, 37
Repentance, 91, 127
Responsa
on abortion, 124
on head covering, 59
on *minyan*, 56
on non-Jews participating in services, 179
on officiating at mixed marriage, 164
function in Reform movement, 117, 119–121, 122
Responsive readings, 74
Resurrection. *See* Afterlife
Revelation
Baeck on, 15
of Bible, 7
as central belief of Judaism, 47, 48
in Columbus Platform, 200
Fackenheim on, 47
Geiger on, 6, 11, 12
halachah as human response to, 49
as incursion of God into time and history, 48
and Israel's destiny, 49, 50
and Jewish law, 49, 118
Jews as people of, 11, 12
meaning in modern times, 1
ongoing, 209
in Pittsburgh Platform, 198
in Statement of Principles, 209
traditional view, 50
Wise on, 37
Reverence for all creation, 209
Revolutions of 1848, 19
Rewards and punishments, 37
Rhea Hirsch School, 193
Right to organize, 147
Ritual of Release, 110, 111
Roe v. Wade, 123
Rosenzweig, Franz, 15, 50, 52
Rosh Chodesh, 96
Rosh HaShanah, 78, 97
Rote prayer, 3

Saadyah Gaon, 36

Sabbath
candlelighting, 82, 86, 118
centrality of, 1, 14, 53, 78, 86, 195
circumcision on, 100
in Columbus Platform, 202
and commitment to freedom, 84
conflicts with work obligations, 78, 87
and covenant with God, 85
in day schools, 186
dwindling observance in 19th cent., 81
enhancing observance of, 84, 89
ethical-religious importance of, 53
and exodus from Egypt, 84
festive meal on, 89
as foretaste of messianic era, 85
Havdalah, 187
Holdheim on, 13, 14
holiness of, 85
home rituals, 82, 83, 86, 87
individual options for, 86
and Jewish peoplehood, 85
and Jewish identity, 85
and Jewish tradition, 78
and Jewish study, 88
joy of, 85
Kiddush, 82, 83, 87
manuals and guides for, 84, 86, 216
meditation for in *Gates of Prayer*, 64
and mixed-marriage families, 88
non-Jew reciting blessings, 166
as opportunity to consecrate oneself, 14
personal experimentation with, 51
Plaut on, 82–83
purposes of, 84
reasons for non-observance, 78, 79, 87
recovering observance of, 51, 82, 86, 87
as remembrance of creation, 14, 84
renewing relationship with prayer, 88
rest on, 85, 210
sanctifying time, 13, 14, 87
seventh day, 14
Shabbatons, 193
"Shabbat Shalom" greeting, 85
during *shivah*, 113
in Statement of Principles, 210
Torah reading on, 58
in *Union Prayer Book*, 63

and unmarried, 87
  See also Home observances;
    Prayer; Public Worship;
    Sunday Sabbath
Sacrificial system, viii, 19, 54,
  196, 198
Saddam Hussein, 160
Salkin, Jeffrey, 187
Sanctity of individual, 148
Sanctuary Movement, 156
Sanitary working conditions,
  146
Saperstein, David, 159
Sarah, 169, 178
Schaalman, Herman E., 41, 127
Schacter-Shalomi, Zalman, 41
Schindler, Alexander M., 165,
  169
Schwarzschild, Steven, 41
Science of Judaism, 6
Secularism, 2, 34, 41, 120
Secular Judaism, 120
Seesen, Westphalia, 2
Segregation, 148
Self-discipline, 51, 91, 126
Sermons, viii, 2, 6, 19
Sexuality/sexual orientation,
  92, 146. *See also* Gays/lesbi-
  ans
Shabbat. *See* Sabbath
Shabbat bereshit, 14
A Shabbat Manual, 84, 86, 126
Shapiro, Mark Dov, 86
Shavuot, 53, 116
Shema, 39, 76, 89
Shivah, 57, 111–114
Shlensky, Evely Laser, 156
Shlonsky, Abraham, 94
Sh'loshim, 115
Sh'mini Atzeret, 116
Shoah. *See* Holocaust
Shofar, x
Shulchan Aruch, 58, 118, 125,
  135
Silberman, Lou, 41
Silver, Abba Hillel, 132, 134,
  136, 137
Single mothers, 104
Sisterhoods, x
Six-Day War, 44, 132, 139
Slavery, ix, 84, 145, 201
Slonimsky, Henry, 38
Social action
  in Columbus Platform, 201,
    202
  difficulty of moral decision-
    making, 159
  and Jewish faith, 156-157
  making Judaism effective be-
    yond synagogue, 83
  and messianic era, 149
  in Pittsburgh Platform, 199
  and Prophetic Judaism, 146-
    147, 154
  Protestant influence on, 145
  Religious Action Center, x

as repairing our fragmented
    selves, 157
  as repairing the world, 24,
    143, 146–147, 160, 193
  in Statement of Principles,
    210
  in UAHC Mission Statement,
    23
  in Yom Kippur haftarah, 91
Social insurance, 147
Soviet Jewry, x, 34, 159
Stahl, Harold, 73
Statement of Principles for Re-
  form Judaism, 208-209
Stern, Chaim, 64
Stern, Jack, 29, 30
Study
  as experiencing the com-
    mandments, 51
  centrality of, 24, 157, 208
  and love for learning, 183
  in Statement of Principles,
    210
  See also Jewish education
Suburbanization, x, 74
Suffering, 40
Suicide, 112
Sukkah, x, 88, 89
Sukkot, 89
Sulzer, Solomon 73, 74
Summer camps, 182–187
Sunday Sabbath, 13, 15, 80, 82
Supplementary Jewish schools,
  182, 183
Supreme Court, U.S., 123
Synagogue
  as center of *avodah,* 76
  centrality of, 212
  in Columbus Platform, 202
  congregational participa-
    tion, 184
  as focus of Jewish life, x
  non-Jewish members, 179,
    180, 181
  as "small sanctuary," 58
  in Statement of Principles,
    212
  suburban, 74
  women's role in, 214
  See also Public worship
Synagogue music
  changing forms over time,
    73, 76
  choirs, 72
  in Columbus Platform, 203
  congregational singing, 2,
    55, 65, 72, 74
  in German reform, 1, 2
  in Jewish education, 183
  modern composers, 73

Tallit, 59
Talmud, vii, 12, 13
Talmud Torah. See Study
Tay Sachs disease, 125
Tefillin, 89, 105

Temple, ancient
  destruction of, 93, 96, 127
  service in, viii, 19, 54, 72,
    196, 198
Temple, contemporary. *See* Synagogue
Ten Commandments, 68
Ten Plagues, 92
Terezin concentration camp,
  15
Terrorism, 160
T'fillah. See Prayer
Theism, 127
Tikkun olam. See Social action
Tishah B'Av, 93
Torah
  in Centenary Perspective, 205
  in Columbus Platform,
    200
  critical view of, 1, 7
  dialectic relation with, 190
  evolution of, 200
  as foundation of Jewish life,
    190, 209
  Geiger on, 7
  human authorship of, 7
  and God's love for Jewish
    people, 210
  and ongoing creation, 205
  in Pittsburgh Platform, 198
  and practice of Judaism, 44.
    See also Halachah
  as record of experience of
    Jewish people, 190
  as revealed text, 1. *See also*
    Revelation
  on Sabbath, 58
  in Statement of Principles,
    208, 210
  study of, 51, 172, 190, 193.
    See also Jewish education
  and Talmud, vii, 13
  in worship service, 58. *See
    also* Torah reading cere-
    mony
*The Torah: A Modern Commen-
  tary* (Plaut), 189
Torah Aura, 188
Torah reading ceremony
  and bar/bat mitzvah, 105.
    See also Bar/bat mitzvah
  and Friday night service,
    106. *See also* Friday night
    service
  and *minyan,* 56, 57
  participation by women, 180
  participation by non-Jew,
    166, 180
  traditional nature of, 76
Totalitarianism, 149
Tower of Babel, 169
Trachtman, Ilana, 101
Trade unions, 147
Tribalism, 169, 173
T'shuvah. See Repentance
T'shuvot. See Responsa

Tur, 118
T'villah. See Immersion
Tzipporah, 101

UAHC. See Union of American Hebrew Congregations
Umansky, Ellen M., 67
Underdeveloped nations, aid to, 149
Unemployment insurance, 147, 202
Union Hymnal, 72, 73
Union of American Hebrew Congregations
on abortion, 123
on aliyah to Israel, 133, 139
Biennial Assemblies, 75, 123, 141
Board of Trustees, 139, 140
in capital punishment, 154
Centenary, 203, 208
congregational autonomy, 22, 23
constitutions, 22, 23
current educational priorities, 192
first general convention, 22
founding of, 21
and Hebrew Union College, 22, 23
on human rights of homosexuals, 155
Long-Range Planning Committee, 24
Mission Statement, 23
on mixed-marriages, 165, 169
number of affiliates, x, xi
outreach programs, 168, 169
presidents
    Eisendrath, 145
    Schindler, 165
    Yoffie, 75, 169, 192
proselytizing campaign, 165
publication program, 150, 158, 189
Religious Action Center, 146
and social activism, 145, 154
Statement of Basic Principles, 147
and suburbanization, x
on Vietnam War, 151
voluntaristic aspects, 141
Wise's role, ix, 21
and World Union for Progressive Judaism, 24
and Zionism, 132, 133, 134, 138
Union Prayer Book
Cohon's critique, 62
formality of, 187
Hoffman on, 65
petitionary prayers, 63
Tishah B'Av, 93
United Nations, 149, 151

Universal health insurance, 147
Universalism
in Centenary Perspective, 204, 207
in German/Classical Reform, 2, 4, 197, 207
intrinsic to Judaism, 29, 42
Jacobson on, 2, 4
Judaism as essence of universal religion, 38
and missionary efforts, 174
and moral law, 48
and outreach, 169
and particularism, ix, 48
particularity, 48
in Philadelphia Principles, 197
Wise on, 38
and Zionism, 133
Vatican II, x
Vernacular hymns, viii
Vernacular sermons, 55
Viability, of fetus, 125
Vietnam War, 145, 150, 153, 159
Vilna Gaon, 60
Visiting the Sick, 70
Vocational choices, 184
Vorspan, Albert, 159

Wacholder, 166, 167
Washofsky, Mark, 121
Welfare reform, 159
Wise, Isaac Mayer
and Central Conference of American Rabbis, 22, 29
role in founding American Reform, ix
and Hebrew Union College, 22, 26
Minhag America, 67
missionary zeal of, 174
"On Judaism," 37
and Sunday Sabbath, 81
theological views of, 37, and Union of American Hebrew Congregations, ix, 22
as visionary and organizer, ix
and worship services, 72, 73–74, 79–80
Wise, Stephen S., 22, 25, 132
Wolf, Arnold Jacob, 41, 52
Women
as circumcisers, 101–102
and Covenant at Sinai, 68
during Egyptian bondage, 92
equality of, 1, 104
and German Reform, 1
and Golden Calf, 96
healing prayers, 70
and Jewish education, 1, 182
in leadership roles, 67, 214
life-cycle events of, 68, 106
in minyan, 57

as rabbis and cantors, xi, 70, 71, 73, 101–102, 214
reciting Kaddish on yahrzeit, 115
in Reform Judaism, 214
and Rosh Chodesh, 96
spirituality of, 68, 70
Torah reading, 180
traditional exclusions of, 67
See also Covenant ceremony for girls; Feminist theology
Women of Reform Judaism, xi
Worker's compensation, 147
World peace, 150, 154, 160, 202
World Union for Progressive Judaism, 15, 22, 24, 32–34
World War I, 146
World War II, 145, 173, 182
World Zionist Organization, 34, 132, 139, 140
Worship service. See Public worship
Wright, Bishop, 153

Yahrzeit, 57, 58, 115, 116
Yarmulke. See Head covering, 59
Yishuv Eretz Yisrael, 143
Yizkor, 116
Yoffie, Eric H., 75, 169, 192
Yom HaAtzma-ut, 95
Yom HaShoah, 94
Yom Kippur, 39, 78
circumcision on, 100
fasting, 91
haftarah, 91
self-denial and fasting, 90
self-searching and introspection, 91
Union Prayer Book, 63
Yizkor, 116
Yom Kippur War, 132
Youth education, 184, 187, 188
Youth groups, x

Zimmerman, Sheldon, 25, 28
Zionism, 120, 128
Ahavat Tzion, 24
centrality of Zion, 143–144
in Classical Reform, viii
in Columbus Platform, 95, 138
and Holocaust, 138
love of Am Yisrael for Eretz Yisrael, 24, 141
opposition to, xiv, 95, 132–134, 196
in Pittsburgh Platform, 198
Silver on, 136–137
support for, 143, 144, 132, 139–141
UAHC Mission Statement, 23
and World Union for Progressive Judaism, 33, 34